3

Date Due

nov 6	12/20/Am		
DEC 17	1/3/Am		
JAN 6			
Dec 19			
DEC 17			
DEC 5			
Dec 8			
DEC 21			
JAN 5			
JAN 6			
JAN 6			
MAR 26			
FEB 9			
MAR 11			
MAR 12 1987	PRINTED IN U. S. A.		

SOCIAL LIFE AT ROME

THE MACMILLAN COMPANY
NEW YORK · CHICAGO
DALLAS · ATLANTA · SAN FRANCISCO
LONDON · MANILA
BRETT-MACMILLAN LTD.
TORONTO

SOCIAL LIFE AT ROME

IN THE AGE OF CICERO

BY

W. WARDE FOWLER, M.A.

FELLOW AND LECTURER OF LINCOLN COLLEGE, OXFORD
AUTHOR OF 'THE CITY-STATE OF THE GREEKS AND ROMANS,'
'THE ROMAN FESTIVALS OF THE PERIOD OF THE REPUBLIC,' ETC.

' Ad illa mihi pro se quisque acriter intendat animum
quae vita, quae mores fuerint.' — LIVY, *Praefatio.*

New York

THE MACMILLAN COMPANY

PREFATORY NOTE

THIS book was originally intended to be a companion to Professor Tucker's *Life in Ancient Athens*, published in Messrs. Macmillan's series of Handbooks of Archaeology and Art; but the plan was abandoned for reasons on which I need not dwell, and before the book was quite finished I was called to other and more specialised work. As it stands, it is merely an attempt to supply an educational want. At our schools and universities we read the great writers of the last age of the Republic, and learn something of its political and constitutional history; but there is no book in our language which supplies a picture of life and manners, of education, morals, and religion in that intensely interesting period. The society of the Augustan age, which in many ways was very different, is known much better; and of late my friend Professor Dill's fascinating volumes have familiarised us with the social life of two several periods of the Roman Empire. But the age of Cicero is in some ways at least as important as any period of the Empire; it is a critical moment in the history of Graeco-Roman civilisation. And in the Ciceronian correspondence, of more than nine hundred contemporary letters, we have the richest treasure-house of social life that has survived from any period of classical antiquity.

Apart from this correspondence and the other literature of the time, my mainstay throughout has been the *Privatleben der Römer* of Marquardt, which forms the last portion of the great *Handbuch der Römischen Altertümer* of Mommsen and Marquardt. My debt is great also to Professors Tyrrell and Purser, whose labours have provided us with a text of Cicero's letters which we can use with confidence; the citations from these letters have all been verified in the new Oxford text edited by Professor Purser. One other name I must mention with gratitude. I firmly believe that the one great hope for classical learning and education lies in the interest which the unlearned public may be brought to feel in ancient life and thought. We have just lost the veteran French scholar who did more perhaps to create and maintain such an interest than any man of his time; and I gladly here acknowledge that it was Boissier's *Cicéron et ses amis* that in my younger days made me first feel the reality of life and character in an age of which I then hardly knew anything but the perplexing political history.

I have to thank my old pupils, Mr. H. E. Mann and Mr. Gilbert Watson, for kind help in revising the proofs.

W. W. F.

CONTENTS

CHAPTER I

CHAPTER II

CHAPTER VI

CHAPTER VII

CHAPTER VIII

CHAPTER IX

CHAPTER X

CHAPTER XI

ILLUSTRATIONS

MAP

Translations of passages in foreign languages in this book will be found in the Appendix following page 362.

CHAPTER I

TOPOGRAPHICAL

THE modern traveller of to-day arriving at Rome by rail drives to his hotel through the uninteresting streets of a modern town, and thence finds his way to the Forum and the Palatine, where his attention is speedily absorbed by excavations which he finds it difficult to understand. It is as likely as not that he may leave Rome without once finding an opportunity of surveying the whole site of the ancient city, or of asking, and possibly answering the question, how it ever came to be where it is. While occupied with museums and picture-galleries, he may well fail "totam aestimare Romam." [1] Assuming that the reader has never been in Rome, I wish to transport him thither in imagination, and with the help of the map, by an entirely different route. But first let him take up the eighth book of the *Aeneid,* and read afresh the oldest and most picturesque of all stories of arrival at Rome; [2] let

[1] Martial iv. 64. 12.
[2] *Aen*. viii. 90 foll. The Capitoline hill, which Virgil means by "arx," is a conspicuous object from the river just below the Aventine,

B

him dismiss all handbooks from his mind, and concentrate it on Aeneas and his ships on their way from the sea to the site of the Eternal City.

Virgil showed himself a true artist in bringing his hero up the Tiber, which in his day was freely used for navigation up to and even above the city. He saw that by the river alone he could land him exactly where he could be shown by his friendly host, almost at a glance, every essential feature of the site, every spot most hallowed by antiquity in the minds of his readers. Rowing up the river, which graciously slackened its swift current, Aeneas presently caught sight of the walls and citadel, and landed just beyond the point where the Aventine hill falls steeply almost to the water's edge. Here in historical times was the dockyard of Rome; and here, when the poet was a child, Cato had landed with the spoils of Cyprus, as the nearest point of the river for the conveyance of that ill-gotten gain to the treasury under the Capitol.[1] Virgil imagines the bank clothed with wood, and in the wood— where afterwards was the Forum Boarium, a crowded haunt—Aeneas finds Evander sacrificing at the Ara maxima of Hercules, of all spots the best starting-point for a walk through the heart of the ancient city.

and would have been much more conspicuous in the poet's time. There is a view of it from this point in Burn's *Rome and the Campagna*, p. 184

[1] Plutarch, *Cato minor* 39. Cato was expected to land at the commercial docks *below* the Aventine (see below, p. 14), where the senate and magistrates were awaiting him, but with his usual rudeness rowed past them to the navalia.

To the right was the Aventine, rising to about a hundred and thirty feet above the river, and this was the first of the hills of Rome to be impressed on the mind of the stranger, by the tale of Hercules and Cacus which Evander tells his guest. In front, but close by, was the long western flank of the Palatine hill, where, when the tale had been told and the rites of Hercules completed, Aeneas was to be shown the cave of the Lupercal; and again to the left, approaching the river within two hundred yards, was the Capitol to be:

> Hinc ad Tarpeiam sedem et Capitolia ducit,
> Aurea nunc, olim silvestribus horrida dumis.

Below it the hero is shown the shrine of the prophetic nymph Carmenta, with the Porta Carmentalis leading into the Campus Martius; then the hollow destined one day to be the Forum Romanum, and beyond it, in the valley of the little stream that here found its way down from the plain beyond, the grove of the Argiletum. Here, and up the slope of the Clivus sacer, with which we shall presently make acquaintance, were the lowing herds of Evander, who then takes his guest to repose for the night in his own dwelling on the Palatine, the site of the most ancient Roman settlement.[1]

What Evander showed to his visitor, as we shall presently see, comprised the whole site of the heart

---

[1] *Aen.* viii. 363. Possibly Virgil meant to put this dwelling on the site of the future Regia, just below the Palatine and between it and the Forum. See Servius *ad loc.*

and life of the city as it was to be, all that lay under
the steep sides of the three almost isolated hills, the
Capitoline, Palatine, and Aventine. The poet knew
that he need not extend their walk to the other so-
called hills, which come down as spurs from the plain
of the Campagna, — Quirinal, Esquiline, Caelian.
Densely populated as those were in his own day,
they were not essential organs of social and political
life; the pulse of Rome was to be felt beating most
strongly in the space between them and the river,
where too the oldest and most cherished associations
of the Roman people, mythical and historical, were
fixed. I propose to take the reader, with a single
deviation, over the same ground, and to ask him to
imagine it as it was in the period with which we are
concerned in this book. But first, in order to take in
with eye and mind the whole city and its position,
let us leave Aeneas, and crossing to the right bank
of the Tiber by the Pons Aemilius,[1] let us climb to the
fort of the Janiculum, an ancient outwork against
attack from the north, by way of the via Aurelia,
and here enjoy the view which Martial has made for
ever famous:

> Hinc septem dominos videre montes
> Et totam licet aestimare Romam,
> Albanos quoque Tusculosque colles
> Et quodcunque iacet sub urbe frigus.

No one who has ever stood on the Janiculum, and

---

[1] The modern visitor would cross by the Ponte Rotto, which is in
the same position as the ancient bridge, just below the Tiber island.

looked down on the river and the city, and across the Latin plain to the Alban mountain and the long line of hills—the last spurs of the Apennines—enclosing the plain to the north, can fail to realise that *Rome was originally an outpost of the Latins,* her kinsmen and confederates, against the powerful and uncanny Etruscan race who dwelt in the undulating hill country to the north. The site was an outpost, because the three isolated hills make it a natural point of defence, and of attack towards the north if attack were desirable; no such point of similar vantage is to be found lower down the river, and if the city had been placed higher up, Latium would have been left open to attack,—the three hills would have been left open to the enemy to gain a firm footing on Latin soil. It was also, as it turned out, an admirable base of operations for carrying on war in the long and narrow peninsula, so awkward, as Hannibal found to his cost, for working out a definite plan of conquest. From Rome, astride of the Tiber, armies could operate on "interior lines" against any combination — could strike north, east, and south at the same moment. With Latium faithful behind her she could not be taken in the rear; the unconquerable Hannibal did indeed approach her once on that side, but fell away again like a wave on a rocky shore. From the sea no enemy ever attempted to reach her till Genseric landed at Ostia in A.D. 455.

Thus it is not difficult to understand how Rome came to be the leading city of Latium; how she came to work her conquering way into Etruria to the north, the land of a strange people who at one time threatened to dominate the whole of Italy; how she advanced up the Tiber valley and its affluents into the heart of the Apennines, and southward into the Oscan country of Samnium and the rich plain of Campania. A glance at the map of Italy will show us at once how apt is Livy's remark that Rome was placed in the centre of the peninsula.[1] That peninsula looks as if it were cleft in twain by the Tiber, or in other words, the Tiber drains the greater part of central Italy, and carries the water down a well-marked valley to a central point on the western coast, with a volume greater than that of any other river south of the Po. A city therefore that commands the Tiber valley, and especially the lower part of it, is in a position of strategic advantage with regard to the whole peninsula. Now Rome, as Strabo remarked, was the only city actually situated on the bank of the river; and Rome was not only on the river, but from the earliest times astride of it. She held the land on both banks from her own site to the Tiber mouth at Ostia, as we know from the fact that one of her most ancient priesthoods[2] had its sacred grove five miles down the river on the northern bank. Thus she had easy access to the sea by the river or by land, and an open way inland up the one great natural entrance from the sea into central Italy.[3] Her position on the Tiber

[1] Livy v. 54.   [2] The Fratres Arvales.
[3] For navigation of the river above Rome see Strabo p. 235.

is much like that of Hispalis (Seville) on the Baetis,
or of Arles on the Rhone, cities opening the way of
commerce or conquest up the basins of two great rivers.
In spite of some disadvantages, to be noticed directly,
there was no such favourable position in Italy for a
virile people apt to fight and to conquer. Capua, in
the rich volcanic plain of Campania, had far greater
advantages in the way of natural wealth; but Capua
was too far south, in a more enervating climate, and
virility was never one of her strong points. Corfinium,
in the heart of the Apennines, once seemed threatening
to become a rival, and was for a time the centre of a
rebellious confederation; but this city was too near
the east coast—an impossible position for a pioneer
of Italian dominion. Italy looks west, not east;
almost all her natural harbours are on her western
side; and though that at Ostia, owing to the amount
of silt carried down by the Tiber, has never been a
good one, it is the only port which can be said to
command an entrance into the centre of the peninsula.

No one, however, would contend that the position
of Rome is an ideal one. Taken in and by itself,
without reference to Italy and the Mediterranean,
that position has little to recommend it. It is too
far from the sea, nearly twenty miles up the valley
of a river with an inconveniently rapid current, to be
a great commercial or industrial centre; and such a
centre Rome has never really been in the whole course
of her history. There are no great natural sources of
wealth in the neighbourhood—no mines like those at

Laurium in Attica, no vast expanse of corn-growing country like that of Carthage. The river too was liable to flood, as it still is, and a familiar ode of Horace tells us how in the time of Augustus the water reached even to the heart of the city.[1] Lastly, the site has never really been a healthy one, especially during the months of July and August,[2] which are the most deadly throughout the basin of the Mediterranean. Pestilences were common at Rome in her early history, and have left their mark in the calendar of her religious festivals; for example, the Apolline games were instituted during the Hannibalic war as the result of a pestilence, and fixed for the unhealthy month of July. Foreigners from the north of Europe have always been liable to fever at Rome; invaders from the north have never been able to withstand the climate for long; in the Middle Ages one German army after another melted away under her walls, and left her mysteriously victorious.

There are some signs that the Romans themselves had occasional misgivings about the excellence of their site. There was a tradition, that after the

---

[1] Horace Od. i. 2. After a bad flood in A.D. 15 proposals were made for diverting a part of the water coming down the Tiber into the Arnus, but this met with fatal opposition from the superstition of the country people (Tacitus, Ann. i. 79). Nissen, Italische Landeskunde, i. p. 324, has collected the records of these floods.

[2] See Nissen, i. p. 407. But it seems likely that the Tiber valley was less malarious then than now (see Nissen's chapter on malaria in Italy, p. 410 foll.). In an interesting paper on Malaria and History, by Mr. W. H. S. Jones (Liverpool University Press), which reached me after this chapter was written, the author is inclined to attribute the ethical and physical degeneracy of the Romans of the Empire partly to this cause.

burning of the city by the Gauls, it was proposed that the people should desert the site and migrate to Veii, the conquered Etruscan city to the north, and that it needed all the eloquence of Camillus to dissuade them. It has given Livy [1] the opportunity of putting into the orator's mouth a splendid encomium on the city and its site ; but no such story could well have found a place in Roman annals if the Capitol had been as deeply set in the hearts of the people as was the Acropolis in the hearts of the Athenians. At a later time of deep depression Horace [2] could fancifully suggest that the Romans should leave their ancient home like the Phocaeans of old, and seek a new one in the islands of the blest. Some idea was abroad that Caesar had meant to transfer the seat of government to Ilium, and after Actium the same intention was ascribed to Augustus, probably without reason; but the third ode of Horace's third book seems to express the popular rumour, and in an interesting paper Mommsen [3] has stated his opinion that the new master of the Roman world may really have thought of changing the seat of government to Byzantium, the supreme convenience and beauty of which were already beginning to be appreciated. [4]

Virgil, on the other hand, though he came from the foot of the Alps and did not love Rome as a place to dwell in, is absolutely true to the great traditions

---

[1] Livy v. 54.   [2] Horace, *Epode* 16.
[3] *Reden und Aufsätze*, p. 173 foll.   [4] *Ib.* p. 175.

of the site. For him "rerum facta est pulcherrima Roma" (*Georg.* ii. 534); and in the *Aeneid* the destiny of Rome is so foretold and expressed as to make it impossible for a Roman reader to think of it except in connexion with the city. He who needs to be convinced of this has but to turn once more to the eighth *Aeneid*, and to add to the charming story of Aeneas' first visit to the seven hills, the splendid picture of the origin and growth of Roman dominion engraved on the shield which Venus gives her son. Cicero again, though he was no Roman by birth, was passionately fond of Rome, and in his treatise *de Republica* praised with genuine affection her "nativa praesidia." [1] He says of Romulus, "that he chose a spot abounding in springs, healthy though in a pestilent region; for her hills are open to the breezes, yet give shade to the hollows below them." And Livy, in the passage already quoted, in language even more perfect than Cicero's, wrote of all the advantages of the site, ending by describing it as "regionum Italiae medium, ad incrementum urbis natum unice locum." It is curious that all these panegyrics were written by men who were not natives of Rome; Virgil came from Mantua, Livy from Padua, Cicero from Arpinum. They are doubtless genuine, though in some degree rhetorical; those of Cicero and Livy can hardly be called strictly accurate. But taken together they may help us to understand that fascination of the site of

---

[1] *De Rep.* ii. 5 and 6.

Rome, to which Virgil gave such inimitable expression.

On this site, which once had been crowded only when the Roman farmers had taken refuge within the walls with their families, flocks, and herds on the threatening appearance of an enemy, by the time of Cicero an enormous population had gathered. Many causes had combined to bring this population together, which can be only glanced at here. As in Europe and America at the present day, so in all the Mediterranean lands since the age of Alexander, there had been a constantly increasing tendency to flock into the towns; and the rise of huge cities, such as Antioch, Alexandria, Carthage, Corinth, or Rhodes, with all the inevitably ensuing social problems and complications, is one of the most marked characteristics of the last three centuries B.C. In Italy in particular, apart from the love of a pleasant social life free from manual toil, with various convenient resorts and amusements, the long series of wars had served to increase the population, in spite of the constant loss by the sword or pestilence; for the veteran soldier who had been serving, perhaps for years, beyond sea, found it hard to return to the monotonous life of agriculture, or perhaps found his holding appropriated by some powerful landholder with whom it would be hopeless to contest possession. The wars too brought a steadily increasing population of slaves to the city, many of whom in course of time would be manumitted, would marry,

and so increase the free population. These are only
a few of the many causes at work after the Punic wars
which crammed together in the site of Rome a population which, in the latter part of the last century
B.C., probably reached half a million or even more.[1]

Let us now descend from the Janiculum, and try
to imagine ourselves in the Rome of Cicero's time,
say in the last year of the Republic, 50 B.C., as we
walk through the busy haunts of this crowded
population. We will not delay on the right bank
of the Tiber, which had probably long been the home
of tradesmen in their gilds,[2] and where farther down
the rich were buying land for gardens[3] and suburban
villas; but cross by the Pons Aemilius, with the
Tiber island on our left, and the opening of the
Cloaca maxima, which drained the water from the
Forum, facing us, as it still does, a little to our right.
We find ourselves close to the Forum Boarium, an
open cattle-market, with shops (tabernae) all around
it, as we know from Livy's record of a fire here,
which burnt many of these shops and much valuable
merchandise.[4] Here by the river was in fact the

---

[1] Beloch, *Die Bevölkerung der griechisch-römischen Welt*, cap. 9, approaching the problem by three several methods, puts it in the first century A.D.
at 800,000, including slaves. In Cicero's time it was, no doubt, considerably
less; but we know that in his last years 320,000 free persons were receiving
doles of corn, apart from slaves and the well-to-do.

[2] Hülsen-Jordan, *Röm. Topographie*, vol. i. part iii. pp. 627, 638.

[3] *Ib.* 643; Cic. *ad Att.* xv. 15. Here, after the death of his daughter
Tullia, Cicero wished to buy land on which to erect a fanum to her (Cic.
ad Att. xii. 19). Here also were the horti Caesaris.

[4] Livy xxxv. 40.

market in the modern sense of the word; the Forum
Romanum, which we are making for, was now the
centre of political and judicial business, and of
social life.

We might go direct to the great Forum, up the
Velabrum, or valley (once a marsh), right in front of
us between the Capitol on the left and the Palatine
on the right. But as we look in the latter direction,
we are attracted by a long low erection almost filling the space between the Palatine and the Aventine,
and turning in that direction we find ourselves at the
lower end of the Circus Maximus, which as yet is the
chief place of amusement of the Roman people. Two
famous shrines, one at each end of it, remind us that
we are on historic ground. At the end where we
stand, and where are the *carceres*, the starting-point
for the competing chariots, was the Ara maxima of
Hercules, which prompted Evander to tell the tale of
Cacus to his guest; at the other end was the subter-
ranean altar of Consus the harvest-god, with which
was connected another tale, that of the rape of the
Sabines. All the associations of this quarter point to
the agricultural character of the early Romans; both
cattle and harvesting have their appropriate myth.
But nothing is visible here now, except the pretty
little round temple of a later date, which is believed
to have been that of Portunus, the god of the landing-
place from the river.[1]

The Circus, some six hundred yards long, at the

[1] Hülsen-Jordan, *op. cit.* p. 143 note.

time of Cicero was still mainly a wooden erection in the form of a long parallelogram, with shops or booths sheltering under its sides ; we shall visit it again when dealing with the public entertainments.[1] Above it on the right is the Aventine hill, a densely populated quarter of the lower classes, crowned with the famous temple of Diana, a deity specially connected with the plebs.[2] The Clivus Patricius led up to this temple ; down this slope, on the last day of his life, Gaius Gracchus had hurried, to cross the river and meet his murderers in the grove of Furrina, of which the site has lately been discovered. If we were to ascend it we should see, on the river-bank below and beyond it, the warehouses and granaries for storing the corn for the city's food-supply, which Gracchus had been the first to extend and organise.

But to ascend the Aventine would take us out of our course. Pushing on to the farther end of the Circus, where the chariots turned at the *metae*, we may pause a moment, for in front of us is a gate in the city wall, the Porta Capena, by which most travellers from the south, using the via Appia or the via Latina, would enter the city.[3] Outside the wall there was then a small temple of Mars, from which

[1] See below, p. 302. Dionysius of Halicarnassus (iii. 68) gives an elaborate account of it in the time of Augustus, when it had been altered and ornamented.—Hülsen-Jordan, p. 120 foll.

[2] Fowler, *Roman Festivals*, p. 199 ; Wissowa in Pauly-Wissowa, *Real-Encyklopädie*, s.v. Diana.

[3] The two roads converged just before arriving at the city. The reader may be reminded that it was by the via Appia that St. Paul entered Rome (Acts xxviii.). Another useful passage for this gate is Juvenal iii. 10 foll.

the procession of the Equites started each year on the
Ides of Quinctilis (July) on its way to the Capitol,
by the same route that we are about to take. We
shall also be following the steps of Cicero on the happy
day, September 4, 57 B.C., when he returned from
exile. " On my arrival at the Porta Capena," he writes
to Atticus, "the steps of the temples were already
crowded from top to bottom by the populace; they
showed their congratulations by the loudest applause,
and similar crowds and applause followed me right
up to the Capitol, and in the Forum and on the
Capitol itself there was again a wonderful throng "
(*ad Att.* iv. 1).

We are now, as the map will show, at the south-
eastern angle of the Palatine, of which, in fact, we are
making the circuit;[1] and here we turn sharp to the
left, by what is now the via di San Gregorio, along a
narrow valley or dip between the Palatine and Caelian
hills—the latter the first we have met of the " hills "
which are not isolated, but spurs of the plain of the
Campagna. The Caelian need not detain us; it was
thickly populated towards the end of the Republican
period, but was not a very fashionable quarter, nor
one of the chief haunts of social life. It held many
of those large lodging-houses (insulae) of which we
shall hear more in the next chapter; one of these
stood so high that it interfered with the view of the
augur taking the auspices on the Capitol, and was

---

[1] It might be useful here to follow the course of the *pomerium*, which
also went round the Palatine, as described in Tacitus, *Annals* xii. 24.

ordered to be pulled down.[1]   Going straight on we
reach the north-eastern angle of the Palatine, where
now stands the arch of Constantine, with the Colosseum
beyond it, and turning once more to the left, we begin
to ascend a gentle slope which will take us to a ridge
between the Palatine and the Esquiline [2]—another of
the spurs of the plain beyond—known by the name
of the Velia.   And now we are approaching the real
heart of the city.

At this point starts the Sacra via,[3] so called
because it is the way to the most sacred spots of the
ancient Roman city,—the temples of Vesta and the
Penates, and the Regia, once the dwelling of the
Rex, now of the Pontifex Maximus; and it will lead
us, in a walk of about eight hundred yards, through
the Forum to the Capitol.   It varied in breadth, and
took by no means a straight course, and later on was
crowded, cramped, and deflected by numerous temples
and other buildings ; but as yet, so far as we can guess,
it was fairly free and open.   We follow it and ascend
the slope till we come to a point known as the *summa
sacra via*, just where the arch of Titus now stands,
and where then was the temple of Jupiter Stator,
and where also a shrine of the public Penates and
another of the Lares (of which no trace is now left)
warn us that we are close on the penetralia of the
Roman State.   Here a way to the left leads up to the

---

[1] Cic. *de Officiis* iii. 16. 66, and the story there related.

[2] Strictly speaking, the Oppius Mons, or southern part of the Esquiline.

[3] See Lanciani's admirable chapter, " A Walk through the Sacra Via," in
his *Ruins and Excavations of Ancient Rome*, p. 190 foll.

Palatine, the residence then of many of the leading men of Rome, Cicero being one of them.

But our attention is not long arrested by these objects; it is soon riveted on the Forum below and in front of us, to which the Sacred Way leads by a downward slope, the Clivus sacer. At the north-western end it is closed in by the Capitoline hill, with its double summit, the arx to the right, and the great temple of Jupiter, Juno, and Minerva facing south-east towards the Aventine. It is of this view that Virgil must have been thinking when he wrote of the happy lot of the countryman who

nec ferrea iura
insanumque forum aut populi tabularia vidit.[1]

For the Forum is crowded with bustling human figures, intent on the business of politics, or of the law-courts (ferrea iura), or of money-making, and just beyond it, immediately under the Capitol, are the record-offices (tabularia) of the Roman Empire. The whole Sacra via from this point is crowded; here Horace a generation later was to meet his immortal "bore," from whom he only escaped when the "ferrea iura" laid a strong hand on that terrible companion. Down below, at the entrance to the Forum by the arch of Fabius (fornix Fabiana), the jostling was great. "If I am knocked about in the crowd at the arch," says Cicero, to illustrate a point in a speech of this time, "I do not accuse

---

[1] *Georg.* ii. 502. Virgil, for all his admiration of Rome, did not love its crowds.

some one at the top of the via Sacra, but the man who jostles me."[1]

The Forum—for from this point we can take it all in, geologically and historically—lies in a deep hollow, to the original level of which excavation has now at last reached. This hollow was formed by a stream which came down between the Esquiline and the Quirinal beyond it, and made its exit towards the river on the other side by way of the Velabrum. As the city extended itself, amalgamating with another community on the Quirinal, this hollow became a common meeting-place and market, and the stream was in due time drained by that Cloaca which we saw debouching into the Tiber near the bridge we crossed. The upper course of this stream, between Esquiline and Quirinal, is a densely populated quarter known as the Argiletum, and higher up as the Subura,[2] where artisans and shops abounded. The lower part of its course, where it has become an invisible drain, is also a crowded street, the vicus Tuscus, leading to the Velabrum, and so to our starting-point at the Forum Boarium.

Let us now descend the Clivus sacer, crossing to the right-hand side of the slope, which the via Sacra now follows, and reach the Forum by the fornix Fabiana. Close by to our left is the round temple of Vesta, where the sacred fire of the State is kept ever

---

[1] Cic. *pro Plancio*, ch. 7.   Cp. Horace, *Sat.* i. 9 ; Lucilius, *Frag.* 9 (ed. Baehrens), which last will be quoted in another context.

[2] On the vexed question of the position of the Subura and its history see Wissowa, *Gesammelte Abhandlungen*, p. 230 foll.

burning by its guardians, the Vestal Virgins, and here too is their dwelling, the Atrium Vestae, and also that of the Pontifex Maximus (Regia), in whose potestas they were; these three buildings, then insignificant to look at, constituted the religious focus of the oldest Rome.[1]   A little farther again to the left is the temple of Castor and the spring of Juturna, lately excavated, where the Twins watered their steeds after the battle of the lake Regillus.   In front of us we can see over the heads of the crowd the Rostra at the farther end of the Forum, where an orator is perhaps addressing a crowd (*contio*) on some political question of the moment, and giving some occupation to the idlers in the throng; and to the right of the Rostra is the Comitium or assembling-place of the people, with the Curia, the ancient meeting-hall of the senate.   In Cicero's day the mere shopman had been got rid of from the Forum, and his place is taken by the banker and money-lender, who do their business in *tabernae* stretching in rows along both sides of the open space.   Much public business, judicial and other, is done in the Basilicae,— roofed halls with colonnades, of which there are already five, and a new one is arising on the south side, of which the ground-plan, as it was extended soon afterwards by Julius Caesar, is now completely laid bare.   But it is becoming evident that the business of the Empire cannot be much longer crowded into this narrow space of the Forum, which is only

---

[1] For excavations here see Lanciani, *op. cit.* p. 221 foll.

about two hundred yards long by seventy; and the next two generations will see new Fora laid out, larger and more commodious, by Julius and Augustus, in the direction of the Quirinal.

Now making our way towards the Capitol, we pass the famous temple or rather gate of the double-headed Janus, standing at the entrance to the Forum from the Argiletum and the Porta Esquilina; then the Comitium and Curia (which last was burnt by the mob in 52 B.C., at the funeral of Clodius), and reach the foot of the Clivus Capitolinus, just where was (and is) the ancient underground prison, called Tullianum, from the old word for a spring (*tullus*), the scene of the deaths of Jugurtha and many noble captives, and of the Catilinarian conspirators on December 5, 63. Here the via Sacra turns, in front of the temple of Concordia, to ascend the Capitol. Behind this temple, extending farther under the slope, is the Tabularium, already mentioned, which is still much as it was then; and below us to the south is the temple of Saturnus, the treasury (*aerarium*) of the Roman people. Thus at this end of the Forum, under the Capitol, are the whole set of public offices, facing the ancient religious buildings around the Vesta temple at the other end.

The way now turns again to the right, and reaches the depression between the two summits of the Capitoline hill. Leaving the arx on the left, we reach by a long flight of steps the greatest of all Roman temples, placed on a long platform with solid substructures of Etruscan workmanship, part of which is still to be seen in the garden of the German Embassy. The temple of Jupiter Optimus Maximus, with his companions Juno and Minerva, was in a very special sense the religious centre of the State and its dominion. Whatever view he might take of the gods and their cults, every Roman instinctively believed that this great Jupiter, above all other deities, watched over the welfare of Rome, and when a generation later Virgil placed the destiny of Rome's mythical hero in the hands of Jupiter, every Roman recognised in this his own inherited con- viction. Here, on the first day of their office, the higher magistrates offered sacrifice in fulfilment of the vows of their predecessors, and renewed the same vows themselves. The consul about to leave the city for a foreign war made it his last duty to sacrifice here, and on his return he deposited here his booty. Here came the triumphal procession along the Sacred Way, the conquering general attired and painted like the statue of the god within the temple; and upon the knees of the statue he placed his wreath of laurel, rendering up to the deity what he had himself deigned to bestow. Here too, from a pedestal on the platform, a statue of Jupiter looked straight over the Forum,[1] the Curia, and the Comitium; and Cicero could declare from the Rostra, and know that in so declaring he was touching the hearts of his hearers, that on that same day on which it had first been

---

[1] Cic. *Cat.* iii. 9. 21 foll.

so placed, the machinations of Catiline and his
conspirators had been detected.[1] " Ille, ille Iupiter
restitit; ille Capitolium, ille haec templa, ille cunctam
urbem, ille vos omnes salvos esse voluit."

The temple had been destroyed by fire in the time
of Sulla, and its restoration was not as yet finally
completed at the time of our imaginary walk.[2] It
faced towards the river and the Aventine, i.e. south-
east, according to the rules of augural lore, like all
Roman public buildings of the Republican period.
From the platform on which it stands we look down
on the Forum Boarium, from which we started,
connected with the Forum by the Velabrum and the
vicus Tuscus; and more to the right below us is the
Campus Martius, with access to the city by that
Porta Carmentalis which Evander showed to Aeneas.
This spacious exercise-ground of Roman armies is
already beginning to be built upon; in fact the
Circus Flaminius has been there for more than a
century and a half, and now the new theatre of
Pompeius, the first stone theatre in Rome, rises
beyond it towards the Vatican hill. But there is
ample space left; for it is nearly a mile from the
Capitol to that curve of the Tiber above which the
Church of St. Peter now stands; and on this large
expanse, at the present day, the greater part of a
population of nearly half a million is housed.

---

[1] Formerly we may assume that it faced south or south-east, like the
temple.

[2] It was completed by Caesar in 46 B.C.

I do not propose to take the reader farther. We have been through the heart of the city, as it was at the close of the Republican period, and from the platform of the great temple we can see all else that we need to keep in mind in these chapters.

CHAPTER II

THE LOWER POPULATION (PLEBS URBANA)

THE walk we have been taking has led us only
through the heart of the city, in which were the
public buildings, temples, basilicas, porticos, etc.,
of which we hear so much in Latin literature. It
was on the hills which are spurs of the plain beyond,
and which look down over the Forum and the Campus
Martius, the Caelian, Esquiline, and Quirinal, with
the hollows lying between them, and also on the
Aventine by the river, that the mass of the population
lived. The most ancient fortification of completed
Rome, the so-called Servian wall and *agger*, enclosed
a singularly large space, larger, we are told, than
the walls of any old city in Italy;[1] it is likely
that a good part of this space was long unoccupied
by houses, and served to shelter the cattle of the
farmers living outside, when an enemy was threatening attack. But in Cicero's time, as to-day, all this
space was covered with dwellings; and as the centre
of the city came to be occupied with public buildings,
erected on sites often bought from private owners, the

---

[1] Beloch, *Bewölkerung*, p. 382.

houses were gradually pushed out along the roads beyond the walls. Exactly the same process has been going on for centuries in the University city of Oxford, where the erection of colleges gradually absorbed the best sites within the old walls, so that many of the dwelling-houses are now quite two miles from the centre of the city. The fact is attested for Rome by the famous municipal law of Julius Caesar, which directs that for a mile outside the gates every resident is to look after the repair of the road in front of his own house.[1]

As a general rule, the heights in Rome were occupied by the better class of residents, and the hollows by the lower stratum of population. This was not indeed entirely so, for poor people no doubt lived on the Aventine, the Caelian, and parts of the Esquiline. But the Palatine was certainly an aristocratic quarter; the Carinae, the height looking down on the hollow where the Colosseum now stands, had many good houses, e.g. those of Pompeius and of Quintus Cicero, and we know of one man of great wealth, Atticus, who lived on the Quirinal.[2] It was in the narrow hollows leading down from these heights to the Forum, such as the Subura between Esquiline and Quirinal, and the Argiletum farther down near the Forum, that we meet in literature with what we may call the working classes; the

---

[1] *C.I.L.* i. 206, and Dessau, *Inscr. Lat. Selectae*, ii. 1. p. 493.

[2] Cic. *ad Q. Fratr.* iii. 1. 14; Suet. *de Grammaticis*, 15; Corn. Nepos, *Atticus*, 13.

Argiletum, for example, was famous both for its booksellers and its shoemakers,[1] and the Subura is the typical street of tradesmen. And no doubt the big lodging-houses in which the lower classes dwelt were to be found in all parts of Rome, except the strictly aristocratic districts like the Palatine.

The whole free population may roughly be divided into three classes, of which the first two, constituting together the social aristocracy, were a mere handful in number compared with the third. At the top of the social order was the governing class, or *ordo senatorius* : then came the *ordo equester*, comprising all the men of business, bankers, money-lenders, and merchants (*negotiatores*) or contractors for the raising of taxes and many other purposes (*publicani*). Of these two upper classes and their social life we shall see something in later chapters ; at present we are concerned with the "masses," at least 320,000 in number,[2] and the social problems which their existence presented, or ought to have presented, to an intelligent Roman statesman of Cicero's time.

Unfortunately, just as we know but little of the populous districts of Rome, so too we know little of its industrial population. The upper classes, including all writers of memoirs and history, were not interested in them. There was no philanthropist, no

---

[1] Hülsen-Jordan, *Röm. Topographie*, vol. i. part iii. p. 323.

[2] This is the number receiving corn gratis when Julius Caesar reformed the corn-distribution.—Suetonius. *Iul.* 41.

devoted inquirer like Mr. Charles Booth, to investi-
gate their condition or try to ameliorate it. The
statesman, if he troubled himself about them at all,
looked on them as a dangerous element of society,
only to be considered as human beings at election
time; at all other times merely as animals that had
to be fed, in order to keep them from becoming an
active peril. The philosopher, even the Stoic, whose
creed was by far the most ennobling in that age,
seems to have left the dregs of the people quite out
of account; though his philosophy nominally took
the whole of mankind into its cognisance, it believed
the masses to be degraded and vicious, and made no
effort to redeem them.[1] The Stoic might profess the
tenderest feeling towards all mankind, as Cicero did,
when moved by some recent reading of Stoic
doctrine; he might say that "men were born for the
sake of men, that each should help the other," or
that "Nature has inclined us to love men, for this
is the foundation of all law";[2] but when in actual
social or political contact with the same masses
Cicero could only speak of them with contempt or
disgust. It is a melancholy and significant fact that
what little we do know from literature about this
class is derived from the part they occasionally
played in riots and revolutionary disorders. It is
fortunately quite impossible that the historian of the

---

[1] See Zeller, *Stoics*, etc., Eng. trans. p. 255 foll.

[2] Cic. *de Legibus*, i. 15. 43. It was not as yet possible to be "poor,
yet making many rich"; to have nothing and yet to possess all things.

future should take account of the life of the educated
and wealthy only; but in the history of the past,
and especially of the last three centuries B.C., we have
to contend with this difficulty, and can only now and
then find side-lights thrown upon the great mass
of mankind.   The crime, the crowding, the occasional
suffering from starvation and pestilence, in the un-
fashionable quarters of such a city as Rome, these
things are hidden from us, and rarely even suggested
by the histories we commonly read.

The three questions to which I wish to make
some answer in this chapter are : (1) how was this
population housed ? (2) how was it supplied with
food and clothing ? and (3) how was it employed ?

1. It was of course impossible in a city like Rome
that each man, married or unmarried, should have
his own house; this is not so even in the great
majority of modern industrial towns, though we in
England are accustomed to see our comparatively
well-to-do artisans dwelling in cottages spreading
out into the country.   At Rome only the wealthy
families lived in separate houses (*domus*), about
which we shall have something to say in another
chapter.   The mass of the population lived, or rather
ate and slept (for southern climates favour an out-
of-door life), in huge lodging-houses called islands
(*insulae*), because they were detached from other
buildings, and had streets on all sides of them, as
islands have water.[1]   These *insulae* were often three

---

[1] See the definition of insula in Festus. p. 111. and for insula generally

or four stories high;[1] the ground-floor was often
occupied by shops, kept perhaps by some of
the lodgers, and the upper floors by single rooms,
with small windows looking out on the street or
into an interior court. The common name for
such a room was *coenaculum*, or dining-room, a
word which seems to be taken over from the
coenaculum of private houses, i.e. an eating-room
on the first floor, where there was one. Once
indeed we hear of an *aedicula* in an insula,
which was perhaps the equivalent of a modern
" flat "; it was inhabited by a young bachelor
of good birth, M. Caelius Rufus, the friend of
Cicero, and in this case the insula was probably
one of a superior kind.[2] The common lodging-
house must have been simply a rabbit-warren,
the crowded inhabitants using their rooms only
for eating and sleeping, while for the most part
they prowled about, either idling or getting such
employment as they could, legitimate or otherwise.

In such a life there could of course have been no
idea of home, or of that simple and sacred family life
which had once been the ethical basis of Roman

Middleton's article " Domus " in the *Dict. of Antiquities*, ed. 2. De Marchi
(*La Religione nella vita domestica*, i. p. 80) compares the big lodging-houses
of the poor at Naples.

[1] Cicero (*Leg. Agr.* ii. 35. 96) describes Rome as being (in comparison with
Capua) " in montibus positam et convallibus, coenaculis (i.e. upper rooms)
sublatam atque suspensam, non optimis viis," etc. Vitruv. ii. 17 is the
locus classicus.

Cic. *pro Caelio* 17.

society.[1] When we read Cicero's thrilling language
about the loss of his own house, after his return from
exile, and then turn to think of the homeless crowds
in the rabbit-warrens of Rome, we can begin to feel
the contrast between the wealth and poverty of that
day. "What is more strictly protected," he says,
"by all religious feeling, than the house of each
individual citizen? Here is his altar, his hearth,
here are his Di Penates: here he keeps all the objects
of his worship and performs all his religious rites:
his house is a refuge so solemnly protected, that no
one can be torn from it by force."[2] The warm-
hearted Cicero is here, as so often, dreaming dreams:
the "each individual citizen" of whom he speaks is
the citizen of his own acquaintance, not the vast
majority, with whom his mind does not trouble itself.

These insulae were usually built or owned by men
of capital, and were often called by the names of
their owners. Cicero, in one of his letters,[3] incidentally mentions that he had money thus invested; and
we are disposed to wonder whether his insulae were
kept in good repair, for in another letter he happens
to tell his man of business that shops (tabernae)
belonging to him were tumbling down and unoccupied. It is more than likely that many of the

---

[1] In *C.I.L.* vi. 65-67 we find a Bona Dea erected "in tutelam insulae," i.e.
a common cult for all the lodgers. De Marchi *l.c.* compares the common
shrine of the Neapolitan lodging-house. Tutela is mentioned as a protecting
deity both of insulae and domus by St. Jerome, *Com. in Isaiam*, 672.

[2] Cic. *de Domo* 109.

[3] Cic. *ad Att.* xv. 17 ; cp. xiv. 9.

insulae were badly built by speculators, and liable to
collapse. The following passage from Plutarch's *Life
of Crassus* suggests this, though, if Plutarch is right,
Crassus did not build himself, but let or sold his sites
and builders to others : " Observing (in Sulla's time)
the accidents that were familiar at Rome, conflagra-
tions and tumbling down of houses owing to their
weight and crowded state, he bought slaves who were
architects and builders. Having collected these to
the number of more than five hundred, it was his
practice to buy up houses on fire, and houses next to
those on fire : for the owners, frightened and anxious,
would sell them cheap. And thus the greater part
of Rome fell into the hands of Crassus : but though
he had so many artisans, he built no house except
his own, for he used to say that those who were fond
of building ruined themselves without the help of an
enemy." [1] The fall of houses, and their destruction
in the frequent fires, became familiar features of life
at Rome about this time, and are alluded to by
Catullus in his twenty-third poem, and later on by
Strabo in his description of Rome (p. 235). It must
indeed have often happened that whole families were
utterly homeless ; [2] and in those days there were no
insurance offices, no benefit societies, no philanthropic
institutions to rescue the suffering from undeserved
misery. As we shall see later on, they were con-

---

[1] Plut. *Crassus* 2 : perhaps from Fenestella.
[2] "Dormientem in taberna," Asconius, ed. Clark, p. 37. Cp. Tacitus,
Hist. i. 86, for persons sleeping in tabernae.

stantly in debt, and in the hands of the money-lender; and against his extortions their judicial remedies were most precarious. But all this is hidden from our eyes: only now and again we can hear a faint echo of their inarticulate cry for help.

2. The needs of these poorer classes in respect of food and drink were very small; it was only the vast number of them that made the supply difficult. The Italians, like the Greeks,[1] were then as now almost entirely vegetarians; cattle and sheep were used for the production of cheese, leather, and wool, or for sacrifices to the gods; the only animal commonly eaten, until luxury came in with increasing wealth, was the pig, and grain and vegetables were the staple food of the poor man, both in town and country. Among the lesser poems ascribed to Virgil there is one, the *Moretum*, which gives a charming picture of the food-supply of the small cultivator in the country. He rises very early, gropes his way to the hearth, and stirs the embers into flame: then takes from his meal-bin a supply of grain for three days and proceeds to grind it in a hand-mill, knead it with water, shape it into round cakes divided into four parts like a "hot-cross bun," and, with the help of his one female slave, to bake these in the embers. He has no sides of smoked bacon, says the poet, hanging from his roof, but only a cheese, so to add to his meal he goes into his garden and gathers thence a number of various herbs and vegetables,

---

[1] Tucker, *Life in Ancient Athens*, p. 10.

which he then makes into the hotch-potch, or *pot-au-feu*, which gives the name to the poem. This bit of delicate genre-painting, which is as good in its way as anything in Crabbe's homely poems, has indeed nothing to tell us of life in an insula at Rome ; but it may serve to show what was the ordinary food of the Italian of that day.[1] The absence of the sides of bacon (" durati sale terga suis," line 57) is interesting. No doubt the Roman took meat when he could get it ; but to have to subsist on it, even for a short time, was painful to him, and more than once Caesar remarks on the endurance of his soldiers in submitting to eat meat when corn was not to be had.[2]

The corn which was at this time the staple food of the Romans of the city was wheat, and wheat of a good kind ; in primitive times it had been an inferior species called *far*, which survived in Cicero's day only in the form of cakes offered to the gods in religious ceremonies. The wheat was not brought from Italy or even from Latium ; what each Italian community then grew was not more than supplied its own inhabitants,[3] and the same was the case with the country villas of the rich, and the huge sheep-farms worked by slaves. By far the greater part of Italy is mountainous, and not well suited to the production

---

[1] The *Moretum* may be a translation from a Greek poet, perhaps Parthenius, but it is certainly as well adapted to the experience of Italians.

[2] e.g. Caesar, *Bell. Civ.* iii. 47. Cp. Tacitus, *Ann.* xiv. 24.

[3] On this point see Salvioli, *Le Capitalisme dans le monde antique*, ch. vi. This is a book with many shortcomings, but written by an Italian who knows his own country

D

of corn on a large scale; and for long past other
causes had combined to limit what production there
was.   Transport too, whether by road or river, was
full of difficulty, while on the other hand a glance at
the map will show that the voyage for corn-ships
between Rome and Sicily, Sardinia, or the province of
Africa (the former dominion of Carthage), was both
short and easy—far shorter and easier than the voyage
from Cisalpine Gaul or even from Apulia, where the
peninsula was richest in good corn-land.   So we are
not surprised to find that, according to tradition, which
is fully borne out by more certain evidence,[1] corn had
been brought to Rome from Sicily as early as 492 B.C.
to relieve a famine, or that since Sicily, Sardinia, and
Africa had become Roman provinces, their vast productive capacity was utilised to feed the great city.

Nor indeed need we be surprised to find that the
State has taken over the task of feeding the Roman
population, and of feeding it cheaply, if only we are
accustomed to think, not merely to read, about life in
the city at this period.   Nothing is more difficult for
the ordinary reader of ancient history than to realise
the difficulty of feeding large masses of human beings,
whether crowded in towns or soldiers in the field.   Our
means of transport are now so easily and rapidly set in
action and maintained, that it would need a war with
some great sea-power to convince us that London
or Glasgow might, under certain untoward circumstances, be starved; and as our attention has never

---

[1] See the author's *Roman Festivals*, p. 76 (Cerealia).

been drawn to the details of food-supply, we do not
readily see why there should have been any such
difficulty at Rome as to call for the intervention of
the State.   Perhaps the best way to realise the problem
is to reflect that every adult inhabitant needed about
four and a half pecks of corn per month, or some three
pounds a day ; so that if the population of Rome be
taken at half a million in Cicero's time, a million and
a half pounds would be demanded as the daily consumption of the people.[1]   I have already said that
in the last three centuries B.C. there was a universal
tendency to leave the country for the towns ; and we
now know that many other cities besides Rome not
only felt the same difficulty, but actually used the
same remedy—State importation of cheap corn.[2]
Even comparatively small cities like Dyrrhachium and
Apollonia in Epirus, as Caesar tells us while narrat-
ing his own difficulty in feeding his army there, used
for the most part imported corn.[3]   And we must
remember that while some of the greatest cities on
the Mediterranean, such as Alexandria and Antioch,
were within easy reach of vast corn-fields, this was
not the case with Rome.   Either she must organise
her corn-supply on a secure basis, or get rid of her
swarms of poor inhabitants ; the latter alternative
might have been possible if she had been willing to

---

[1] Marquardt, *Staatsverwaltung*, ii. pp. 107, 110 foll.   A modius, which
=nearly a peck, contained about 20 lb. of wheat (Pliny, *N. H.* xviii. 66).
Four and a half modii × 20 = 90 lb.

[2] Hirschfeld, *Verwaltungsbeamten*, ed. 2, p. 231 ; Strabo, p. 652 (Rhodes).

[3] Caesar, *B. C.* iii. 42. 3.

let them starve, but probably in no other way. To attempt to put them out upon the land again was hopeless ; they knew nothing of agriculture, and were unused to manual labour, which they despised.

Thus ever since Rome had been a city of any size it had been the duty of the plebeian aediles to see that it was adequately supplied with corn, and in times of dearth or other difficulty these magistrates had to take special measures to procure it. With a population steadily rising since the war with Hannibal, and after the acquisition of two corn-growing provinces, to which Africa was added in 146 B.C., it was natural that they should turn their attention more closely to the resources of these ; and now the provincial governors had to see that the necessary amount of corn was furnished from these provinces at a fixed price, and that a low one.[1] In 123 B.C. Gaius Gracchus took the matter in hand, and made it a part of his whole far-reaching political scheme. The plebs urbana had become a very awkward element in the calculations of a statesman, and to have it in a state of starvation, or even fearing such a state, was dangerous in the extreme, as every Roman statesman had to learn in the course of the two following centuries. The aediles, we may guess, were quite unequal to the work demanded of them ; and at times victorious provincial governors would bring home great quantities of corn and give it away gratis for their private purposes, with bad results both economic and

[1] Marquardt, op. cit. p. 110.

moral.   Gracchus saw that the work of supply needed
a thorough organisation in regard to production,
transport, warehousing, and finance, and set about it
with a delight in hard work such as no Roman statesman had shown before, believing that if the people
could be fed cheaply and regularly, they would cease
to be "a troublesome neighbour."[1]   We do not
know the details of his scheme of organisation except
in one particular, the price at which the corn was to
be sold per *modius* (peck) : this was to be six and
one-third *asses*, or rather less than half the normal
market-price of the day, so far as it can be made out.
Whether he believed that the cost of production
could be brought down to this level by regularity of
demand and transport we cannot tell; it seems at
any rate probable that he had gone carefully into
the financial aspect of the business.[2]   But there can
hardly be a doubt that he miscalculated, and that
the result of the law by which he sought to effect his
object was a yearly loss to the treasury, so that after
his time, and until his law was repealed by Sulla, the
people were really being fed largely at the expense
of the State, and thus lapsing into a state of semi-
pauperism, with bad ethical consequences.

One of these consequences was that inconsiderate
statesmen would only too readily seize the chance of
reducing the price of the corn still lower, as was done
by Saturninus in 100 B.C., for political purposes.   To

---

[1] For Gracchus' motives see a paper by the present writer in the *English
Historical Review* for 1905, p. 221 foll.   [2] Cic. *Tusc. Disp.* iii. 20. 48.

prevent this Sulla abolished the Gracchan system *in toto*; but it was renewed in 73 B.C., and in 58 the demagogue P. Clodius made the distribution of corn gratuitous. In 46 Caesar found that no less than 320,000 persons were receiving corn from the State for nothing; by a bill, of which we still possess a part,[1] he reduced the number to 150,000, and by a rigid system of rules, of which we know something, contrived to ensure that it should be kept at that point. With the policy of Augustus and his successors in regard to the corn-supply (*annona*) I am not here concerned; but it is necessary to observe that with the establishment of the Empire the plebs urbana ceased to be of any importance in politics, and could be treated as a petted population, from whom no harm was to be expected if they were kept comfortable and amused. Augustus seems to have found himself compelled to take up this attitude towards them, and he was able to do so because he had thoroughly reorganised the public finance and knew what he could afford for the purpose. But in the time of Cicero the people were still powerful in legislation and elections, and the public finance was disorganised and in confusion; and the result was that the corn-supply was mixed up with politics,[2] and handled by reckless politicians in a way that was as ruinous to the treasury as it was to the moral

---

[1] Lex Julia municipalis, 1-20, compared with Suetonius, *Jul.* 41.

[2] A good example will be found in Cic. *ad Att.* iv. 1. 6 foll. ; the first letter written by Cicero after his return from exile.

welfare of the city. The whole story, from Gracchus onwards, is a wholesome lesson on the mischief of granting "outdoor relief" in any form whatever, without instituting the means of inquiry into each individual case. Gracchus' intentions were doubtless honest and good; but "ubi semel recto deerratum est, in praeceps pervenitur."

The drink of the Roman was water, but he mixed it with wine whenever he had the chance. Fortunately for him he had no other intoxicating drink; we hear neither of beer nor spirits in Roman literature. Italy was well suited to the cultivation of the vine; and though down to the last century of the Republic the choice kinds of wine came chiefly from Greece, yet we have unquestionable proof that wine was made in the neighbourhood of Rome at the very outset of Roman history. In the oldest religious calendar [1] we find two festivals called Vinalia, one in April and the other in August; what exactly was the relation of each of them to the operations of viticulture is by no means clear, but we know that these operations were under the protection of Jupiter, and that his priest, the Flamen Dialis, offered to him the first-fruits of the vintage. The production of rough wine must indeed have been large, for we happen to know that it was at times remarkably cheap. In 250 B.C., in many ways a wonderfully productive year, wine was sold at an *as* the *congius*, which is nearly three quarts; [2] under the early

---

[1] See my *Roman Festivals*, pp. 85 and 204.   [2] Pliny, *Nat. Hist.* xviii. 17.

Empire Columella (iii. 3. 10) reckoned the amphora (nearly 6 gallons) at 15 sesterces, i.e. about eightpence. That the common citizen did expect to be able to qualify his water with wine seems proved by a story told by Suetonius, that when the people complained to Augustus that the price of wine was too high, he curtly and wisely answered that Agrippa had but lately given them an excellent water-supply.[1] It looks as though they were claiming to have wine as well as grain supplied them by the government at a low price or gratuitously; but this was too much even for Augustus.

For his water the Roman, it need hardly be said, paid nothing. On the whole, at the time of which we are speaking he was fairly well supplied with it; but in this, as in so many other matters of urban administration, it was under Augustus that an abundant supply was first procured and maintained by an excellent system of management. Frontinus, to whose work *de Aqueductibus* we owe almost all that we know about the Roman water-supply, tells us that for four hundred and forty-one years after the foundation of the city the Romans contented themselves with such water as they could get from the Tiber, from wells, and from natural springs, and adds that some of the springs were in his day still held in honour on account of their health-giving qualities.[2] Cicero describes Rome, in his idealising

---

[1] Suet. *Aug.* 42.
[2] Frontinus i. 4. The date of his work is towards the end of the first century A.D.

way, as "locum fontibus abundantem," and twenty-three springs are known to have existed ; but as early as 312 B.C. it was found necessary to seek elsewhere for a purer and more regular supply. More than six miles from Rome, on the via Collatina, springs were found and utilised for this purpose, which have lately been re-discovered at the bottom of some stone quarries ; and hence the water was brought by underground pipes along the line of the same road to the city, and through it to the foot of the Aventine, the plebeian quarter. This was the Aqua Appia, named after the famous censor Appius Claudius Caecus, whom Mommsen has shown to have been a friend of the people.[1] Forty years later another censor, Manius Curius Dentatus, brought a second supply, also by an underground channel, from the river Anio near Tibur (Tivoli), the water of which, never of the first quality, was used for the irrigation of gardens and the flushing of drains. In 144 B.C. it was found that these two old aqueducts were out of repair and insufficient, and this time a praetor, Q. Marcius Rex (probably through the influence of a family clique), was commissioned to set them in order and to procure a fresh supply. He went much farther than his predecessors had gone for springs, and drew a volume of excellent and clear cold water from the Sabine hills beyond Tibur, thirty-six miles from the city, which had the highest repu-

---

[1] See Lanciani, *Ruins and Excavations*, p. 48 ; Mommsen, *Hist.* vol. i. Appendix.

tation at all times; and for the last six miles of its course it was carried above ground upon a series of arches.[1] One other aqueduct was added in 125 B.C., the Aqua Tepula, so called because its water was unusually warm; and the whole amount of water entering Rome in the last century of the Republic is estimated at more than 700,000 cubic metres per diem, which would amply suffice for a population of half a million. At the present day Rome, with a population of 450,000, receives from all sources only 379,000.[2] Baths, both public and private, were already beginning to come into fashion; of these more will be said later on. The water for drinking was collected in large *castella*, or reservoirs, and thence distributed into public fountains, of which one still survives—the "Trofei di Mario," in the Piazza Vittorio Emmanuele on the Esquiline.[3] When the supply came to be large enough, the owners of insulae and domus were allowed to have water laid on by private pipes, as we have it in modern towns; but it is not certain when this permission was first given.

3. But we must return to the individual Roman of the masses, whom we have now seen well supplied with the necessaries of life, and try to form some

---

[1] Frontinus i. 7, whose account is confirmed by the recently discovered Epitomes of Livy's lost books.—Grenfell and Hunt, *Oxyrhynchus Papyri*, iv. 113.

[2] See the useful table in Lanciani, *op. cit.* 58.

[3] This dates from the reign of Domitian. The nature of the public fountain may be realised at Pompeii. See Mau, *Pompeii, its Life and Art*, p. 224 foll.

idea of the way in which he was employed, or earned a living. This is by no means an easy task, for these small people, as we have already seen, did not interest their educated fellow-citizens, and for this reason we hear hardly anything of them in the literature of the time. Not only a want of philanthropic feeling in their betters, but an inherited contempt for all small industry and retail dealing, has helped to hide them away from us : an *inherited* contempt, because it is in fact a survival from an older social system, when the citizen did not need the work of the artisan and small retailer, but supplied all his own wants within the circle of his household, i.e. his own family and slaves, and produced on his farm the material of his food and clothing. And the survival was all the stronger, because even in the late Republic the abundant supply of slaves enabled the man of capital still to dispense largely with the services of the tradesman and artisan.

Cicero expresses this contempt for the artisan and trading classes in more than one striking passage. One, in his treatise on Duties, is probably paraphrased from the Greek of Panaetius, the philosopher who first introduced Stoicism to the Romans, and modified it to suit their temperament, but it is quite clear that Cicero himself entirely endorses the Stoic view. "All gains made by hired labourers," he says, " are dishonourable and base, for what we buy of them is their labour, not their artistic skill : with them the very gain itself does but increase the slavishness of the work. All retail dealing too may be put in the same category, for the dealer will gain nothing except by profuse lying, and nothing is more disgraceful than untruthful huckstering. Again, the work of all artisans (*opifices*) is sordid; there can be nothing honourable in a workshop."[1]

If this view of the low character of the work of the artisan and retailer should be thought too obviously a Greek one, let the reader turn to the description by Livy[2]—a true gentleman—of the low origin of Terentius Varro, the consul who was in command at Cannae; he uses the same language as Cicero. "He sprang from an origin not merely humble but sordid: his father was a butcher, who sold his own meat, and employed his son in this slavish business." The story may not be true, and indeed it is not a very probable one, but it well represents the inherited feeling towards retail trade of the Roman of the higher classes of society,—a feeling so tenacious of life, that even in modern England, where it arose from much the same causes as in the ancient world, it has only within the last century begun to die out.[3]

Yet in Rome these humble workers existed and made a living for themselves from the very beginning, as far as we can guess, of real city life. They are the necessary and inevitable product of the growth of a town population, and of the resulting

[1] Cic. *de Officiis*, i. 42. 150.   [2] Livy xxii. 25 *ad fin.*
[3] It is very conspicuous, e.g., in the novels of Jane Austen.

division of labour. The following passage from a
work on industrial organisation in England may be
taken as closely representing the same process in
early Rome :[1] "The town arose as a centre in which
the surplus produce of many villages could be profitably disposed of by exchange. Trade thus became
a settled occupation, and trade prepared the way for
the establishment of the handicrafts, by furnishing
capital for the support of the craftsmen, and by
creating a regular market for their products. It was
possible for a great many bodies of craftsmen,—the
weavers, tailors, butchers, bakers, etc., to find a liveli-
hood, each craft devoting itself to the supply of a
single branch of those wants which the village household had attempted very imperfectly to satisfy by its
own labours."

As in mediaeval Europe, so in early Rome, the
same conditions produced the same results : we find
the craftsmen of the town forming themselves into
gilds, not only for the protection of their trade, but
from a natural instinct of association, and providing
these gilds, on the model of the older groups of
family and gens, with a religious centre and a patron
deity. The gilds (*collegia*) of Roman craftsmen were
attributed to Numa, like so many other religious
institutions ; they included associations of weavers,
fullers, dyers, shoemakers, doctors, teachers, painters,
etc.,[2] and were mainly devoted to Minerva as the

---

[1] G. Unwin, *Industrial Organisation*, etc., p. 2.
[2] Plutarch, *Numa*, 17 ; Ovid, *Fasti*, iii 810 foll

deity of handiwork. "The society that witnessed the coming of Minerva from Etruria . . . little knew that in her temple on the Aventine was being brought to expression the trade-union idea." [1] These *collegia opificum*, most unfortunately, pass entirely out of our sight, until they reappear in the age of Cicero in a very different form, as clubs used for political purposes, but composed still of the lowest strata of the free population (*collegia sodalicia*). [2] The history and causes of their disappearance and metamorphosis are lost to us; but it is not hard to guess that the main cause is to be found in the great economic changes that followed the Hannibalic war,—the vast number of slaves imported, and the consequent resuscitation of the old system of the economic independence of the great households; the decay of religious practice, which affected both public and private life in a hundred different ways; and that steady growth of individualism which is characteristic of eras of town life, and especially of the last three centuries B.C. It is curious to notice that by the time these old gilds emerge into light again as clubs that could be used for political purposes, a new source of gain, and one that was really sordid, had been placed within the reach of the Roman plebs urbana : it was possible to make money by your vote in the election of magistrates. In that degenerate

[1] J. B. Carter, *The Religion of Numa*, p. 48.
[2] Marq. iii. p. 138. See also Kornemann's article "Collegium" in Pauly. Wissowa, *Real-Encykl.*, and Waltzing, *Corporations professionelles chez les Romains*, i. p. 78 foll.

age, when the vast accumulation of capital made it
possible for a man to purchase his way to power, in
spite of repeated attempts to check the evil by
legislation, the old principle of honourable association
was used to help the small man to make a living by
choosing the unprincipled and often the incompetent
to undertake the government of the Empire.

Apart, however, from such illegal means of making
money, there was beyond doubt in the Rome of the last
century B.C. a large amount of honest and useful labour
done by free citizens. We must not run away with the
idea that the whole labour of the city was performed
by slaves, who ousted the freeman from his chance
of a living. There was indeed a certain number of
public slaves who did public work for the State;
but on the whole the great mass of the servile population worked entirely within the households and on
the estates of the rich, and did not interfere to any
sensible degree with the labour of the small freeman.
As has been justly observed by Salvioli,[1] never at any
period did the Roman proletariat complain of the
competition of slave labour as detrimental to its own
interests. Had there been no slave labour there, the
small freeman might indeed have had a wider field of
enterprise, and have been better able to accumulate
a small capital by undertaking work for the great
families, which was done, as it was, by their slaves.
But he was not aware of this, and the two kinds of
labour, the paid and the unpaid, went on side by side

[1] *Le Capitalisme*, etc., p. 144 foll.

without active rivalry. No doubt slavery helped to foster idleness, as it did in the Southern States of America before the Civil War ;[1] no doubt there were plenty of idle ruffians in the city, ready to steal, to murder, or to hire themselves out as the armed followers of a political desperado like Clodius; but the simple necessities of the life of those who had no slaves of their own gave employment, we may be certain, to a great number of free tradesmen and artisans and labourers of a more unskilled kind.

To begin with, we may ask the pertinent question, how the corn sold cheap by the State was made into bread for the small consumer. Pliny gives us very valuable information, which we may accept as roughly correct, that until the year 171 B.C. there were no bakers in Rome.[2] "The Quirites," he says, "made their own bread, which was the business of the women, as it is still among most peoples." The demand which was thus supplied by a new trade was no doubt caused by the increase of the lower population of the city, by the return of old soldiers, often perhaps unmarried, and by the manumission of slaves, many of whom would also be inexperienced in domestic life and its needs ; and we may probably connect it with the growth of the system of insulae, the great lodging-houses in which it would not be convenient either to grind your corn or to bake your bread. So the bakers, called *pistores* from the old practice of pounding the

---

[1] Cairnes, *Slave Power*, pp. 78, 143 foll.   See below, p. 235.
[2] Pliny, *Nat. Hist.* xviii. 107.

grain in a mortar (*pingere*), soon became a very important and flourishing section of the plebs, though never held in high repute; and in connexion with the distributions of corn some of them probably rose above the level of the small tradesman, like the *pistor redemptor*, Marcus Vergilius Eurysaces, whose monument has come down to us.[1] It should be noted that the trade of the baker included the grinding of the corn; there were no millers at Rome. This can be well illustrated from the numerous bakers' shops which have been excavated at Pompeii.[2] In one of these, for example, we find the four mills in a large apartment at the rear of the building, and close by is the stall for the donkeys that turned them, and also the kneading-room, oven, and store-room. Small bakeries may have had only hand-mills, like the one with which we saw the peasant in the *Moretum* grinding his corn; but the donkey was from quite early times associated with the business, as we know from the fact that at the festival of Vesta, the patron deity of all bakers, they were decorated with wreaths and cakes.[3]

The baking trade must have given employment to a large number of persons. So beyond doubt did the supply of vegetables, which were brought into the city from gardens outside, and formed, after the corn, the staple food of the lower classes. We have

---

[1] *C.I.L.* i. 1013. The date is possibly pre-Augustan.

[2] Mau's *Pompeii*, p. 380.

[3] See my *Roman Festivals*, p. 148. For the mills of various kinds see also Marquardt, *Privatleben*, p. 405.

already seen in the *Moretum* the countryman adding
to his store of bread by a hotch-potch made of
vegetables, and the reader of the poem will have
been astonished at the number mentioned, including
garden herbs for flavouring purposes. The ancients
were fully alive to the value of vegetable food and
of fruit as a healthy diet in warm climates, and
the wonderfully full information we have on this
subject comes from medical writers like Galen, as well
as from Pliny's *Natural History*, and from the writers
on agriculture. The very names of some Roman
families, e.g. the Fabii and Caepiones, carry us back
to a time when beans and onions, which later on were
not so much in favour, were a regular part of the
diet of the Roman people. The list of vegetables
and herbs which we know of as consumed fills a
whole page in Marquardt's interesting account of this
subject, and includes most of those which we use at
the present day.[1] It was only when the consumption
of meat and game came in with the growth of capital
and its attendant luxury, that a vegetarian diet came
to be at all despised. This is another result of
the economic changes caused by the Hannibalic war,
and is curiously illustrated by the speech of the cook
of a great household in the *Pseudolus* of Plautus,
who prides himself on not being as other cooks are,
who make the guests into beasts of the field, stuffing
them with all kinds of food which cattle eat, and
even with things which cattle would refuse![2] But

---

[1] *Privatleben*, p. 409.   [2] *Pseudolus*, 810 foll.

we may take it that at all times the Roman of the
lower class consumed fruit and vegetables largely,
and thus gave employment to a number of market-
gardeners and small purveyors.   Fish he did not eat ;
like meat, it was too expensive ; in fact fish-eating
only came in towards the end of the republican
period, and then only as a luxury for those who could
afford to keep fish-ponds on their estates.   How far
the supply of other luxuries, such as butchers' meat,
gave employment to freemen, is not very clear ; and
perhaps we need here only take account of such
few other products, e.g. oil and wine, as were in
universal demand, though not always procurable by
the needy.   There were plenty of small shops in
Rome where these things were sold ; we have a
picture of such a shop (*caupona*) in another of the
minor Virgilian poems, the *Copa*, i.e. hostess, or perhaps in this case the woman who danced and sang
for the entertainment of the guests.   She plied her
trade in a smoky tavern (fumosa taberna), all the
contents of which are charmingly described in the
poem.[1]

Let us now see how the other chief necessity of
human life, the supply of clothing, gave employment
to the free Roman shopkeeper.

The clothing of the whole Roman population was
originally woollen ; both the outer garment, the *toga*,
and the inner (*tunica*) were of this material, and the

---

[1] Cp. the uncta popina of Horace, *Epist.* i. 14. 21 foll.   Scene in a wine-
shop at Pompeii, Mau, p. 395.

sheep which supplied it were pastured well and conveniently in all the higher hilly regions of Italy. Other materials, linen, cotton, and silk, came in later with the growth of commerce, but the manufacture of these into clothing was chiefly carried on by slaves in the great households, and we need not take any account of them here. The preparation of wool too was in well regulated households undertaken even under the Empire by the women of the family, including the materfamilias herself, and in many an inscription we find the *lanificium* recorded as the honourable practice of matrons.[1] But as in the case of food, so with the simple material of clothing, it was soon found impossible in a city for the poorer citizens to do all that was necessary within their own houses; this is proved conclusively by the mention of gilds of fullers [2] (*fullones*) among those traditionally ascribed to Numa. Fulling is the preparation of cloth by cleansing in water after it has come from the loom; but the fuller's trade of the later republic probably often comprised the actual manufacture of the wool for those who could not do it themselves. He also acted as the washer of garments already in use, and this was no doubt a very important part of his business, for in a warm climate heavy woollen material is naturally apt to get frequently impure and unwholesome. Soap was

---

[1] See, e.g., the Laudatio Turiae, *C.I.L.* vi. i. 1527, line 30.

[2] Only very rich families employed their own fullers.—Marq. *Privat-leben*, p. 512.

not known till the first century of the Empire, and
the process of cleansing was all the more lengthy
and elaborate; the details of the process are known
to us from paintings at Pompeii, where they adorn
the walls of fulleries which have been excavated.
A plan of one of them will be found in Mau's
Pompeii, p. 388. The ordinary woollen garments
were simply bleached white, not dyed; and though
dyers are mentioned among the ancient gilds by
Plutarch, it is probable that he means chiefly fullers
by the Greek word βαφεῖς.

Of the manufacture of leather we do not know so
much. This, like that of wool, must have originally
been carried on in the household, but it is mentioned
as a trade as early as the time of Plautus.[1] The
shoemakers' business was, however, a common one
from the earliest times, probably because it needs
some technical skill and experience; the most natural
division of labour in early societies is sure to produce
this trade. The shoemakers' gild was among the
earliest, and had its centre in the *atrium sutorium*;[2]
and the individual shoemakers carried on their trade
in booths or shops. The Roman shoe, it may be
mentioned here, was of several different kinds,
according to the sex, rank, and occupation of the
wearer; but the two most important sorts were the
calceus, the shoe worn with the toga in the city, and

---

[1] *Menaechmi*, 404: this may, however, be only a translation from the
Greek.

[2] *C.I.L.* i. p. 389.

the mark of the Roman citizen ; and the *pero* or high boot, which was more serviceable in the country.

Among the old gilds were also those of the smiths (*fabri ferrarii*) and the potters (*figuli*), but of these little need be said here, for they were naturally fewer in num¹er than the vendors of food and clothing, and the raw material for their work had, in later times at least, to be brought from a distance. The later Romans seem to have procured their iron-ore from the island of Elba and Spain, Gaul, and other provinces,[1] and to have imported ware of all kinds, especially the finer sorts, from various parts of the Empire ; the commoner kinds, such as the *dolia* or large vessels for storing wine and oil, were certainly made in Rome in the second century B.C., for Cato in his book on agriculture[2] remarks that they could be best procured there. But both these manufactures require a certain amount of capital, and we may doubt whether the free population was largely employed in them ; we know for certain that in the early Empire the manufacture of ware, tiles, bricks, etc., was carried on by capitalists, some of them of noble birth, including even Emperors themselves, and beyond doubt the "hands" they employed were chiefly slaves.[3]

But industries of this kind may serve to remind

[1] Marquardt, *Privatleben*, p. 693 and reff.

[2] Cato, *de re rustica*, 135 ; a very interesting chapter, which shows that of the farmer's "plant," clothing, rugs, carts as well as dolia, were best purchased at Rome.

[3] Marq. *Privatleben*, p. 645.

us of another kind of employment in which the lower classes of Rome and Ostia may have found the means of making a living. The importation of raw materials, and that of goods of all kinds, which was constantly on the increase throughout Roman history, called for the employment of vast numbers of porters, carriers, and what we should call dock hands, working both at Ostia, where the heavier ships were unladed or relieved of part of their cargoes in order to enable them to come up the Tiber,[1] and also at the wharves at Rome under the Aventine. We must also remember that almost all porterage in the city had to be done by men, with the aid of mules or donkeys; the streets were so narrow that in trying to picture what they looked like we must banish from our minds the crowds of vehicles familiar in a modern city. Julius Caesar, in his regulations for the government of the city of Rome, forbade waggons to be driven in the streets in the day-time.[2] Even supposing that a large amount of porterage was done by slaves for their masters, we may reasonably guess that free labour was also employed in this way at Rome, as was certainly the case at Ostia, and also at Pompeii, where the pack-carriers (*saccarii*) and mule-drivers (*muliones*) are among the corporations of free men who have left in the form of *graffiti* appeals to voters to support a particular candidate for election to a magistracy.[3]

---

[1] Strabo, p. 231.   [2] Lex Julia Municipalis, line 56 foll.

[3] Mau, *Pompeii*, p. 377.

Thus we may safely conclude that there was a very considerable amount of employment in Rome available for the poorer citizens, quite apart from the labour performed by slaves. But before closing this chapter it is necessary to point out the precarious conditions under which that employment was carried on, as compared with the industrial conditions of a modern city. It is true enough that the factory system of modern times, with the sweating, the long hours of work, and the unwholesome surroundings of our industrial towns, has produced much misery, much physical degeneracy; and we have also the problem of the unemployed always with us. But there were two points in which the condition of the free artisan and tradesman at Rome was far worse than it is with us, and rendered him liable to an even more hopeless submersion than that which is too often the fate of the modern wage-earner.

First, let us consider that markets, then as now, were liable to fluctuation,—probably more liable then than now, because the supply both of food and of the raw material of manufacture was more precarious owing to the greater difficulties of conveyance. Trade would be bad at times, and many things might happen which would compel the man with little or no capital to borrow money, which he could only do on the security of his stock, or indeed, as the law of Rome still recognised, of his person. Money-lenders were abundant, as we shall find in the next chapter, interest was high, and to fall into the hands of a money-lender was only another step on the way to destruction. At the present day, if a tradesman fails in business, he can appeal to a merciful bankruptcy law, which gives him every chance to satisfy his creditors and to start afresh; or in the case of a single debt, he can be put into a county court where every chance is given him to pay it within a reasonable time. All this machinery, most of which (to the disgrace of modern civilisation) is quite recent in date, was absent at Rome. The only magistrates administering the civil law were the praetors, and though since the reforms of Sulla there were usually eight of these in the city, we can well imagine how hard it would be for the poor debtor in a huge city to get his affairs attended to. Probably in most cases the creditor worked his will with him, took possession of his property without the interference of the law, and so submerged him, or even reduced him to slavery. If he chose to be merciful he could go to the praetor, and get what was called a *missio in bona*, i.e. a legal right to take the whole of his debtor's property, waiving the right to his person. And it must be noted that no more humane law of bankruptcy was introduced until the time of Augustus. No wonder that at least three times in the last century of the Republic there arose a cry for the total abolition of debts (*tabulae novae*): in 88 B.C., after the Social War; in 63, during Cicero's consulship, when political and social revolutionary projects were combined in the conspiracy of Catiline; and in

48, when the economic condition of Italy had been disturbed by the Civil War, and Caesar had much difficulty in keeping unprincipled agitators from applying violent and foolish remedies. But to this we shall return in the next chapter.

Secondly, let us consider that in a large city of to-day the person and property of all, rich or poor, are adequately protected by a sound system of police, and by courts of first instance which are sitting every day. Assault and murder, theft and burglary, are exceptional. It might be going too far to say that at Rome they were the rule; but it is the fact that in what we may call the slums of Rome there was no machinery for checking them. No such machinery had been invented, because according to the old rules of law, still in force, a father might punish his children, a master his slaves, and a murderer or thief might be killed by his intended victim if caught red-handed. This rude justice would suffice in a small city and a simple social system; but it would be totally inadequate to protect life and property in a huge population, such as that of the Rome of the last century B.C. Since the time of Sulla there had indeed been courts for the trial of crimes of violence, and at all times the consuls with their staff of assistants had been charged with the peace of the city; but we may well ask whether the poor Roman of Cicero's day could really benefit either by the consular imperium or the action of the Sullan courts. A slave was the object of his master's care, and theft from a slave was theft from his owner,—if injured or murdered satisfaction could be had for him. But in that age of slack and sordid government it is at least extremely doubtful whether either the person or the property of the lower class of citizen could be said to have been properly protected in the city. And the same anarchy prevailed all over Italy,—from the suburbs of Rome, infested by robbers, to the sheep-farm of the great capitalist, where the traveller might be kidnapped by runaway slaves, to vanish from the sight of men without leaving a trace of his fate.

It is the great merit of Augustus that he made Rome not only a city of marble, but one in which the person and property of all citizens were fairly secure. By a new and rational bankruptcy law, and by a well-organised system of police, he made life endurable even for the poorest. If he initiated a policy which eventually spoilt and degraded the Roman population, if he failed to encourage free industry as persistently as it seems to us that he might have done, he may perhaps be in some degree excused, as knowing the conditions and difficulties of the problem before him better than we can know them.

CHAPTER III

THE highest class in the social scale at Rome was divided, roughly rather than exactly, into two sections, according as they did or did not aim at being elected to magistracies and so entering the senate. To the senatorius ordo, which will be dealt with in the next chapter, belonged all senators, and all sons of senators whether or no they had as yet been elected to the quaestorship, which after Sulla was the magistracy qualifying for the senate. But outside the senatorial ranks there were numbers of wealthy and well educated men, most of whom were engaged in one way or another in business; by which term is here meant, not so much trading and mercantile operations, as banking, money-lending, the undertaking of State contracts, and the raising of taxes. The general name for this class was, strange to say, *equites*, or knights, as they are often but unfortunately called in modern histories of Rome. They were in fact at this time the most unmilitary part of the population, and they inherited the title only because the property qualification for the equites

equo privato, i.e. the cavalry who served with their
own horses, had been taken as the qualification also
for equestrian judices, to whom Gaius Gracchus had
given the decision of cases in the quaestio de repetundis.[1] This law of Gracchus had had the result of
constituting an ordo equester alongside of the ordo
senatorius, with a property qualification of 400,000
sesterces, or about £3200, not of income but of
capital. Any one who had this sum could call
himself an eques, provided he were not a senator,
even if he had never served in the cavalry or
mounted a horse.

We are concerned here with the business which
these men carried on, not with their history as a
body in the State ; this latter difficult subject has
been handled by Dr. Greenidge in his *Roman Public
Life*, and by many other writers. We have to take
them here as the representatives of capital and the
chief uses to which it was put in the age of Cicero ;
for, as a matter of fact, they were then doing by far
the greatest part of the money-making of the Empire.
They were not indeed always doing it for themselves ;
they often represented men of senatorial rank, and
acted as their agents in the investment of money and
in securing the returns due. For the senator was not
allowed, by the strict letter of the law, to engage in
business which would take him out of Italy :[2] his
services were needed at home, and if indeed he had

---

[1] See Greenidge, *Roman Public Life*, p. 225.
[2] Lex Claudia ; Livy xxi. 63.

performed his proper work with industry and energy he never could have found time to travel on his own business. At the time of which we are speaking there were ways in which he could escape from his duties,—ways only too often used; but many senators did undoubtedly employ members of the equestrian order to transact their business abroad, so that it is not untrue to say that the equites had in their hands almost the whole of the monetary business of the Empire.

The property qualification may seem to us small enough, but it is of course no real index to the amount of capital which a wealthy eques might possess. Nothing is more astonishing in the history of the last century of the republic than the vast sums of money in the hands of individuals, and the enormous sums lent and borrowed in private by the men whose names are familiar to us as statesmen. It is told of Caesar that as a very young man he owed a sum equivalent to about £280,000; of Crassus that he had 200 million sesterces invested in land alone.[1] Cicero, though from time to time in difficulties, always found it possible to borrow the large sums which he spent on houses, libraries, etc. These are men of the ordo senatorius; of the equites proper, the men who dealt rather in lending than borrowing, we have not such explicit accounts, because they were not in the same degree before the public. But of Atticus, the type of the best and highest

[1] Plut. *Crassus*, 2; Pliny, *N. H.* xxxiii. 134 : equivalent to about £160,000.

section of the ordo equester, and of the amount and the sources of his wealth, we happen to know a good deal from the little biography of him written by his contemporary and friend Cornelius Nepos, taken together with Cicero's numerous letters to him. His father had left him the moderate fortune of £16,000. With this he bought land, not in Italy but in Epirus, where it was probably to be had cheap. The profits arising from this land, with which he took no doubt much trouble and pains, he invested again in other ways. He lent money to Greek cities: to Athens indeed without claiming any interest; to Sicyon without much hope of repayment; but no doubt to many others at a large profit. He also undertook the publishing of books, buying slaves who were skilled copyists; and in this, as in so many other ways, his friendship was of infinite value to Cicero. When we reflect that every highly educated man at this time owned a library and wished to have the last new book, we can understand how even this business might be extensive and profitable, and are not astonished to find Cicero asking Atticus to see that copies of his Greek book on his own consulship were to be had in Athens and other Greek towns.[1] This shrewd man also invested in gladiators, whom he could let out at a profit, as no doubt he would let out his library slaves.[2] Lastly, he owned houses in Rome; in fact he must have been making money in many different ways, spending but little himself, and attending personally and in-

---

[1] Cic. *ad Att.* ii. 1. 2.   [2] *Ib.* iv. 4.

defatigably to all his business, as indeed with true and
disinterested friendship he attended to that of Cicero.
In him we see the best type of the Roman business-
man : not the bloated millionaire living in coarse
luxury, but the man who loved to be always busy for
himself or his friends, and whose knowledge of men
and things was so thorough that he could make a
fortune without anxiety to himself or discomfort to
others.   What amount of capital he realised in these
various ways we do not know, but the mass of his
fortune came to him after he had been pursuing them
for many years, in the form of a legacy from an uncle.
This uncle was a typical capitalist and money-lender
of a much lower and coarser type than his nephew;
Nepos aptly describes him as " familiarem L. Luculli,
divitem, *difficillima natura*."   The nephew was the
only man who could get on with this Peter Feather-
stone of Roman life, and this simple fact tells us as
much about the character and disposition of Atticus
as anything in Cicero's correspondence with him.
The happy result was that his uncle left him a sum
which we may reckon at about £80,000 (centies
sestertium),[1] and henceforward he may be reckoned, if
not as a millionaire, at any rate as a man of large
capital, soundly invested and continually on the
increase.

There is no doubt then as to the fact of the
presence of capital on a large scale in the Rome of the
last century B.C., or of the business talents of many

---

[1] Corn. Nepos, *Atticus*, 5.

of its holders, or again of the many profitable ways in which it might be invested.   But in order to learn a little more of the history of capital at Rome, which is of the utmost importance for a proper understanding not only of the economic, but of the social and ethical characteristics of the age, it is necessary to go as far back as the war with Hannibal at least.

That there had been surplus capital in the hands of individuals long before the war with Hannibal is a well known fact, proved by the old Roman law of debt, and by the traditions of the unhappy relations of debtor and creditor.   But in order not to go back too far, we may notice a striking fact which meets us at the very outset of that momentous war.   In 215 B.C., and again the next year, the treasury was almost empty; then for the first time, so far as we know, private individuals came to the rescue, and lent large sums to the State;[1] these were partners in certain associations to be described later on in this chapter, which had made money by undertaking State contracts in the previous wars.   The presence of Hannibal in Italy strained the resources of the State to the utmost in every way; it cut the Romans off from their supply of the precious metals, forced them to reduce the weight of the *as* to one ounce, and, curiously enough, also to issue gold coins for the first time,—a measure probably taken on account of the dearth of silver,—and to make use of the uncoined gold in the treasury or in private hands.   At the end

---

[1] Livy xxiii. 49.

F

of the war the supply of silver was recovered; hence-forward all reckonings were made in silver, and the gold coinage was not long continued.

At this happy time, when Rome felt that she could breathe again after the final defeat of her deadly enemy, began the great inpouring of wealth of which the capitalism of Cicero's time is the direct result. The chief sources of this wealth, so far as the State was concerned, were the indemnities paid by conquered peoples, especially Carthage and Antiochus of Syria, and the booty brought home by victorious generals. Of these Livy has preserved explicit accounts, and the best example is perhaps that of the booty brought by Scipio Asiaticus from Asia Minor in 189 B.C., of which Pliny remarks that it first introduced luxury into Italy.[1] It has been roughly computed that the total amount from indemnities may be taken at six million of our pounds, in the period of the great wars of the second century B.C., and from booty very much the same sum. Besides this we have to take account of the produce of the Spanish silver mines, of which the Romans came into possession with the Carthaginian dominions in Spain; the richest of these were near Carthago Nova, and Polybius tells us that in his day they employed 40,000 miners, and produced an immense revenue.[2]

---

[1] Pliny, *N. H.* xxxiii. 148; Livy xxxvii. 59.

[2] Polyb. xxxiv. 9, quoted by Strabo, p. 148. Cp. Livy xlv. 18 for valuable mines in Macedonia.

All this went into the aerarium, except what was distributed out of the booty to the soldiers, both Romans and socii, the former naturally taking as a rule double the amount paid to the latter. But the influx of treasure into the State coffers soon began to tell upon the financial welfare of the whole citizen community; the most striking proof of this is the fact that, in 167 B.C., after the second Macedonian war, the *tributum* or property-tax was no longer imposed upon all citizens. Henceforward the Roman citizen had hardly any burdens to bear except the necessity of military service, and there are very distinct signs that he was beginning to be unwilling to bear even that one. He saw the prominent men of his time enriching themselves abroad and leading luxurious lives, and the spirit of ease and idleness began inevitably to affect him too. Polybius indeed, writing about 140–130 B.C., declines to state positively that the great Romans were corrupt or extortionate,[1] and those who were his intimate friends, Aemilius Paullus and his sons, were distinguished for their " abstinentia " : but the mere occurrence of this word " abstinentia " in the epitomes of Livy's lost books which dealt with this time, betrays the fact too obviously. In 149 was passed the first of the long series of laws intended, but in vain, to check the tendency of provincial governors to extort money from their subjects; and as this law established for the first time a standing court to try

[1] Polyb. xviii. 35.   For the unwillingness to serve, Livy, Epit. 48 and 55.

offences of this kind, the inference is inevitable that such offences were common and on the increase.

The remarkable fact about this inpouring of wealth is its extraordinary suddenness.   Within the lifetime of a single individual, Cato the Censor, who died an old man in 149 B.C., the financial condition of the State and of individuals had undergone a complete change.   Cato loved to make money and knew very well how to do it, as his own treatise on agriculture plainly shows ; but he wished to do it in a legitimate way, and to spend profitably the money he made, and he spared no pains to prevent others from making it illegally and spending it unprofitably.   He saw clearly that the sudden influx of wealth was disturbing the balance of the Roman mind, and that the desire to make money was taking the place of the idea of duty to the State.   He knew that no Roman could serve two masters, Mammon and the State, and that Mammon was getting the upper hand in his views of life.   If the accumulation of wealth had been gradual instead of sudden, natural instead of artificial, this could hardly have happened; as in England from the fourteenth century onwards, the steady growth of capital would have produced no ethical mischief, no false economic ideas, because it would have been an *organic* growth, resting upon a sound and natural economic basis.[1]   As the French historian has said with singular felicity,[2] " Money is

[1] Cunningham, *Western Civilisation* (*Modern*), p. 162 foll.
[2] Duruy, *Hist. de Rome*, vol. ii. p. 12.

like the water of a river : if it suddenly floods, it devastates ; divide it into a thousand channels where it circulates quietly, and it brings life and fertility to every spot."

It was in this period of the great wars, so un-wholesome and perilous economically, that the men of business, as defined at the beginning of this chapter —the men of capital outside the ordo senatorius— first rose to real importance.   In the century that followed, and as we see them more especially in Cicero's correspondence, they became a great power in the State, and not only in Rome, but in every corner of the Empire.   We have now to see how they gained this importance and this power, and what use they made of their capital and their opportunities. This is not usually explained or illustrated in the ordinary histories of Rome, yet it is impossible with-out explaining it to understand either the social or the public life of the Rome of this period.

The men of business may be divided into two classes, according as they undertook work for the State or on their own account entirely.   It does not follow that these two classes were mutually exclusive ; a man might very well invest his money in both kinds of undertaking, but these two kinds were totally distinct, and called by different names.   A public undertaking was called *publicum*,[1] and the men who undertook it *publicani* ; a private under-taking was *negotium*, and all private business men

[1] Cic. *de Provinciis consularibus*. v. 12.

were known as *negotiatores*. The publicani were always organised in joint-stock companies (*societates publicanorum*); the negotiatores might be in private partnership with one or more partners,[1] but as a rule seem to have been single individuals. We will deal first with the publicani.

In a passage of Livy quoted just now it is stated that at the beginning of the Hannibalic war money was advanced to the State by societates publicanorum; Livy also happens to mention that three of these competed for the privilege. Thus it is clear that the system of getting public work done by contract was in full operation before that date, together with the practice on the part of the contractors of uniting in partnerships to lessen the risk. System and practice are equally natural, and it needs but a little historical imagination to realise their development. As the Roman State became involved in wars leading to the conquest of Italy, and in due time to the acquisition of dominions beyond sea, armies and fleets had to be equipped and provisioned, roads had to be made, public rents to be got in, new buildings to be erected for public convenience or worship, corn had to be procured for the growing population, and, above all, taxes had to be collected both in Italy and in the provinces as these were severally acquired.[2] The government had no ap-

---

[1] Cic. *pro Quinctio* 3. 12 ; a good case of partnership in a res pecuaria et rustica in Gaul.

[2] Examples in Livy xxiii. 49 ; xxxii. 7 (portoria) ; xxxviii. 35 (corn-supply) ; xliv. 16 (army) ; xlii. 9 (revenue of ager Campanus).

paratus for carrying out these undertakings itself;
it had not, as we have, separate departments or
bureaux with a permanent staff of officials attached
to each, and even if it had been so provided, it would
still have found it most convenient, as modern
governments also do, to get the necessary work
carried out in most cases by private contractors.
Every five years the censors let the various works by
auction to contracting companies, who engaged to
carry them out for fixed sums, and make what profit
they could out of the business (*censoria locatio*).
This saved an immense amount of trouble to the
senate and magistrates, who were usually busily
engaged in other matters; nor was there at first any
harm in the system, so long as the Romans were
morally sound, and incapable of jobbing or scamping
their work. The very fact that they united into
companies for the purpose of undertaking these
contracts shows that they were aware of the risk
involved, and wished as far as possible to neutralise
it; it did not mean greed for money, but rather
anxiety not to lose the capital invested.

But as Rome advanced her dominion in the second
century B.C., and had to see to an ever-increasing
amount of public business, it was discovered that the
business of contracting was one which might indeed
be risky, but with skill and experience, and especially
with a trifle of unscrupulousness, might be made a
perfectly safe and paying investment. This was
especially the case with the undertakings for raising

the taxes in the newly acquired provinces as well as in Italy, more particularly in those provinces, viz. Sicily and Asia, which paid their taxes in the form of tithe and not in a lump sum.   The collection of these revenues could be made a very paying concern, seeing that it was not necessary to be too squeamish about the rights and claims of the provincials.   And, indeed, by the time of the Gracchi all these joint-stock companies had become the one favourite investment in which every one who had any capital, however small, placed it without hesitation.   Polybius, who was in Rome at this time for several years, and was thoroughly acquainted with Roman life, has left a valuable record in his sixth book (ch. xvii.) of the universal demand for shares in these companies; a fact which proves that they were believed to be both safe and profitable.

These societates were managed by the great men of business, as our joint-stock companies are directed by men of capital and consequence.   Polybius tells us that among those who were concerned, some took the contracts from the censors : these were called *mancipes*, because the sign of accepting the contract at the auction was to hold up the hand.[1]   Others, Polybius goes on, were in association with these mancipes, and, as we may assume, equally responsible with them ; these were the *socii*.   It was of course necessary that security should be given for the fulfilment of the contract, and Polybius does not omit

[1] Festus, ed. Müller, p. 151.

to mention the *praedes* or guarantors.[1] Lastly, he
says that others again gave their property on behalf
of these official members of the companies, or in
their name, for the public purpose in hand. These
last words admit of more than one interpretation,
but as in the same passage Polybius tells us that all
who had any money put it into these concerns, we
may reasonably suppose that he means to indicate
the *participes*, or small holders of shares, which were
called *partes*, or if very small, *particulae*.[2] The
socii and participes seem to be distinguished by
Cicero in his Verrine orations (ii. 1. 55), where he
quotes an addition made by Verres illegally as
praetor to a lex censoria : " qui de censoribus red-
emerit, eum socium ne admittito neve partem dato."
If this be so, we may regard the socius as having a
share both in the management and the liability,
while the particeps merely put his money into the
undertaking.[3] The actual management, on which
Polybius is silent, was in Rome in the hands of a
magister, changing yearly, like the magistrates of
the State, and in the provinces of a *pro-magister*
answering to the pro-magistrate, with a large staff
of assistants.[4] Communications between the manage-

---

[1] e.g. Livy xxii. 60 praedibus et praediis cavere populo.

[2] Cicero, in his defence of Rabirius Postumus, 2. 4, says that Rabirius'
father magnas *partes* habuit publicorum.   One Aufidius (Val. Max. vi. 9. 7)
"Asiatici publici exiguam admodum *particulam* habuit."   Cp. Cic. *in Vat.*
12. 29.

[3] This is the view of Deloume, *Les Manieurs d'argent à Rome*,
p. 119 foll.

[4] Marq. *Staatsverwaltung*, ii. p. 291.

ment at home and that in the provinces were kept
up by messengers (*tabellarii*), who were chiefly
slaves; and it is interesting incidentally to notice
that these, who are constantly mentioned in Cicero's
letters, also acted as letter-carriers for private persons
to whom their employers were known.

Such a business as this, involving the interests of
so many citizens, must have necessitated something
very like the Stock Exchange or Bourse of modern
times; and in fact the basilicas and porticoes which
we met with in the Forum during our walk through
Rome did actually serve this purpose.[1] The reader
of Cicero's letters will have noticed how often the
Forum is spoken of as the centre of life at Rome—
going down to the Forum was indeed the equivalent
of "going into the City," as well as of "going down
to Westminster." All who had investments in the
societates would wish to know the latest news
brought by *tabellarii* from the provinces, e.g. of the
state of the crop in Sicily or Asia, or of the disposition
of some provincial governor towards the publicani
of his province, or again of the approach of some
enemy, such as Mithridates or Ariovistus, who by
defeating a Roman army might break into Roman
territory and destroy the prospects of a successful
contractual enterprise. Assuredly Cicero's love for
the Forum was not a political one only; he loved it
indeed as the scene of his great triumphs as an
advocate, but also no doubt because he was concerned

---

[1] Deloume, *Manieurs d'argent*, p. 317 foll.

in some of the companies which had their head-
quarters there. When urging the people to give
Pompeius extraordinary powers to drive Mithridates
out of reach of Roman Asia, where he had done
incalculable damage, he dwells both with knowledge
and feeling on the value of the province, not only to
the State, but to innumerable private citizens who
had their money invested in its revenues.[1] " If
some," he pleads, " lose their whole fortunes, they will
drag many more down with them. Save the State
from such a calamity : and believe me (though you
see it well enough) that the whole system of credit
and finance which is carried on here at Rome in the
Forum, is inextricably bound up with the revenues
of the Asiatic province. If those revenues are
destroyed, our whole system of credit will come down
with a crash. See that you do not hesitate for a
moment to prosecute with all your energies a war
by which the glory of the Roman name, the safety
of our allies, our most valuable revenues, and the
fortunes of innumerable citizens, will be effectually
preserved."[2]

This is a good example of the way in which
political questions might be decided in the interests
of capital, and it is all the more striking, because
a few years earlier Sulla had done all he could to
weaken the capitalists as a distinct class. Pompeius
went out with abnormal powers, and might be considered for the time as their representative; the

---

[1] *pro lege Manilia*, 7. 18.   [2] *Ib.* 7. 19.

result in this case was on the whole good, for the
work he did in the East was of permanent value to
the Empire.   But the constitution was shaken and
never wholly recovered, and nothing that he was
able to do could restore the unfortunate province of
Asia to its former prosperity.   Four years later the
company which had contracted for raising the taxes in
the province sought to repudiate their bargain.   This
was disgraceful, as Cicero himself expressly says ;[1]
but it is quite possible that they had great difficulty
in getting the money in, and feared a dead loss,[2]
owing to the impoverishment of the provincials.
This matter again led to a political crisis ; for the
senate, urged by Cato, was disposed to refuse the
concession, and the alliance between the senatorial
class and the business men (*ordinum concordia*),
which it had been Cicero's particular policy to confirm, in order to mass together all men of property
against the dangers of socialism and anarchy, was
thereby threatened so seriously that it ceased to be
a factor in politics.

These companies and their agents were indeed
destined to be a thorn in Cicero's side as a provincial
governor himself.   When called upon to rule Cilicia
in 51 B.C. he found the people quite unable to pay
their taxes and driven into the hands of the middle-

---

[1] *ad Att.* i. 17. 9.   Crassus, no doubt a large shareholder, urged them on.
[2] In a letter to his brother, then governor of this province, Cicero con-
templates the possibility of contracts being taken at a loss (*ad Q. F.* i. 1. 33),
"publicis male redemptis." And in a letter of introduction in 46, he alludes
to heavy losses suffered in this way, *ad Fam.* xiii. 10.

man in order to do so;[1] his sympathies were thus
divided between the unfortunate provincials, for whom
he felt a genuine pity, and the interests of the company for collecting the Cilician taxes, and of those
who had invested their money in its funds.   In his
edict, issued before his entrance into the province, he
had tried to balance the conflicting interests; writing
of it to Atticus, who had naturally as a capitalist been
anxious to know what he was doing, he says that he
is doing all he can for the publicani, coaxing them,
praising them, yielding to them—but taking care
that they do no mischief;[2] words which perhaps
did not altogether satisfy his friend.   All honest
provincial governors, especially in the Eastern
provinces, which had been the scene of continual
wars for nearly three centuries, found themselves in
the same difficulty.   They were continually beset by
urgent appeals on behalf of the tax-companies and
their agents—appeals made without a thought of the
condition of a province or its tax-paying capacity—
so completely had the idea of making money taken
possession of the Roman mind.   Among the letters
of Cicero are many such appeals, sent by himself
to other provincial governors, some of them while
he was himself in Cilicia.   We may take two as
examples, before bringing this part of our subject to
a close.

The first of these letters is to P. Silius Nerva,
propraetor of Bithynia, a province recently added to

---

[1] *ad Att.* v. 16. 2.   [2] *Ib* vi. 1. 16.

the Empire by Pompeius. Cicero here says that he is himself closely connected with the partners in the company for collecting the pasture-dues (scriptura) of the province, "not only because that company as a body is my client, but also because I am very intimate with most of the individual partners." Can we doubt that he was himself a shareholder? He urges Nerva to do all he can for Terentius Hispo, the pro-magister of the company, and to try to secure for him the means of making all the necessary arrangements with the taxed communities—relying, we are glad to find, on the tact and kindness of the governor.[1]   The second letter, to his own son-in-law, Furius Crassipes, quaestor of Bithynia, shall be quoted here in full from Mr. Shuckburgh's translation : [2]

"Though in a personal interview I recommended as earnestly as I could the publicani of Bithynia, and though I gathered that by your own inclination no less than from my recommendation, you were anxious to promote the advantage of that company in every way in your power, I have not hesitated to write you this, since those interested thought it of great importance that I should inform you what my feeling towards them was. I wish you to believe that, while I have ever had the greatest pleasure in doing all I can for the order of publicani generally, yet this particular company of Bithynia has my special

---

[1] *ad Familiares*, xiii. 65.
[2] *Ib.* xiii. 9.   I have not adhered quite closely to his translation.

good wishes. Owing to the rank and birth of its members, this company constitutes a very important part of the state : for it is made up of members of the other companies : and it so happens that a very large number of its members are extremely intimate with me, and especially the man who is at present at the head of the business, P. Rupilius, its pro-magister. Such being the case, I beg you with more than common earnestness to protect Cn. Pupius, an employé of the company,[1] by every sort of kindness and liberality in your power, and to secure, as you easily may, that his services shall be as satisfactory as possible to the company, while at the same time securing and promoting the property and interests of the partners—as to which I am well aware how much power a quaestor possesses. You will be doing me in this matter a very great favour, and I can myself from personal experience pledge you my word that you will find the partners of the Bithynia company gratefully mindful of any services you can do them."

If Cicero, the most tender-hearted of Roman public men, could urge the claims of the companies so strongly, and, as in this last letter, without any allusion to the interests of the province and its people, we may well imagine how others, less scrupulous, must have combined with the capitalists to work havoc in regions that only needed peace and mild government to recover from centuries of misery.

---

[1] "Qui est in operis ejus societatis," i.e. engaged as a subordinate agent. —Marquardt, *Staatsverwaltung*, ii. p. 291.

Such a letter is the best comment we can have on the pernicious system of raising taxes by contract, —a system which was to be modified, regulated, and eventually reduced to harmless dimensions under the benevolent and scientific government of the early Empire.

We must now turn to the other department of the activity of the men of business, that of banking and money-lending (*negotiatores*).

On the north or sunny side of the Forum we noticed in our walk round the city the shops of the bankers (*tabernae argentariae*). The *argentarii* were originally, as their name suggests, only money-changers, a class of small business men that arose in response to a need felt as soon as increasing commerce and extended empire brought foreign coin in large quantities to Rome. The Italian communities outside the Roman State issued their own coinage until they were admitted to the civitas after the Social War,—a fact which alone is sufficient to show the need of men who made it their business to know the current value of various coins in Roman money; and as Rome became involved in the affairs of the East, there were always circulating in the city the tetradrachms of Antioch and Alexandria, the Rhodian drachmas, and the cistophori of the kings of Pergamus, afterwards coined in the province of Asia.[1] No doubt the money-changing business was a profitable one, and itself led to the formation of capital which could be

[1] Marq. ii. p. 35 foll.

used in taking deposits and making advances ; and, as Professor Purser puts it,[1] the mere possession of a quantity of coin for purposes of change would be likely to develop spontaneously the profession of banking.   In the same way the *nummularii*, or assayers of the coin, having a mass of it in their hands, would tend to develop a private business as well as their official public one.   All these, argentarii or nummularii, might be called *foeneratores*, from the interest (*foenus*) which they charged in their trans- actions.   The profession was a respectable one, for honesty and exactness in accounts were absolutely necessary to success in it.[2]   If the reader will turn to Cicero's speech in defence of Caecina (6. 16), he will find these accounts appealed to, though apparently not actually produced in court ; but in the *Noctes Atticae* of Aulus Gellius (xiv. 2) a judge who is describing a civil case which came before him, mentions, among the documents pro- duced, *mensae rationes*, i.e. the accounts kept by the banker.

Your argentarius seems to have been ready to undertake for you almost all that a modern banker will do for his customer.   He would take deposits of money, either for the depositor's use or to bear interest, and would make payments on his behalf on

---

[1] See his article in *Dict. of Antiq.* ed. 2, s.v. argentarii.

[2] Augustus' grandfather was an argentarius (Suet. *Aug.* 2), yet his son could marry a Julia, and be elected to the consulship, which, however, he was prevented by death from filling.

G

receipt of a written order, answering to our cheque ;[1] this was a practice probably introduced from Greece, for in the Eastern Mediterranean the whole business of credit and exchange had long been reduced to a system. Again, if you wished to be supplied with money during a journey, or to pay a sum to any one at a distance, e.g. in Greece or Asia, your argentarius would arrange it for you by giving you letters of credit or bills of exchange on a banker at such towns as you might mention, and so save you the trouble of carrying a heavy weight of coin with you. When Cicero sent his son to the University of Athens, he wished to give him a generous allowance,—too generous, as we should think, for it amounted to about £640 a year,—and he asked Atticus whether it could be managed for him by *permutatio*, i.e. exchange, and received an affirmative answer.[2] So too when his beloved freedman secretary Tiro fell ill of fever at Patrae, Cicero finds it easy to get a local banker there to advance him all the money he needed, and to pay the doctor, engaging himself to repay the money to any agent whom the banker might name.[3]

Your argentarius would also attend for you, or appoint an agent to attend, at any public auction in which you were interested as seller or purchaser, and would pay or receive the money for you,—a practice which must have greatly helped him in getting to

---

[1] The word for this cheque is *perscriptio*. Cp. Cic. *ad Att.* ix. 12. 3 viri boni usuras perscribunt, i.e. draw the interest on their deposits.

[2] Cic. *ad Att.* xii. 24 and 27. [3] Cic. *ad Fam.* xvi. 4 and 9.

know the current value of all kinds of property, and
indeed in learning to understand human nature on its
business side.   In the passage from the *pro Caecina*
quoted just now, a lady, Caesennia, wished to buy an
estate ; she employs an agent, Aebutius, no doubt
recommended by her banker, and to him the estate is
knocked down.   He undertakes that the argentarius
of the vendor, who is present at the auction, shall
be paid the value, and this is ultimately done by
Caesennia, and the sum entered in the banker's books
(tabulae).

But perhaps the most important part of the
business was the finding money for those who were
in want of it, i.e. making advances on interest.   The
poor man who was in need of ready money could get
it from the argentarius in coin if he had any security
to offer, and, as we saw in the last chapter, might
get entangled more and more hopelessly in the nets
of the money-lender.   Whether the same argentarius
did this small business and also the work of supplying
the rich man with credit, we do not know ; it may
have been the case that the great money-lenders like
Atticus themselves employed argentarii, and so kept
them going.   That Atticus would undertake, anyhow,
for a friend like Cicero, any amount of money-finding,
we know well from many letters of Cicero, written
when he was anxious to buy a piece of land at any
cost on which to erect a shrine to his beloved
daughter ; [1] and we may be pretty sure that Atticus

---

[1] Cic. *ad Att.* xiii. contains many letters of interest in this connexion.

could not have done all that Cicero importunately pressed upon him if he had not had a number of useful professional agents at command.   From these same letters we also learn that finding money by no means necessarily meant finding coin ; in a society where every one was lending or borrowing, and probably doing both at the same time, what actually passed was chiefly securities, mortgages, debts, and so on. If you wanted to hand over a hundred thousand or so to a creditor, what your agent had as often as not to do was to persuade that creditor to accept as payment the debts owing to yourself from others, i.e. you would hand over to him, if he would accept them, the bonds or other securities given you by your own debtors.[1]

It is plain then that the money-lenders had an enormous business, even in Rome alone, and risky as it undoubtedly was, it must often have been a profitable one.   And it was not only at Rome that men were borrowing and lending, but over the whole Empire.   For reasons which it would need an economic treatise to explain, private men, cities, and even kings were in want of money ; it was needed to meet the increased cost of living and the constantly increasing standard of living among the educated ;[2] it was needed by the cities of Greece and

---

[1] Cic. *ad Att.* xiii. 2. 3.   Cp. xii. 25.   In xii. 12 Cicero's divorced wife Terentia wishes to pay a debt by transferring to her creditor a debt of Cicero's to herself.   Another way in which actual payment could be avoided was by paying interest on purchase-money instead of the lump sum. Cp. xii. 22.

[2] A good example of this in Velleius ii. 10 (house-rent).

the East to repair the damages done in the wars of
the last three hundred years; it was needed by the
poorer provincials to pay the taxes for which neither
the publicani nor the Roman government could
afford to wait; and it was needed by the kings who
had come within the dismal shadow of the Roman
Empire, in order to carry on their own government,
or to satisfy the demands of the neighbouring
provincial governor, or to bribe the ruling men at
Rome to get some decree passed in their favour.
Cicero, at the end of his life, looking back to his own
consulship in 63, says that at no time in his recol-
lection was the whole world in such a condition of
indebtedness,[1] and in a famous passage in his second
Catilinarian oration he has drawn a picture of the
various classes of debtors in Rome and Italy at that
time (*Cat.* ii. § 18 foll.).   He tells us of those who
have wealth and yet will not pay their debts; of
those who are in debt and look to a revolution to
absolve them; of the veterans of the Sullan army,
settled in colonies such as Faesulae, who had rushed
into debt in order to live luxurious lives; of old
debtors of the city, getting deeper and deeper into
the quagmire, who joined the conspiracy as a last
desperate venture.   There was in fact in that famous
year a real social fermentation going on, caused by
economic disturbance of the most serious kind; the
germs of the disease can be traced back to the
Hannibalic war and its effects on Italy, but all the

[1] Cic. *de Officiis*, ii. 24, 84.

symptoms had been continually exacerbated by the negligence and ignorance of the government, and brought to a head by the Social and Civil Wars in 90–82 B.C. In 63 the State escaped an economic catastrophe through the vigilance of Cicero and the alliance of the respectable classes under his leadership. In 49, and again in 48, it escaped a similar disaster through the good sense of Caesar and his agents, who succeeded in steering between Scylla and Charybdis by saving the debtors without ruining the lenders.[1]

Wonderful figures are given by later writers, such as Plutarch, of the debts and loans of the great men of this time, and they may stand as giving us a general impression of private financial recklessness. But the only authentic information that has come down to us is what Cicero drops from time to time in his correspondence about his own affairs,[2] and even this needs much explanation which we are unable to apply to it. What is certain is that Cicero never had more than a very moderate income on which he could depend, and that at times he was hard up for money, especially of course after his exile and the confiscation of his property; and that on the other hand he never had any difficulty in getting the sums he needed, and never shows the smallest real anxiety about his finances. His profession as a barrister

[1] Caesar, *de Bell. Civ.* iii. 1 and 20 foll.

[2] Deloume in his *Manieurs d'argent* has a chapter on this (p. 58 foll.), but his details are not wholly to be relied on. Boissier's sketch in *Cicéron et ses amis*, 83 foll., is quite accurate.

only brought him a return indirectly in the form of
an occasional legacy or gift, since fees were forbidden
by a lex Cincia; his books could hardly have paid
him, at least in the form of money; his inherited
property was small, and his Italian villas were not
profitable farms, nor was it the practice to let such
country houses, as we do now, when not occupying
them; he declined a provincial government, the
usual source of wealth, and when at last compelled
to undertake one, only realised what was then a
paltry sum,—some £17,500, all of which, while in
deposit at Ephesus, was seized by the Pompeians in
the Civil War.[1] Yet even early in life he could afford
the necessary expenses for election to successive
magistracies, and could live in the style demanded
of an important public man. Immediately after his
consulship he paid £28,000 for Crassus' house on the
Palatine, and it is here that we first discover how he
managed such financial operations. Here are his own
words in a letter to a friend of December 62 B.C. :[2]
"I have bought the house for 3,500 sestertia . . . so
you may now look on me as so deeply in debt as to
be eager to join a conspiracy if any one would admit
me ! . . . Money is plentiful at 6 per cent, and the
success of my measures (in the consulship) has caused
me to be regarded as a good security."

The simple fact was that Cicero was always
regarded as a safe man to lend money to, by the
business men and the great capitalists; partly

[1] *ad Fam.* v. 20 fin.   [2] *Ib.* v. 9.

because he was an honest man,—a *vir bonus* who would never dream of repudiation or bankruptcy; partly because he knew every one, and had a hundred wealthy friends besides the lender of the moment, and among them, most faithful of all, the prudent and indefatigable Atticus.   Undoubtedly then it was by borrowing, and regularly paying interest on the loans, that he raised money whenever he wanted it. He may have occasionally made money in the companies of tax-collectors; we have seen that he probably had shares in some of their ventures.   But there is no clear evidence in his letters of this source of wealth,[1] and there is abundant evidence of the borrowing.   After his return from exile, though the senate had given him somewhat meagre compensation for the loss of his property, he began at once to borrow and to build: "I am building in three places," he writes to his brother,[2] "and am patching up my other houses.   I live somewhat more lavishly than I used to do; I am obliged to do so."   Here again we know from whom he borrowed,—it was this same brother, who of course had no more certain income than his own, probably less.   But he had been governor of Asia for three years (61–58 B.C.), and must have realised large sums even in that exhausted province; and at this moment he was legatus to Pompeius as special commissioner for organising the

---

[1] Deloume's attempt to prove that Cicero speculated with enormous profits seems to me to miss the mark.

[2] *ad Q. Fratr.* ii. 4. 3.   Cp. *ad Att.* iv. 2.

supply of corn, and thus was in immediate contact
with one of the greatest millionaires of the day. In
order to repay his brother all Marcus had to do was
to borrow from other friends. " In regard to money
I am crippled. But the liberality of my brother I
have repaid, in spite of his protests, by the aid of
my friends, that I might not be drained quite dry
myself" (*ad Att.* iv. 3). Two years later an unwary
reader might feel some astonishment at finding that
Quintus himself was now deep in debt;[1] but as he
continues to read the correspondence his astonishment will vanish. With the prospect before him of
a prolonged stay in Gaul with Caesar, Quintus might
doubtless have borrowed to any extent; and in fact
with Caesar's help—the proceeds of the Gallic wars—
both brothers found themselves in opulence. The
Civil War, and the repayment of his debts to Caesar,
nearly ruined Marcus towards the end of his life,
but nothing prevented his contriving to find money
for any object on which he had set his heart;
when in his grief for the loss of his daughter he
wishes to buy suburban gardens where a shrine to her
memory may (strange to say) attract public notice,
he tells Atticus to buy what is necessary *at any
cost*. "Manage the business your own way; do
not consider what my purse demands—about that
I care nothing—but what I *want*."[2]

---

[1] *ad Q. Fratr.* ii. 14. 3.

[2] *ad Att.* xii. 22. I may add in a footnote a final startling example of
the recklessness we have been noting. Decimus Brutus had, in March

Such being the financial method of Cicero and his brother, we cannot be surprised to find that the younger generation of the family followed faithfully in the footsteps of their elders. We have seen that the young Marcus had a large allowance at Athens, and on the whole he seems to have kept fairly well within it, in spite of some trouble; but his cousin the younger Quintus, coming to see his uncle in December 45, showed him a gloomy countenance, and on being asked the meaning of it, said that he was going with Caesar to the Parthian war in order to avoid his creditors, and presumably to make money to pay them with.[1] He had not even enough money for the journey out. His uncle did not offer to give him any, but he does not seem to have thought very seriously of the young man's embarrassments.

One more example of the financial dealings of the business men of this extraordinary age, and we will bring this chapter to an end. It is a story which has luckily been preserved in Cicero's speech in defence of a certain Rabirius Postumus in the year 54, who was accused under Caesar's law de pecuniis repetundis (extortion in the provinces). It is a remarkable revelation of all the most striking methods of making and using money in the last years of the Republic.

44 B.C., a capital of £320,000, yet next year he writes to Cicero that so far from any part of his private property being unencumbered, he had encumbered all his friends with debt also (ad Fam. xi. 10. 5). But this was in order to maintain troops.

[1] ad Att. xiii. 42. Cp. xvi. 5.

The father of this Rabirius, says Cicero, had been a distinguished member of the equestrian order, and "fortissimus et maximus publicanus"; not greedy of money, but most liberal to his friends—in other words, he was not a miser, for that character was rare in this age, but lent his money freely in order to acquire influence and consideration. The son took up the same line of business, and engaged in a wide sphere of financial operations. He dealt largely in the stock of the tax-companies; he lent money to cities in several provinces; he lent money to Ptolemy Auletes, King of Egypt, both before he was expelled from his kingdom by sedition, and afterwards when he was in Rome in 59 and 58, intriguing to induce the senate to have him restored. Rabirius never doubted that he would be so restored, and seems to have failed to see the probability of such a policy being contested or quarrelled about, as actually happened in the winter of 57–56. He lent, and persuaded his friends to lend:[1] he represented the king's cause as a good investment; and then, like the investing agent of to-day who slips so easily from carelessness into crime, he had to go on lending more and more, because he feared that if he stopped the king might turn against him.

He had staked the mass of his substance on a desperate venture. But time went on and Ptolemy

---

[1] What the king really wanted the money for, was to bribe the senate to restore him.—Cic. *ad Fam.* i. 1.

was not restored, and without the revenues of his
kingdom he of course could not pay his creditors.
At last, at the end of the year 56, Gabinius, then
governor of Syria, had pressure put on him by the
creditors—among them perhaps both Caesar and Pompeius—to march into Egypt without the authority
of the senate. He took Rabirius with him, and, in
order to secure the re-payment, the latter was made
superintendent (διοικητής) of the Egyptian revenues.[1]
Unluckily for him, his wily debtor did after all turn
against him, and he escaped from Egypt with
difficulty and with the loss of all his wealth. When
Gabinius was accused de repetundis and found guilty
of accepting enormous sums from Ptolemy, Rabirius
was involved in the same prosecution as having
received part of the money; Cicero defended him,
and as it seems with success, on the plea that equites
were not liable to prosecution under the lex Julia.
Towards the end of his speech he drew a clever
picture of his unlucky client's misfortunes, and declared that he would have had to quit the Forum, i.e.
to leave the Stock Exchange in disgrace, if Caesar
had not come to his rescue by placing large sums at
his disposal.

What Rabirius did was simply to gamble on a
gigantic scale, and get others to gamble with him.
The luck turned against him, and he came utterly
to grief. There seems indeed to have been a
perfect passion for dealing with money in this wild

[1] Cic. pro Rab. Post. 8. 22.

way among the men of wealth and influence; it was the fancy of the hour, and no disgrace attached to it if a man could escape ruin. Thus the vast capital accumulated — the sources of which were almost entirely in the provinces and the kingdoms on the frontiers — was hardly ever used productively. It never returned to the region whence it came, to be used in developing its resources; the idea of using it even in Italy for industrial undertakings was absent from the mind of the gambler. Those numberless villas, of which we shall speak in another chapter, were homes of luxury and magnificence, not centres of agricultural industry. There are indeed some signs that in this very generation the revival of Italian agriculture was beginning, and more especially the cultivation of the olive and the vine; Varro, some twenty years later, could claim that Italy was the best cultivated country in the world.[1] It may be that the din of the " insanum forum" and its wild speculation has prevented our hearing of the quiet efforts in the country to put capital to a legitimate productive use. But of the social life of the city the Forum was the heart, and of any prudent

---

[1] Varro, *R. R.* i. 2. Ferrero (*Greatness and Decline of Rome*) has the merit of having discerned the signs of the regeneration of Italian agriculture at this time, but he is apt to push his conclusions further than the evidence warrants. See the translation of his work by A. E. Zimmern, i. p. 124 ; ii. p. 131 foll. The statement of Pliny quoted by him (xv. 1. 3) that oil was first exported from Italy in the year 52 B.C., is, however, of the utmost importance.

or scientific use of capital the Forum knew hardly anything.

Of the two classes of business men we have been describing, the tax-farmers and the money-lenders, it is hard to say which wrought the most mischief in the Empire; they played into each other's hands in wringing money out of the helpless provincials. Together too they did incalculable harm, morally and socially, among the upper strata of Roman society at home. Economic maladies react upon the mental and moral condition of a State. Where the idea of making money for its own sake, or merely for the sake of the pleasure derivable from excitement, is paramount in the minds of so large a section of society, moral perception quickly becomes warped. The sense of justice disappears, because when the fever is on a man he does not stop to ask whether his gains are ill-gotten; and in this age the only restriction on the plundering of the subjects of the Empire was a legal one, and that of no great efficacy. There are many repulsive things in the exquisite poetry of Catullus, but none of them jar on the modern mind quite so sharply as his virulent attacks on a provincial governor in whose suite he had gone to Bithynia in the hope of enriching himself, and under whose just administration he had failed to do so. There is lost also the sense of a duty arising out of the possession of wealth—the feeling that it should do some good in the world, or at least be in part applied to some useful purpose. Lastly, the exciting pursuit

of wealth helps to produce a curious restlessness
and instability of character, of which we have many
examples in the age we are studying. " Unstable as
water, thou shalt not excel," are words that might
be applied to many a young man among Cicero's
acquaintance, and to many women also.

No sudden operation could cure these evils—they
needed the careful and gradual treatment of a wise
physician. As in so many other ways, so here
Augustus showed his wonderful instinct as a social
reformer. The first requisite of all was an age of
comparative peace—a healthy atmosphere in which
the patient could recover his natural tone. Next in
importance was the removal of the incitement to
enrich yourself and to spend illegally or unprofitably,
and the revival of a sense of duty towards the State
and its rulers. Provincial governors were made more
really responsible, and a scientific census revealed the
actual tax-paying capacity of the provincials; tax-
farming was more closely superintended and gradually
disappeared. It is true enough that even under the
Empire great fortunes were made and lost, but the
gambling spirit, the wild recklessness in monetary
dealings, are not met with again. The Roman Forum
ceased to be insane, and Italy became once more the
home of much happy and useful country life. The
passionate and reckless self-consciousness of Catullus
is succeeded in the next generation by the calm
sweet hopefulness of Virgil; in passing from the one
poet to the other, we feel that we are leaving behind

us an age of over-sensitive self-seeking and entering on one in which duty and honour, labour on the land and hard work for the State, may be reckoned as things more likely to make life worth living than all the accumulated capital of a Crassus.

CHAPTER IV

THE GOVERNING ARISTOCRACY

ABOVE the men of business of equestrian rank, in social standing though not necessarily in wealth, there was in Cicero's time an aristocracy which a Roman of that day would perhaps have found it a little difficult to explain or define to a foreigner. Fortunately all foreigners coming to Rome would know what was meant by the senate, the great council which received envoys from all nations outside the Empire; and the stranger might be told in the first place that all members of that august assembly, with their families, were considered as elevated above the equestrian order, and as forming the main body of the aristocracy proper. But if the informant were by chance a conservative Roman of old family, he might proceed to qualify this definition. "There are now in the senate," he might say, "plenty of men who are only there because they have held the quaestorship, which Sulla made the qualification for a seat, and there are many equites whom Sulla made into senators by the form of a vote of the people; such men, even the great orator Cicero himself, I do

not reckon as really members of the nobility, because
they do not belong to old families who have done the
State good service in past time. They have no images
of their ancestors in their houses; they come from
municipal towns, or spring from some low family in
the city; they may have raised themselves by their
talents, perhaps only by their money, but they have
no guarantee of antiquity, their names are not in our
annals. All we true conservative Romans (and a
Roman is hardly a Roman if not conservative) profoundly believe that a man whose family has once
attained to high public honour and done good public
service, will be a safer person to elect as a magistrate
than one whose family is unknown and untried—a
belief which is surely based on a truth of human
nature. I should count a man who happens not to be
in the senate himself, for want of wealth or inclination, but whose family has its images and its traditions
of great ancestors, as far more truly an "optimate" than
most of these new men. Fortunately our most famous
families, whose names are known all over the Empire,
are still to be found in the senate, and indeed form a
powerful body there, capable of resisting to the last
the revolutionary dangers that threaten us. The
people still elect to magistracies the Aemilii, Lutatii,
Claudii, Cornelii, Julii, and many more families that
have been famous in our history, and will, I trust, continue to elect them so long as our Republic lasts." [1]

[1] The Republic was not to last long; but among the consuls of the last
years of its existence were several members of the old families.

There was indeed a glamour about these splendid names, as there is about the titles of our ancient noble families; their holders may almost be said to have claimed high office as a right, like the Whig families of the Revolution for a century after their triumph. Though we may use the word in a wider sense in this chapter, these grand old families were the true aristocracy, and inspired just that respect in the minds of men outside their circle which is still so familiar to us in England. Cicero was to such men an "outsider," a *novus homo*; and the close reader of Cicero's letters, if he is looking out (as he should be) for Cicero's constantly changing attitude of mind as he addresses himself to various correspondents, cannot fail to see how comparatively awkward and stilted he often is when writing to one of these great nobles, with whom he has never been really intimate; and how easily his pen glides along when he is letting himself talk to Atticus, or Poetus, or M. Marius, men who were outside the pale of nobility. It is true that he is sometimes embarrassed in other ways when writing to great personages, as, for example, Lentulus Spinther, consul in 57, or to Appius Claudius, consul in 53; but had they been men of his own kind he never would have felt that embarrassment in the same degree. When writing to such men he rarely or never indulges in those little sportive jokes or allusions which enliven his more intimate correspondence, nor does he tell the truth so strictly, for they might not always care to hear it.

Here is a specimen which will give some idea of his manner in writing to an aristocrat: he is congratulating L. Aemilius Paullus, who secured his election to the consulship in the summer of 51 B.C. :

"Though I never doubted that the Roman people, considering your eminent services to the Republic and *the splendid position of your family*, would enthusiastically elect you consul by a unanimous vote, yet I felt extreme delight when the news reached me ; and I pray the gods to render your official career fortunate, and to make the administration of your office worthy of your own position and *that of your ancestors.* . . . And would that it had been in my power to have been at home to see that wished-for day, and to have given you the support which your noble services and kindness to me deserved ! But since the unexpected and unlooked-for accident of my having to take a province has deprived me of that opportunity, yet, that I may be enabled to see you as consul actually administering the state in a manner worthy of your position, I earnestly beg you to take care to prevent my being treated unfairly, or having additional time added to my year of office. If you do that, you will abundantly crown your former acts of kindness to me." [1]

This Aemilius Paullus, like Spinther and many

---

[1] *ad Fam.* xv. 12. This rather stilted letter is nearly identical with one to the other consul-designate, another aristocrat, Claudius Marcellus. Cicero is in each case trying to do his own business, while writing to a man of higher social rank than his own.

others, belonged to a respectable but somewhat characterless type of aristocrat ; these formed a considerable and a powerful section of the senate, where they were an obstacle to reform and administrative efficiency. They were really a survival from the old type of Roman noble, which had done excellent work in its day ; men in whom the individual had been kept in strict subordination to the State, and whose personal idiosyncrasies and ambitions only excited suspicion. But towards the end of the Republican period the individual had free play ; at no time in ancient history do we meet with so many various and interesting kinds of individuality, even among the nobilitas itself. This is not merely the result of the abundant literature in which their traits have come down to us ; it was a fact of the age, in which the idea of the State had fallen into the background, and the individual found no restraint on his thoughts and little on his actions, no hindrance to the development of his capacity either for good or evil. Sulla, Catiline, Pompeius, Cato, Clodius, Caesar, all have their marked characteristics, familiar to all who read the history of the Roman revolution. Caesar is the most remarkable example of strong character among the men of high aristocratic descent, and it is interesting to notice how entirely he was without the exclusive tendency which we associate with aristocrats. He was intimate with men of all ranks ; his closest friends seem to have been men who were not noble. While the high aristocrats looked down

as a rule on Cicero the novus homo, and for some
years positively hated him,[1] Caesar, though differing from him *toto coelo* in politics, was always on
pleasant terms of personal intercourse with him; he
had a charm of manner, a literary taste, and a genuine
admiration for genius, which was invariably irresistible to the sensitive "novus homo." With Pompey, though he trusted him politically as he never
trusted Caesar, Cicero was never so intimate. They
had not the same common interests; Cicero could
laugh at Pompey behind his back, but hardly once in
his correspondence does he attempt to raise a jest
about Caesar.

Thus in the governing or senatorial aristocracy
we find men of a great variety of character, from
the old-fashioned nobilis, exclusive in society and
obstructive in politics, to the man of individual
genius and literary ability, whether of blue blood
like Caesar, or like Cicero the scion of a municipal
family which has never gained or sought political
distinction. But for the purposes of this chapter we
may discern and discuss two main types of character
in this aristocracy: first, that on which the new
Greek culture had worked to advantage, not destroying the best Roman qualities, but drawing them into

[1] The letters of the years 58 to 54 are full of bitter allusions to the
invidia of these men, which culminate in the long and windy one to
Lentulus Spinther of October 54, where he actually accuses them of taking
up Clodius in order to spite him. In a confidential note to Atticus in the
spring of 56, he told him that they hated him for buying the Tusculan
villa of the great noble Catulus.—*ad Fam.* i. 9 ; *ad Att.* iv. 5.

usefulness in new ways; secondly, that on which
the same culture had worked to its harm by taking
advantage of weak points in the Roman armour,
sapping the true Roman quality without substituting
any other excellence. We will briefly trace the
growth of these two types, and take an example of
each among Cicero's intimate friends, not from the
famous personages familiar to every one, but from
eminent and interesting men of whom the ordinary
student knows comparatively little.

Ever since the Hannibalic war, and probably even
before it, Roman nobles had felt the power of Greek
culture; they had begun to think, to learn about
peoples who were different from themselves in habits
and manners, and to advance, the best of them at
least, in wisdom and knowledge; and this is true
in spite of the unquestioned fact that it was in this
same era that the seeds were sown of moral and
political degeneracy. We shall have abundant opportunity of noting the effects of this degeneracy in the
last age of the Republic, but it is pleasant to dwell
for a moment on that more wholesome Greek
influence which enticed the finer minds among the
Roman nobility into a new region of culture,
stimulating thought and strengthening the springs
of conduct.

Even the old Cato himself, most rigid of Roman
conservatives, was not unmoved by this influence,[1]
and it was to him that Rome owed the introduction

[1] Plutarch, *Cato major* 2 and 12.

of Ennius, the greatest literary figure of that age, into Roman society.[1] But the first genuine example of the new culture, of the Hellenic enthusiasm of the age, is to be found in Aemilius Paullus, the conqueror of Macedonia, a true Roman aristocrat who was delighted to learn from Greeks. Plutarch's *Life* of this man is a valuable record of the tendencies of the time. After his failure to obtain a second consulship, Plutarch tells us[2] that he retired into private life, devoting himself to religious duties and to the education of his children, training these in the old Roman habits in which he had himself been trained, but also in Greek culture, and that with even greater enthusiasm. He had about them Greek teachers, not only of grammar, rhetoric, and philosophy, but of the fine arts, and even of out-door pursuits, such as hunting (to which the Romans were not greatly addicted), and of the care of horses and dogs; and he made a point of being present himself at all their exercises, bodily and mental. The result of this wholesome Xenophontic education is seen in his son, the great Scipio Aemilianus, who was adopted into the family of the Scipios in the lifetime of his father. Whatever view we may take of this great man's conduct in war and politics, there can hardly be a doubt that the Romans themselves were right in treasuring his memory as one of the best of

[1] Corn. Nepos, *Cato* 1. 4, who remarks that Cato's return from his quaestorship in Sardinia with Ennius in his train was as good as a splendid triumph.

[2] Plut. *Aem. Paul.* 6 *ad fin.*

their race. When we put all the facts of his life
together, from his early youth, of which his friend
Polybius has left us a most beautiful picture,[1] to his
sudden and probably violent death in the maturity
of his powers, we are compelled to believe that he
was really a man of wide sympathies, a strong sense
of justice which guided him steadily through good
report and ill, perfect purity of life, and hatred of all
that was low and bad, whether in rich or poor. He
was not, like his father, a Roman aristocrat patronising Greek culture ;[2] in him we see a perfectly natural
and mature combination of the noblest qualities of
the Roman and the wholesomest qualities of the
Greek. "It was an awakening truth," says a great
authority, "in the minds of Romans like Scipio, that
intellectual culture must be built upon a foundation
of moral rectitude : and such a foundation they could
find in the storehouse of their own domestic traditions."[3] When Cicero, who held him to be the
greatest of Romans, wrote his dialogue on the State
(de Republica), with the new idea pervading it of
the moral and political ascendancy of a single man,
he made Scipio the hero and the one ascendant
figure in his work, and ended it with an imitation of
the Platonic "myth," in the form of a "dream of
Scipio."

Scipio gathered round him a circle of able and

---

[1] Polybius, xxxii. 9–16.

[2] The difference between him and his father, especially in politics, is
sketched in Plutarch's *Life* of the latter, ch. xxxviii.

[3] F. Leo, in *Die griechische und lateinische Literatur*, p. 337.

cultured men, both Roman and Greek, including
almost every living Roman of ability, and among the
Greeks the historian Polybius and the philosopher
Panaetius, of whom we shall have more to learn in
the course of this volume. Of this circle the best
and ablest men of Cicero's earlier days were mentally
the children, and his own views both of literature
and politics were largely formed upon the Scipionic
tradition. Indeed to understand the mental and moral
furniture of the Roman mind in the Ciceronian age, it
is absolutely necessary to study that of the generation
which made that mind what it was ; but here space
can only be found to point out how the enlighten-
ment of the Scipionic circle opened out new ways in
manners, in literature, in philosophical receptivity,
and lastly in the study of the law, which was destined
to be Rome's greatest contribution to civilisation.

Manners, the demeanour of the individual in social
intercourse, are a valuable index, if not an entirely
conclusive one, of the mental and moral tone of
society in any age. Ease and courteousness of
bearing mean, as a rule, that the sense of another's
claims as a human being are always present to the
mind. Whatever be the shortcomings of the last
age of the Republic, we must give due credit to the
fact that in their outward demeanour towards each
other the educated men of that age almost invariably
show good breeding. It is true enough that public
vituperation, in senate or law-courts, was a fact of
every day, and the wealth of violent personal abuse

which a gentleman like Cicero could expend on one
whom for the time he hated, or who had done him
some wrong, passes all belief.[1] But the history of
this vituperation is a curious one ; it was a traditional
method of hostile oratory, and sprang from an old
Roman root, the tendency to defamation and satire,
which may itself be attributed in part to the Italian
custom of levelling abuse at a public man (e.g. at his
triumph) in order to avert evil from him.[2] To single
out a man's personal ugliness, to calumniate his
ancestry in the vilest terms,—these were little more
than traditional practices, oratorical devices, which
the rhetorical education of the day encouraged, and
which no one took very seriously.[3] But we are
concerned in this chapter mainly with private life ;
and there we find almost universal consideration
and courtesy. In the whole of the Ciceronian correspondence there is hardly a letter that does not show
good breeding, and there are many that are the natural
result of real kindly feeling and true sympathy.

A good example of the best type of Roman
manners is to be found in Plutarch's *Life* of Gaius
Gracchus, the younger contemporary of Scipio, who
had married his sister. Plutarch draws a picture of
him so vivid that by common consent it is ascribed to

[1] The best specimens, or rather the worst, are to be found in the speeches
in Pisonem, in Vatinium, and in the *Second Philippic*.

[2] The most instructive passage on vituperatio is Cicero's defence of Caelius,
ch. 3. Cp. Quintilian iii. 7. 1 and 19. On the custom at triumphs, etc., see
Munro's *Elucidations of Catullus*, p. 75 foll. for most valuable remarks.

[3] We have courteous letters from Cicero both to Piso and Vatinius, only
a few years after he had depicted them in public as monsters of iniquity.

the memoirs of some one who knew him.   " In all his
dealings with men," says the biographer, " he was
always dignified yet always courteous " ; that is, while
he inspired respect, men felt also that he would do
anything in his power for them.   That this was said
of him by a Roman, and not invented for him by
Plutarch, seems probable because the combination is
one peculiarly Roman ; so Livy, when he wishes to
describe the finest type of Roman character, says
that a certain man was "haud minus libertatis
alienae quam suae dignitatis memor." [1]   This same
combination meets us also in the little pictures of the
social life of cultivated men which Cicero has left us
in some of his dialogues.   There the speakers are
usually of the nobility, often distinguished members
of senatorial families, as in the *de Oratore*, where the
chief *personae* are Crassus, Antonius, and Scaevola,
the conservative triumvirate of the day.   They all
seem grave, or but seldom gently jocular, respectful to
each other, and perhaps a trifle tedious ; they never
quarrel, however deeply they may differ, and we
may guess that they did not hold their opinions
strongly enough to urge them to open rupture.   We
seem to see the same grave faces, with rather long
noses and large mouths, which meet us in the
sculptures of Augustus' Ara Pacis,[2]—full of dignity,
but a little wanting in animation.

[1] Plut. *C. Gracchus*, ch. 6 *ad fin.*   Cp. Livy vii. 33.
[2] These characteristic figures may be most conveniently seen in Mrs.
Strong's interesting volume on Roman sculpture, p. 42 foll.

There is one singular exception to the good manners of the period; but as the result rather of affectation than of nature, it may help to prove our rule. Again and again in Plutarch's *Life* of Cato the younger the mention of his rudeness proves the strength of the tradition about him. It was said that this lost him the consulship, as he declined to make himself agreeable in the style expected from candidates.[1] Even in a letter to Cicero, an old friend, though not actually rude, he is absurdly patronising and impertinent to a man many years his senior, and writes in very bad taste. Probably the enmity between him and Caesar arose or was confirmed in this way, as Cato always made a point of being rudest to those whom he most disliked. He fancied that he was imitating his great ancestor, and asserting the virtue of good old Roman bluntness against modern Greek affectation; he did not in the least see that he was himself a curious example of Roman affectation, shown up by the real amenities of intercourse, for which Romans had largely to thank Greece.[2]

In literature too the average capacity of this aristocracy was high, though the greatest literary figures of the age, if we except Caesar, do not, strictly speaking, belong to it; Cicero was a novus homo, and Lucretius and Catullus were not of the senatorial

---

[1] Plut. *Cato*, ch. 1. *ad fin.* Blanditia was the word for civility in a candidate: "opus est magnopere blanditia," says Quintus Cicero, *de pet. cons.* § 41.

[2] There is a pleasanter picture of Cato, sitting in Lucullus' library and in his right mind, in Cic. *de Finibus* iii. 2. 7.

order. But the new education, as we shall see later
on, was admirably calculated to train men in the art
of speaking and writing, if not in the habit of
independent thinking; and among the nobles who
reaped the full fruits of this education every one
could write in Latin and probably also in Greek, and
if he aimed at public distinction, could speak without disgracing himself in the senate and the courts.
Oratory was, in fact, the staple product of the age,
and the chief *raison d'être* of its literary activity.
Long ago the practice had begun of writing out
successful speeches delivered in the senate, in the
courts, or at funerals; the means of publication were
easy, as a consequence of the number of Greek slaves
who could act as copyists, and thus oratory formed
the basis of a prose literature which is essentially
Roman,[1] rooted in the practical necessities of the life
of the Roman noble, though deeply tinged with the
Greek ideas and forms of expression acquired in the
process of education in vogue. Treatises on rhetoric,
the art of effective expression in prose, form an
important part of it; two of them still survive from
the time of Sulla,—the *Rhetorica ad Herennium*
of an unknown author, and Cicero's early treatise
de Inventione. Later on Cicero wrote his admirable dialogue *de Oratore* and other works on the
same subject, ending with his *Brutus,* a catalogue
raisonnée, invaluable to us, of all the great Roman
orators down to his own time.

[1] See Leo, in work already cited, p. 338 foll.

In history writing the standard was not so high. The rhetorical education made men good professional orators, but indifferent and dilettante historians, and the example of more accurate historical investigation and reflection set by Polybius was not followed, except perhaps by Caelius Antipater in the Gracchan age.[1] History was affected for the worse by the rhetorical art, as indeed poetry was destined also to be ; Sallust, though we owe much to him, was in fact an amateur, who thought more of style and expression than of truth and fact. Caesar, who did not profess to be a historian, but only to provide the materials for history,[2] stands alone in making facts more important than words, and rarely troubles his reader with speeches or other rhetorical superfluities.[3] Biographies and autobiographies were fashionable ; of the former only those of Cornelius Nepos, one of Cicero's many friends, have come down to us, and none of the latter, but we know a long list of eminent men who wrote their own memoirs, including Catulus the elder, Rutilius the famous victim of equestrian judges, Sulla, and Lucullus. But far above all other prose writers of the age stand two men, neither of them Roman by birth, but yet members of the

[1] For this remarkable writer, of whose work only a few fragments survive, see Leo, *op. cit.* p. 340, and Schanz, *Gesch. der röm. Literatur,* i. p. 278 foll.

[2] Cicero, *Brutus,* 75, 262.

[3] The other Caesarian writers followed him more or less successfully ; Hirtius, who wrote the eighth book of the Gallic War, and the authors of the Alexandrian, African, and Spanish Wars (the first possibly by Asinius Pollio).

senatorial order; the one a man of encyclopaedic
learning, with what we may almost call a scientific
interest in the subjects which he treated in awkward
and homely Latin, the other a man of comparatively
little learning, but gifted with so exquisite a sense of
the beautiful in expression, and at the same time
with a humanity so real and in that day so rare, that
it is not without good cause that he has recently
been called the most highly cultured man of all
antiquity.[1] Of Varro's numerous works we have
unluckily but few survivals; of Cicero's we have
still such a mass as will for ever provide ample
material for studying the life, the manners, the
thought of his day.

A large part of this mass consists of the correspondence of which we are making such frequent
use in these chapters. Letter-writing is perhaps the
most pleasing and genuine of all the literary activities
of the time; men took pains to write well, yet not
with any definite prospect of publication, such as was
the motive a century later in the days of Seneca and
Pliny. The nine hundred and odd letters of the
Ciceronian collection are most of them neither mere
communications nor yet rhetorical exercises, but real
letters, the intercourse of intimate friends at a
distance, in which their inmost thoughts can often
be seen. Cicero is indeed apt to become rhetorical
even in his letters, when writing under excitement
about politics; but the most delightful letters in the

[1] Leo, *op. cit.* p. 355.

collection are those in which he writes to his friends in happy and natural language of his daily life and occupations, his books, his villas, his children, his joys and sorrows. It is strange that the great historian of Rome in our time entirely failed to see the charm and the value of these letters, as of all Cicero's writings; his countrymen have now agreed to differ from him, and to restore a great writer to his true position.

In philosophical receptivity too the brightest and finest minds among this aristocracy show an ability which is almost astonishing, when we consider that there had been no education in Rome worth the name until the second century B.C.[1] I use the word receptivity, because the Romans of our period never really learnt to think for themselves; they never grappled with a problem, or struck out a new line of thought. But so far as we can judge by Cicero's philosophical works, the only ones of his age which have come down to us, the power to read with understanding and to reproduce with skill was unquestionably of a high order. The opportunities for study were not wanting; private libraries were numerous, and all Cicero's friends who had collected books were glad to let him have the use of them.[2] Greek philosophers were often domesticated in wealthy families, and could discourse with the statesman when

---

[1] See below, ch. vi.

[2] The passage just cited from the *de Finibus* (iii. 27) introduces us to the library of Lucullus at Tusculum, whither Cicero had gone to consult books, and where he found Cato sitting surrounded by volumes of Stoic treatises.

he had leisure from public business. Much of this
was no more than fashion, and real endeavour and
earnestness were rare ; but the fact remains that one
philosophical system, more especially on its ethical
side, took real possession of the best type of Roman
mind, and had permanent and saving influence
on it.

Stoicism was brought to Rome by Panaetius of
Rhodes, the intimate friend of Scipio, a mild and
tactful Greek whose Rhodian birth gave him perhaps
some advantage in associating with the old allies of
his state. He came to Rome at a critical moment,
when even the best men were drifting into pure
material self-seeking ; and the results of his teaching
were during two centuries so wholesome and inspiring
that we may almost think of him as a missionary.
The ground had been prepared for him in some sense
by Polybius, who introduced him to Scipio and his
circle, and who was then engaged in writing his
history. From Polybius the Romans, the best of
them at least, first learnt to realise their own empire
and the great change it had wrought in the world ;
to think about what they had done and the qualities
that enabled them to do it. From Panaetius they
were to learn a philosophical creed which might
direct and save them in the future, which might
serve as ballast in public and private life, just when
the ship was beginning to drift in moral helplessness.
He was the founder of a school of practical wisdom,
singularly well adapted to the Roman character and

intellect, which were always practical rather than speculative; and far better suited to ordinary human life than the old rigid and austere Stoic ethics, of which the younger Cato was the only eminent Roman disciple. From what we know of Panaetius' ethical teaching,—and in the first two books of Cicero's work, *de Officiis*, we have a fairly complete view of it,—we do not find the old doctrine that absolute wisdom and justice are the only ends to pursue, and everything else indifferent; a doctrine which put the old-fashioned Stoic out of court in public life. The relative element, the useful, played a great part in the teaching of Panaetius. Though his system is based on the highest principles to which moral teaching could then appeal, it did not exclude the give and take, the compromise without which no practical man of affairs can make way, nor yet the wealth and bodily comforts that secure leisure for thought.[1]

Panaetius' mission was carried on by another Rhodian philosopher, the famous Posidonius, who lived long enough to know Cicero himself and many of his contemporaries; a man less inspiring perhaps than Panaetius, but of greater knowledge and attainment; a traveller, geographer, and a man of the world, whose writings on many subjects, though lost to us, really lie at the back of a great part of the

---

[1] The fragments of Panaetius are collected by H. N. Fowler, Bonn, 1885. The best account of his teaching known to me is in Schmekel, *Philosophie der Mittleren Stoa*, p. 18 foll. But all can read the two first books of the *de Officiis*.

Roman literary output of his time.[1] He was the disciple of Panaetius; envoy from Rhodes to Rome in the terrible year 86; and later on the inmate of Roman families, and the admired friend of Cicero, Pompeius, and Varro. Philosophy was only one of the many pursuits of this extraordinary man, whose literary and historical influence can be traced in almost every leading Roman author for a century at least; but his philosophical importance was during his lifetime perhaps predominant. The generation that knew him was rich in Stoics; for example, Aelius Stilo, the master of Varro, "doctissimus eorum temporum," as Gellius calls him;[2] Rutilius, who was mentioned just now as having written memoirs; and among others probably the great lawyer Mucius Scaevola. Cato, as we have seen, was not a follower of the Roman school of Stoicism, but of the older and uncompromising doctrine; but Cicero, though never a professed Stoic, was really deeply influenced, and towards the end of his life almost fascinated, by a creed which suited his humanity whi'e it stimulated his instinct for righteousness.[2] And, like Cicero, many other men of serious character felt the power of Stoicism almost unconsciously, without openly professing it.

Stoicism then was in several ways congenial to the Roman spirit, but in one direction it had an

---

[1] Leo, *op. cit.* p. 360. Schmekel deals comprehensively with Posidonius' philosophy, as reflected in Varro and Cicero, p. 85 foll.

[2] See Professor Reid's introduction to Cicero's *Academica*, p. 17. Cicero considered Posidonius the greatest of the Stoics.—*Ib.* p. 5.

inspiring influence which has been of lasting moment
to the world.   Up to the time of Panaetius and the
Scipionic circle the Roman idea and study of law had
been of a crabbed practical character, wanting in
breadth of treatment, destitute of any philosophical
conception of the moral principles which lie behind
all law and government.   The Stoic doctrine of
universal law ruling the world—a divine law, emanating from the universal Reason—seems to have
called up life in these dry bones.   It might be held
by a Roman Stoic that human law comes into existence when man becomes aware of the divine law,
and recognises its claim upon him.   Morality is thus
identical with law in the widest sense of the word,
for both are equally called into being by the Right
Reason, which is the universal primary force.[1]   It is
not possible here to show how this grand and elevating
idea of law may have affected Roman jurisprudence,
but we will just notice that the first quasi-philo-
sophical treatment of law is found following the age
of Panaetius and the Scipionic circle ; that the phrase
ius gentium then begins to take the meaning of
general principles or rules common to all peoples, and
founded on " natural reason ";[2] and that this led by
degrees to the later idea of the Law of Nature, and
to the cosmopolitanism of the Roman legal system,

[1] Cic. *de Legibus* i. affords many examples of this view, which was apparently that of Posidonius, e.g. 6. 18 and 8. 25.   Cp. *de Republica*, iii. 22. 33.

[2] Gaius i. 1 ; Cic. *de Officiis* iii. 5. 23 ; Mommsen, *Staatsrecht*, iii. p. 604,
based on the research of H. Nettleship in *Journal of Philology*, vol. xiii.
p. 175.   See also Sohm, *Institutes of Roman Law*, ch. ii.

which came to embrace all peoples and degrees in its
rational and beneficent influence. If the Greek had
a genius for beauty, and the Jew for righteousness,
the Roman had a genius for law; and the power
of Stoicism in ennobling and enriching his native
conception of it is probably not to be easily over-
estimated.

Thus behind the stormy scenes of public life in
this period there is a process going on which will
be of value not only to the Roman Empire but to
modern civilisation. It was carried on more especially
by two men of the highest character, Q. Mucius
Scaevola, Cicero's adviser in his early days, and
often his model in later life; and Servius Sulpicius
Rufus, his exact contemporary and lifelong friend.
Neither Scaevola nor Sulpicius were, so far as we
know, professed disciples of Stoicism; but that they
applied perhaps half unconsciously the principles of
Stoicism to their own legal studies is almost certain.
The combination of legal training and Stoic influence
(whether direct or unconscious) seems to have been
capable of bringing the Roman aristocratic character
to a high pitch of perfection; and it will be pleasant
to take this friend of Cicero, whose public career we
can clearly trace, and one or two of whose letters we
still possess, as our example of a really well spent life
in an age when time and talent were constantly
abused and wasted.

Sulpicius and Cicero were born in the same year,
106; they went hand in hand in early life, and

remained friends till their deaths in 43, Sulpicius
dying a few months before Cicero. They were
both attached in early youth to the Scaevola just
mentioned, the first of the great series of scientific
Roman lawyers. But the consulship of Cicero made
a wide divergence in their lives. In that year
Sulpicius was a candidate for the consulship and
failed; and then, resigning further attempts to obtain
the highest honour, he retired for the next twelve
years into private life, devoting himself to the work
which has made his name immortal. His writings
are lost; nothing remains of them but a few chance
fragments and allusions; but he was reckoned the
second of the great writers on legal subjects, and
it is probable that he contributed as much as any of
them to the work of making Roman law what it has
been as a power in the world, a factor in modern
civilisation. For he treated it, as his friend said of
him,[1] with the hand and mind of an artist, laying
out his whole subject and distributing it into its
constituent parts, by definition and interpretation
making clear what seemed obscure, and distinguishing
the false from the true in legal principle. In the
splendid panegyric pronounced on him in the senate
after his death,[2] Cicero again emphatically declared
him to be unrivalled in jurisprudence. In beautiful
but untranslatable language he claims that he was

---

[1] *Brutus* 41. 151, where he plainly ranks him above Scaevola. The
passage is a most interesting one, deserving careful attention.

[2] The *Ninth Philippic*: the passage referred to in the text is 5. 10 foll.

"non magis iuris consultus, quam iustitiae,"—an encomium which all great lawyers might well envy ; he aimed rather at enabling men to be rid of litigation than at encouraging them to engage in it.

From such passages we might conjecture, even if we knew nothing more about him, that Sulpicius was a man of very fine clay, of real *humanitas* in the widest sense of that expressive word ; and this is entirely borne out in other ways.[1] Emerging at last from retirement, he stood again for the consulship in 52 B.C., and was elected. The year of his office, 51, was the first in which the enemies of Caesar, with Cato at their head, began to attack his position and clamour for his recall from his command ; this violent hostility Sulpicius tried, not without temporary success, to restrain, and the fact that a man of so just a mind should have taken this line is one of the best arguments for the reasonableness of Caesar's cause.[2] When war broke out he was greatly perplexed how to act ; his breadth of view made decision difficult, and he seems to have been at all times more a student than a man of action. With some heart-burnings he joined Caesar in the struggle, and accepted from him the government of Achaia ; it was at this time that he wrote the famous letter of consolation to Cicero on the death of his beloved daughter Tullia, which

[1] I omit *pro Murena*, chs. vii. and xxi., for want of space. Sulpicius was opposing Cicero in this case, and the latter's allusions to him are useful specimens of the good breeding spoken of above.

[2] See Dio Cassius xl. 59 ; and Cic. *ad Fam.* iv. 1 and 3, to Sulpicius, with allusions to his consulship.

is full of true feeling and kindliness, though evidently composed with effort, if not with difficulty. After Caesar's death he of course acted with Cicero against Antony, and in the spring of 43, making always for peace and good-will, he gave his life for his country in a way that claims our admiration more really than the suicide of Cato the professional Stoic ; he headed an embassy to Antony, though dangerously ill at the time, and died in this last effort to obtain a hearing for the voice of justice. He has a *monumentum aere perennius* in the speech of his old friend urging the senate to vote him a public funeral and a statue, as one who had laid down his life for his country.

We must now turn to consider how the mischievous side of the new Greek culture, in combination with other tendencies of the time, found its way into weak points in the armour of the Roman aristocracy.

The pursuit of ease and pleasure, to which the attainment of wealth and political power were too often merely subordinated, is a leading characteristic of the time. It is seen in many different forms, in many different types of character ; but at the root of the whole corruption is the spirit of the coarser side of Epicureanism. As with Roman Stoicism, so too with Roman Epicureanism, it is not so much the professed holding of philosophical tenets that affected life ; in the case of the latter system, it was the coincidence of its popularity with the decay of the old Roman faith and morality, and with the abnormal opportunities of self-indulgence.   Cato as a professed Stoic, Lucretius as an enthusiastic Epicurean, stand quite apart from the mass of men who were actuated one way or the other by these philosophical creeds. The majority simply played with the philosophy, while following the natural bent of their individual character; but such dilettanteism was often quite enough to affect that character permanently for good or evil.

"Epicureanism popularised inevitably turns to vice."   Was it really popular at Rome?   Cicero tells us in a valuable passage [1] that one Amafinius had written on it, and that a great number of copies of his book were sold, partly because the arguments were easy to follow, partly because the doctrine was pleasant, and partly too because men failed to get hold of anything better.   The date of this Amafinius is uncertain, but it is probable that Cicero is here speaking of the latter part of the second century B.C. ; and he goes on to say that other writers took up the same line of teaching, and established it over the whole of Italy (Italiam totam occupaverunt).   If this was in the time of the Social and Civil Wars, of the proscriptions, of increasing crime and self-seeking, we can well understand that the doctrine was popular.   We have a remarkable example of it in the life of a public man of Cicero's own time, the object of the most

[1] *Tusc. Disp.* iv. 3. 6.

envenomed invective that he ever uttered.[1] We
cannot believe a tithe of what he says about this man,
Calpurnius Piso, consul in 58 ; but in this particular
matter of the damage done him by Epicurean teaching we have independent evidence which confirms it.
Piso, then a young man, made acquaintance with a
Greek of this school of thought, learnt from him
that pleasure was the sole end of life, and failing to
appreciate the true meaning and bearing of the
doctrine, fell into the trap. It was a dangerous
doctrine, Cicero says, for a youth of no remarkable
intelligence ; and the tutor, instead of being the
young man's guide to virtue, was used by him as
an authority for vice.[2] This Greek was a certain
Philodemus, a few of whose poems are preserved in
the *Greek Anthology* ; and a glance at them will show
at once how dangerous such a man would be as the
companion of a Roman youth. He may not himself
have been a bad man—Cicero indeed rather suggests
the contrary, calling him *vere humanus*—but the air
about him was poisonous. In his pupil, if we can
trust in the smallest degree the picture drawn of
him by Cicero, we may see a specimen of the young
men of the age whose talents might have made them

[1] The speech *in Pisonem* ; cp. the *de Provinciis consularibus*, 1-6. This
Piso was the father of Caesar's wife Calpurnia, who survives in Shakespeare.

[2] The difficult passage in which Cicero describes the perversion of this
character under the influence of Philodemus, has been skilfully translated
by Dr. Mahaffy in his *Greek World under Roman Sway*, p. 126 foll.; and the
reader may do well to refer to his whole treatment of the practical result of
Epicureanism.

useful in the world, but for the strength of the current that drew them into self-indulgence.

Not only the pursuit of pleasure, but its correlative, the avoidance of work and duty, can be abundantly illustrated in this age; and this too may have had a subtle connexion with Epicurean teaching, which had always discouraged the individual from distraction in the service of the State, as disturbing to the free development of his own virtue. Sulla did much hard work, but made the serious blunder of retiring to enjoy himself just when his new constitutional machinery needed the most careful watching and tending. Lucullus, after showing a wonderful capacity for work and a greater genius for war than perhaps any man of his time, retired from public life as a millionaire and a quietist, to enjoy the wealth that has become proverbial, and a luxury that is astonishing, even if we make due allowance for the exaggeration of our accounts of it. To his library we have already been introduced; those who would see him in his banqueting-hall, or rather one of the many in his palace, may turn to the fortieth chapter of Plutarch's most interesting *Life* of him, and read the story there told of the dinner he gave to Cicero and Pompeius in the "Apollo" dining-room.[1]

The same cynical carelessness about public affairs and neglect of duty, as compared with private ease or advantage, seems to have been characteristic of the

---

[1] This chapter is also useful as illustrating the urbanity of manners, for Lucullus and Pompeius were political enemies.

ordinary senator. Active and busy in his own interest, he was indifferent to that of the State. There are distinct signs that the attendance in the senate was not good. When Cicero was away in Cilicia his correspondent writes of difficulties in getting together a sufficient number even for such important business as the settlement of provincial governments.[1] On the other hand, much private business was done, and many jobs perpetrated, in a thin senate; in 66 a tribune proposed that no senator should be dispensed from the action of a law unless two hundred were present.[2] It was in such a thin senate, we may be sure, that the virtuous Brutus was dispensed from the law which forbade lending to foreign borrowers in Rome, and thus was enabled to lend to the miserable Salaminians of Cyprus at 48 per cent, and to recover his money under the bond.[3] Writing to his brother in December 57, Cicero speaks of business done in a senate full for the time of year, which was midwinter, just before the Saturnalia, when only two hundred were present out of about six hundred. In February 54, a month when the senate had always much business to get through, it was so cold one day that the few members present clamoured for dismissal and obtained it.[4] And when the senate did meet there was a constant tendency to let things go. No reform of procedure is mentioned as even thought of, at a

---

[1] *ad Fam.* viii. 5 *fin.* ; viii. 9. 2.
[2] See the introduction of Asconius to Cicero *pro Cornelio*, ed. Clark, p. 58.
[3] *ad Att.* v. 21. 11, 13.   [4] *ad Q. frat.* ii. 1. 1 ; ii. 10. 1.

time when it was far more necessary than in our Parliament; business was talked about, postponed, obstructed, and personal animosities and private interests seem, so far as we can judge from the correspondence of the time, to have been predominant. With wearisome iteration the letters speak of nothing done, of business postponed, or of the passing of some senatus consultum, the utter futility of which is obvious even now.[1]   Even the magistrates seem to have been growing careless; we hear of a praetor presiding in the court de repetundis who had not taken the trouble to acquaint himself with the text of the law which governed its procedure;[2] and that praetors were worse than careless about their action in civil cases is proved by another law of the same tribune Cornelius mentioned just now, "that praetors should abide by the rules laid down in their edicts."[3]

But all these futilities, and much of the same kind outside of the senate, together with the quarrels of individuals, the chances and incidents of elections, and all such gossip as forms the staple commodity of the society papers of to-day, were a source of infinite delight to another type of pleasure-loving public man, the last to be illustrated here.

If the older noble families were apathetic and idle,

---

[1] The letters written immediately after Cicero's return from exile are the best examples of this paralysis of business, e.g. *ad Fam.* i. 4; *ad Q. F.* ii. 3. See a useful paper by P. Groebe in *Klio*, vol. v. p. 229.

[2] This appears from a letter of Caelius to Cicero in 51.—*ad Fam.* viii. 8. 3.

[3] Asconius *in Cornelianum*, ed. Clark, p. 59.   "Ut praetores ex edictis suis perpetuis ius dicerent."

there were plenty of young men, rising most often
from the class below, whose minds were intensely
active—active in the pursuit of pleasure, but pleasure
in the comparatively harmless form of amusement and
excitement. One of these, the son of a banker at
Puteoli, Marcus Caelius Rufus, stands out as a living
portrait in his own letters to Cicero, of which no
fewer than seventeen are preserved.[1] Of his early
years too we know a good deal, told us in the speech
in defence of him spoken by Cicero in the year 56;
and these combined sources of information make him
the most interesting figure in the life of his age.
M. Boissier has written a delightful essay on him
in his *Cicéron et ses amis*, and Professor Tyrrell has
done the like in the introduction to the fourth
volume of his edition of Cicero's letters; but they have
treated him less as a type of the youth of his day
than as the friend and pupil of Cicero. Caelius will
always repay fresh study; he was amusing and
interesting to his contemporaries, and so he will be
for ever to us. He is a veritable Proteus—you
never know what shape he will take next;

Omnia transformat sese in miracula rerum—

we can trace no less than six such transformations
in the story of his life. And this instability, let
us note at once, was not the restlessness of a jaded
roué, but the coruscation of a clever mind wholly
without principle, intensely interested in his *monde*,

---

[1] All his letters are in the eighth book of those *ad Familiares*.

in the life in which he moved, with all its enjoyment and excitement.

Caelius' father brought his son to Cicero, as soon as he had taken his toga virilis, to study law and oratory, and Cicero was evidently attracted by the bright and lively boy; he never deserted him, and the last letter of Caelius to his old preceptor was written only just before his own sad end. But Cicero was not the man to keep an unstable character out of mischief; he loved young men, especially clever ones, and was apt to take an optimistic view of them, as he did of his own son and nephew. Caelius, always attracted by novelty, left Cicero and attached himself to Catiline; and for this vagary, as well as for his own want of success in controlling his pupil, Cicero rather awkwardly and amusingly apologises in the early chapters of his speech in his defence. Wild oats must be sown, he says; when a youth has given full fling to his propensities to vice, they will leave him, and he may become a useful citizen,—a dangerous view of a preceptor's duty, which reminds us of the treatment of the boy Nero by his philosopher guardian long afterwards.[1]

Caelius escaped the fate of Catiline and his crew only to fall into the hands of another clique not less dangerous for his moral welfare. He became one of a group of brilliant young men, among whom were probably Catullus and Calvus the poets, who were lovers, and passionate lovers, of the infamous Clodia;

[1] Tacitus, *Annals* xiii. 2: "voluptatibus concessis."

they were needy, she found them money, and they hovered about her like moths about a candle. In such a life of passion and pleasure quarrels were inevitable. If the Lesbia of Catullus be Clodia, as we may believe, she had thrown the poet over with a light heart. It was apparently of his own free will that Caelius deserted her : in revenge she turned upon him with an accusation of theft and attempt to poison. What truth there was in the charges we do not really know, but Cicero defended him successfully, and in this way we come to know the details of this unsteady life.

In gratitude, and possibly in shame, Caelius now returned to his old friend, and abandoned the whole ring of his vicious companions for diligent practice in the courts, where he obtained considerable fame as an orator. A fragment of a speech of his preserved by Quintilian shows, as Professor Tyrrell observes, wonderful power of graphic and picturesque utterance.[1] Cicero, writing of him after his death,[2] says that he was at this time on the right side in politics, and that as tribune of the plebs in 56 he successfully supported the good cause, and checked revolutionary and seditious movements. All was going well with him until Cicero went as governor to Cilicia in 51. Cicero seems to have felt complete confidence in him, and invited him to become his confidential political correspondent ; fifteen out of his seventeen letters were written in this capacity. These letters show

[1] Quintil. iv. 2. 123.   [2] *Brutus* 79. 273.

K

us the man as clearly as if we had his diary before
us.   Caelius is no idle scamp or lazy Epicurean;
his mind is constantly active : nothing escapes his
notice : the minutest and most sordid things delight
him.   He is bright, happy, witty, frivolous, and
doubtless lovable.   It is amusing to see how Cicero
himself now and again catches the infection, and
tries (in vain) to write in the same frivolous manner.[1]
Caelius has some political insight ; he sees civil war
approaching, but he takes it all as a game, and on
the eve of events which were to shake the world he
trifles with the symptoms as though they were the
silliest gossip of the capital.[2]   In none of these
letters is there the smallest vestige of principle to be
found.   On the very eve of civil war he tells Cicero[3]
that as soon as war breaks out the right thing to do
is to join the stronger side.   Judging Caesar's side
to be the stronger, he joined it accordingly, and did
his best to induce Cicero to do the same.   As
M. Boissier happily says, he never cared to " ménager
ses transitions."

He had, however, to discover that if to change
over to Caesar was the safer course, to turn a political
somersault once more, to try and undermine the
work of the master, meant simply ruin.   We have
the story of his sixth and last transformation from

[1] e.g. ad Fam. ii. 13. 3.

[2] Exactly the same combination of real interest in, and frivolous treatment of, politics is to be found in the early letters of Horace Walpole to Sir
H. Mann, especially those of the year 1742.

[3] ad Fam. viii. 14. 3.

Caesar himself, who was not, however, in Italy at the time.[1] Credit in Italy had been seriously upset by the outbreak of Civil War, and Caesar had been at much pains to steady it by an ordinance which has been alluded to in the last chapter.[2] In 48 Caelius was praetor; in the master's absence he suddenly took up the cause of the debtors, and tried to evoke appeals against the decisions of his colleague Trebonius,—a great lawyer and a just man. Failing in this, he started as a downright revolutionary, proposing first the abolition of house-rent, and finally the abolition of all debts; and Milo, in exile at Massilia, was summoned to help him to raise Italy against Caesar. This was too much, and both were quickly caught and killed as they were stirring up gladiators and other slave-bands among the latifundia of South Italy.

Caelius' letters give us a chance of seeing what that life of the Forum really was which so fascinated the young men of the day, and some of the old, such as Cicero himself. We can see these children playing on the very edge of the crater, like the French noblesse before the Revolution. In both cases there was a semi-consciousness that the eruption was not far off,—but they went on playing. What was it that so greatly amused and pleased them?

What Caelius is always writing of is mainly elections and canvassing, accusations and trials, games and shows. Elections he treats as pure sport, as a

---

[1] Caesar, *Bell. Civ.* iii. 20 foll.   [2] See above, p. 86 ; cp. p. 58.

kind of enjoyable gambling, or as a means of spiting some one whom you want to annoy. With elections accusations were often connected : if a man were accused before his election he could not continue to stand ; if condemned after it he was disqualified ; here were ways in which personal spite might deprive him of success at the last moment.[1] Accusations, too, were of course the best means by which an ambitious young man could come to the front. The whole number of trials mentioned by Caelius is astonishing ; sometimes there is such a complication of them as is difficult to follow. Every one is ready to lay an accusation, without the smallest regard for truth. Young Appius Claudius accuses Servilius, and makes a mess of the attack, while the praetor mismanages the conduct of the trial, so that nothing comes of it ; but finally Appius is himself accused by the Servilii *de vi*, in order to keep him from further attacks on Servilius![2] Appius the father quarrelled with Caelius and egged on others to accuse him, though he was curule aedile at the time. "Their impudence was so boundless that they secured that an information should be laid against me for a very serious crime (under the Scantinian law). Scarcely had Pola got the words out of his mouth, when I laid an information under the same law against the censor, Appius. I never saw a more successful stroke !"[3]

Of the games, and the panthers to be exhibited at

---

[1] So for example Servaeus is disqualified, *ad Fam.* viii. 4. 1.
[2] *Ib.* viii. 8. 2.   [3] *Ib.* 8. 12.

them, about which Caelius is for ever worrying his
friend in Cilicia, we shall see something in another
chapter. There is plenty of other gossip in these
letters, and gossip often about unsavoury matters
which need not be noticed here. It lets in a flood of
light upon the causes of the general incompetence
and inefficiency ; the life of the Forum was a demoral-
ising one :

> Uni se atque eidem studio omnes dedere et arti
> uerba dare ut caute possint, pugnare dolose :
> blanditia certare, bonum simulare uirum se :
> insidias facere, ut si hostes sint omnibus omnes.[1]

From what has been said in this sketch it should
be clear that we have in the aristocracy of this period
a complicated society, the various aspects of which
can hardly be united in a single picture. It is partly
a hereditary aristocracy, with all the pride and
exclusiveness of a group of old families accustomed
to power and consequence. It is in the main a
society of gentlemen, dignified in manner, and kindly
towards each other, and it is also a society of high
culture and literary ability, though poor in creative
genius, and unimaginative. On the other hand, it
is a class which has lost its interest in the State, and
is energetic only when pursuing its own interests :
pleasure-loving, luxurious, gossiping, trifling with
serious matters, short-sighted in politics because
anxious only for personal advance. " Rari nantes in
gurgite vasto " are the men who are really in earnest,

---

[1] Lucilius, *Fragm.* 9, ed. Baehrens.

but they are there; we must not forget that in Lucretius and Cicero this society produced one of the greatest poets and one of the most perfect prose writers that the world treasures; in Sulpicius a lawyer of permanent value to humanity, and in Caesar not only an author and a scholar but a man of action unrivalled in capacity and industry.

CHAPTER V

MARRIAGE : AND THE ROMAN LADY

In order to appreciate the position of women of various types in the society we are examining, it is necessary to make it clear what Roman marriage originally and ideally meant. In any society, it will be found that the position and influence of woman can be fairly well discerned from the nature of the marriage ceremony and the conditions under which it is carried out. At Rome, in all periods of her history, a *iustum matrimonium*, i.e. a marriage sanctioned by law and religion, and therefore entirely legal in all its results, was a matter of great moment, not to be achieved without many forms and ceremonies. The reason for this elaboration is obvious, at any rate to any one who has some acquaintance with ancient life in Greece or Italy. As we shall see later on, the house was a residence for the divine members of the family, as well as the human ; the entrance, therefore, of a bride into the household,—of one, that is, who had no part nor lot in that family life—meant some straining of the relation between the divine and

human members.   The human part of the family
brings in a new member, but it has to be assured that
the divine part is willing to accept her before the step
taken can be regarded as complete.   She has to enter
the family in such a way as to be able to share in its
sacra, i.e. in the worship of the household spirits, the
ancestors in their tombs, or in any special cult
attached to the family.   In order to secure this
eligibility, she was in the earliest times subjected to
a ceremony which was clearly of a sacramental
character, and which had as its effect the transference
of the bride from the hand (*manus*) of her father,
i.e. from absolute subjection to him as the head
of her own family, to the hand of her husband, i.e.
to absolute subjection to him as the head of her new
family.

This sacramental ceremony was called *confarreatio*, because a sacred cake, made of the old Italian
grain called *far*, and offered to Jupiter Farreus,[1] was
partaken of by bride and bridegroom, in the presence
of the Pontifex Maximus, the Flamen Dialis, and ten
other witnesses.   At such a ceremony the auspices
had of course been taken, and apparently a victim
was also slain, and offered probably to Ceres, the
skin of which was stretched over two seats (*sellae*),

---

[1] This probably means that the deity was believed to reside in the cake,
and that the communicants not only entered into communion with each
other in eating of it, but also with him.   It is in fact exactly analogous to
the sacramental ceremony of the Latin festival, in which each city partook
of the sacred victim, in that case a white heifer.   See Fowler, *Roman
Festivals*, p. 96 and reff.

on which the bride and bridegroom had to sit.[1]
These details of the early form of patrician marriage
are only mentioned here to make the religious character of the Roman idea of the rite quite plain ; in
other words, to prove that the entrance of a bride
into a family from outside was a matter of very great
difficulty and seriousness, not to be achieved without
special aid and the intervention of the gods. We
may even go so far as to say that the new materfamilias was in some sort a priestess of the household,
and that she must undergo a solemn initiation before
assuming that position. And we may still further
illustrate the mystical religious nature of the whole
rite, if we remember that throughout Roman history
no one could hold the priesthood of Jupiter (fla-
minium diale), or that of Mars or Quirinus, or of the
Rex sacrorum, who had not been born of parents
wedded by confarreatio, and that in each case the
priest himself must be married by the same ceremony.[2]
This last mentioned fact may also serve to remind
us that it was not only the family and its sacra, its
life and its maintenance, that called for the ceremonies making up a iustum matrimonium, but also
the State and its sacra, its life and its maintenance.[3]
As confarreatio had as its immediate object the
providing of a materfamilias fully qualified in all

---

[1] This interesting custom is recorded by Servius (*ad Aen.* iv. 374). For
the whole ceremony of confarreatio see De Marchi, *La Religione nella vita
domestica*, p. 155 foll. ; Marquardt, *Privatleben*, p. 32 foll.   Cp. also
Gaius i. 112.
[2] Gaius *l.c.*   [3] Cic. *de Off.* i. 17. 54.

her various functions, and as its further object the
providing of persons legally qualified to perform the
most important sacra of the state; so marriage, in
whatever form, had as its object at once the maintenance of the family and its sacra and the production of men able to serve the State in peace
and war. To be a Roman citizen you must be the
product of a iustum matrimonium. From this
initial fact flow all the *iura* or rights which together
make up citizenship; whether the private rights,
which enable you to hold and transfer and to inherit
property under the shelter of the Roman law,[1] or
the public rights, which protect your person against
violence and murder, and enable you to give your
vote in the public assembly and to seek election to
magistracies.[2]

Marriage then was a matter of the utmost importance in Roman life, and in all the forms of it we find
this importance marked by due solemnity of ritual.
In two other forms, besides confarreatio, the bride
could be brought under the hand of her husband,
viz., *coemptio* and *usus*, with which we are not here
specially concerned ; for long before the last century
of the Republic all three methods had become practically obsolete, or were only occasionally used for
particular purposes. In the course of time it had
been found more convenient for a woman to remain

[1] i.e. ius commercii and ius connubii : the former enabling a man to
claim the protection of the courts in all cases relating to property, the latter
to claim the same protection in cases of disputed inheritance.

[2] i.e. ius provocationis, ius suffragii, ius honorum.

after her marriage in the hand of her father, or if he were dead, in the "tutela" of a guardian (tutor), than to pass into that of her husband; for in the latter case her property became absolutely his. The natural tendency to escape from the restrictions of marital *manus* may be illustrated by a case such as the following: a woman under the *tutela* of a guardian wishes to marry; if she does so, and passes under the *manus* of her husband, her *tutor* loses all control over her property, which may probably be of great importance for the family she is leaving; he therefore naturally objects to such a marriage, and urges that she should be married without *manus*.[1] In fact the interests of her own family would often clash with those of the one she was about to enter, and a compromise could be effected by the abandonment of marriage *cum manu*.

Now this, the abandonment of marriage *cum manu*, means simply that certain legal consequences of the marriage ceremony were dropped, and with them just those parts of the ceremony which produced these consequences. Otherwise the marriage was absolutely as valid for all purposes private and public as it could be made even by confarreatio itself. The sacramental part was absent, and the survival of the features of marriage by purchase, which we may

---

[1] This is how I understand Cuq, *Institutions juridiques des Romains*, p. 223. In the well known Laudatio Turiae we have a curious case of a re-marriage by coemptio with manus, for a particular purpose, connected of course with money matters. See Mommsen's Commentary, reprinted in his *Gesammelte Schriften*, vol. i.

see in the form of coemptio, was also absent; but in all other respects the marriage ceremony was the same as in marriage *cum manu*. It retained all essential religious features, losing only a part of its legal character. It will be as well briefly to describe a Roman wedding of the type common in the last two centuries of the Republic.

To begin with, the boy and girl—for such they were, as we should look on them, even at the time of marriage—have been betrothed, in all probability, long before. Cicero tells us that he betrothed his daughter Tullia to Calpurnius Piso Frugi early in 66 B.C.; the marriage took place in 63. Tullia seems to have been born in 76, so that she was ten years old at the time of betrothal and thirteen at that of marriage. This is probably typical of what usually happened; and it shows that the matter was really entirely in the hands of the parents. It was a family arrangement, a *mariage de convenance*, as has been and is the practice among many peoples, ancient and modern.[1] The betrothal was indeed a promise rather than a definite contract, and might be broken off without illegality; and thus if there were a strong dislike on the part of either girl or boy a way of escape could be found.[2] However this may be, we may be sure that the idea of the marriage was not that of a union for love, though it was distinguished

---

[1] Westermarck, *History of Human Marriage*, ch. x.

[2] See, however, the curious passage quoted by Gellius (iv. 4. 2) from Serv. Sulpicius, the great jurist (above, p. 118 foll.), on *sponsalia* in Latium down to 89 B.C.

from concubinage by an "affectio maritalis" as well as
by legal forms, and though a true attachment might,
and often did, as in modern times in like circumstances, arise out of it. It was the idea of the
service of the family and the State that lay at the
root of the union. This is well illustrated, like so
many other Roman ideas, in the *Aeneid* of Virgil.
Those who persist in looking on Aeneas with modern
eyes, and convict him of perfidy towards Dido, forget
that his passion for Dido was a sudden one, not
sanctioned by the gods or by favourable auspices,
and that the ultimate union with Lavinia, for whom
he forms no such attachment, was one which would
recommend itself to every Roman as justified by the
advantage to the State. The poet, it is true, betrays
his own intense humanity in his treatment of the
fate of Dido, but he does so in spite of his theme,—
the duty of every Roman to his family and the State.
A Roman would no doubt fall in love, like a youth
of any other nation, but his passion had nothing to
do with his life of duty as a Roman. This idea of
marriage had serious consequences, to which we shall
return later on.

When the day for the wedding arrives, our bride
assumes her bridal dress, laying aside the toga
praetexta of her childhood and dedicating her dolls
to the Lar of her family; and wearing the reddish
veil (*flammeum*) and the woollen girdle fastened
with a knot called the knot of Hercules,[1] she awaits

---

[1] For the other details of the dress, see Marq. *Privatleben*, p. 43.

the arrival of the bridegroom in her father's house. Meanwhile the auspices are being taken;[1] in earlier times this was done by observing the flight of birds, but now by examination of the entrails of a victim, apparently a sheep. If this is satisfactory the youthful pair declare their consent to the union and join their right hands as directed by a pronuba, i.e. a married woman, who acts as a kind of priestess. Then after another sacrifice and a wedding feast, the bride is conducted from her old home to that of her husband, accompanied by three boys, sons of living parents, one carrying a torch while the other two lead her by either hand; flute-players go before, and nuts are thrown to the boys. This *deductio*, charmingly described in the beautiful sixty-fifth poem of Catullus, is full of interesting detail which must be omitted here. When the bridegroom's house is reached, the bride smears the doorposts with fat and oil and ties a woollen fillet round each : she is then lifted over the threshold, is taken by her husband into the partnership of fire and water—the essentials of domestic life—and passes into the atrium. The morrow will find her a materfamilias, sitting among her maids in that atrium, or in the more private apartments behind it :

Claudite ostia, virgines
Lusimus satis. At boni
Coniuges, bene vivite, et
Munere assiduo valentem
Exercete iuventam.

[1] Cic. *de Div.* i. 16. 28.

Even the dissipated Catullus could not but treat the subject of marriage with dignity and tenderness, and in this last stanza of his poem he alludes to the duties of a married pair in language which would have satisfied the strictest Roman. He has also touched another chord which would echo in the heart of every good citizen, in the delicious lines which just precede those quoted, and anticipate the child— a son of course—that is to be born, and that will lie in his mother's arms holding out his little hands, and smiling on his father.[1] Nothing can better illustrate the contrast in the mind of the Roman between passionate love and serious marriage than a comparison of this lovely poem with those which tell the sordid tale of the poet's intrigues with Lesbia (Clodia). The beauty and *gravitas* of married life as it used to be are still felt and still found, but the depths of human feeling are not stirred by them. Love lies beyond, is a fact outside the pale of the ordered life of the family or the State.

No one who studies this ceremonial of Roman marriage, in the light of the ideas which it indicates and reflects, can avoid the conclusion that the position of the married woman must have been one of substantial dignity, calling for and calling out a corresponding type of character. Beyond doubt the position of the Roman materfamilias was a much more dignified one than that of the Greek wife. She

---

[1] These lines suggested to Virgil the famous four at the end of the fourth Eclogue. See *Virgil's " Messianic Eclogue,"* p. 72.

was far indeed from being a mere drudge or squaw; she shared with her husband in all the duties of the household, including those of religion, and within the house itself she was practically supreme.[1] She lived in the atrium, and was not shut away in a women's chamber; she nursed her own children and brought them up; she had entire control of the female slaves who were her maids; she took her meals with her husband, but sitting, not reclining, and abstaining from wine; in all practical matters she was consulted, and only on questions political or intellectual was she expected to be silent. When she went out arrayed in the graceful *stola matronalis*, she was treated with respect, and the passers-by made way for her; but it is characteristic of her position that she did not as a rule leave the house without the knowledge of her husband, or without an escort.[2]

In keeping with this dignified position was the ideal character of the materfamilias. Ideal we must call it, for it does not in all respects coincide with the tradition of Roman women even in early times; but we must remember that at all periods of Roman history the woman whose memory survives is apt to be the woman who is not the ideal matron, but one who forces herself into notice by violating the

[1] She was addressed as *domina* by all members of the family. See Marquardt, *Privatleben*, p. 57 note 3. It should be noted that she had brought a contribution to the family resources in the form of a dowry (dos), given her by her father to maintain her position.

[2] These details are drawn chiefly from the sixth book of Valerius Maximus, *de Pudicitia*

traditions of womanhood. The typical matron would assuredly never dream of playing a part in history; her influence was behind the scenes, and therefore proportionally powerful. The legendary mother of Coriolanus (the Volumnia of Shakespeare), Cornelia the mother of the Gracchi, Aurelia, Caesar's mother, and Julia his daughter, did indirectly play a far greater part in public life than the loud and vicious ladies who have left behind them names famous or infamous; but they never claimed the recognition of their power.

This peculiar character of the Roman matron, a combination of dignity, industry, and practical wisdom, was exactly suited to attract the attention of a gentle philosopher like Plutarch, who loved, with genuine moral fervour, all that was noble and honest in human nature. Not only does he constantly refer to the Roman ladies and their character in his *Lives* and his *Morals*, but in his series of more than a hundred "Roman questions" the first nine, as well as many others, are concerned with marriage and the household life; and in his treatise called *Coniugalia praecepta* he reflects many of the features of the Roman matron. From him, in Sir Thomas North's translation, Shakespeare drew the inspiration which enabled him to produce on the Elizabethan stage at least one such typical matron. In Coriolanus he has followed Plutarch so closely that the reader may almost be referred to him as an authority; and in the contrast between the austere and dignified

L

Volumnia and the passionate and voluptuous Cleopatra of the later play, the poet's imagination seems to have been guided by a true historical instinct.

We need not doubt that the austere matron of the old type survived into the age we are specially concerned with ; but we hardly come across her in the literature of the time, just because she was living her own useful life, and did not seek publicity. Chance has indeed preserved for us on stone the story of a wonderful lady, whose early years of married life were spent in the trying time of the civil wars of 49-43 B.C., and who, if a devoted husband's praises are to be trusted, as indeed they may be, was a woman of the finest Roman cast, and endowed with such a combination of practical virtues as we should hardly have expected even in a Roman matron. But we shall return to this inscription later on.

The ladies whom we meet with in Cicero's letters and in the other literature of the last age of the Republic are not of this type. Since the second Punic war the Roman lady has changed, like everything else Roman. It is not possible here to trace the history of the change in detail, but we may note that it seems to have begun within the household, in matters of dress and expense, and later on affected the life and bearing of women in society and politics. Marriages cum manu became unusual : the wife remained in the potestas of her father, who in most cases, doubtless, ceased to trouble himself about her, and as her property did not pass to her husband, she could not but obtain a new position of independence. Women began to be rich, and in the year 169 B.C. a law was passed (lex Voconia) forbidding women of the highest census[1] (who alone would probably be concerned) to inherit legacies. Even before the end of the great war, and when private luxury would seem out of place, it had been proposed to abolish the Oppian law, which placed restrictions on the ornaments and apparel of women; and in spite of the vehement opposition of Cato, then a young man, the proposal was successful.[2] At the same time divorce, which had probably never been impossible though it must have been rare,[3] began to be a common practice. We find to our surprise that the virtuous Aemilius Paullus, in other respects a model paterfamilias, put away his wife, and when asked why he did so, replied that a woman might be excellent in the eyes of her neighbours, but that only a husband could tell where the shoe pinched.[4] And in estimating the changed position of women within the family we must not forget the fact that in the course of the long and unceasing wars of the second century B.C., husbands were away from home for

[1] This is proved by an allusion to Cato's speech in support of the law, in Gellius, *Noct. Att.* vi. 13.

[2] Livy xxxiv. 1 foll., where the speech of Cato is reproduced in Livy's language and with "modern" rhetoric.

[3] De Marchi, *op. cit.* p. 163 ; Marq. *Privatleben*, p. 87 foll. Confarreatio was only dissoluble by diffarreatio, but this was perhaps used only for penal purposes. Other forms of marriage did not present the same difficulty, not being of a sacramental character.

[4] Plutarch, *Aem. Paull.* 5.

years together, and in innumerable cases must have
perished by the sword or pestilence, or fallen into
the hands of an enemy and been enslaved. It was
inevitable that as the male population diminished, as
it undoubtedly did in that century, the importance
of woman should proportionately have increased.
Unfortunately too, even when the husbands were at
home, their wives sometimes seem to have wished
to be rid of them.   In 180 B.C. the consul Piso was
believed to have been murdered by his wife, and
whether the story be true or not, the suspicion is at
least significant.[1]   In 154 two noble ladies, wives of
consulares, were accused of poisoning their husbands
and put to death by a council of their own relations.[2]
Though the evidence in these cases is not by any
means satisfactory, yet we can hardly doubt that
there was a tendency among women of the highest
rank to give way to passion and excitement; the
evidence for the Bacchanalian conspiracy of 186 B.C.,
in which women played a very prominent part, is
explicit, and shows that there was a "new woman"
even then, who had ceased to be satisfied with
the austere life of the family and with the mental
comfort supplied by the old religion, and was ready
to break out into recklessness even in matters which
were the concern of the State.[3]   That they had
already begun to exercise an undue influence over
their husbands in public affairs seems suggested by
old Cato's famous dictum that "all men rule over

[1] Livy xl. 37.   [2] Livy, *Epit.* 48.   [3] Livy xxxix. 8–18.

women, we Romans rule over all men, and our
wives rule over us."[1]

But it would be a great mistake to suppose that
the men themselves were not equally to blame.
Wives do not poison their husbands without some
reason for hating them, and the reason is not difficult
to guess. It is a fact beyond doubt that in spite of
the charm of family life as it has been described
above, neither law nor custom exacted conjugal
faithfulness from a husband.[2] Old Cato represents
fairly well the old idea of Roman virtue, yet it is
clear enough, both from Plutarch's *Life* of him (e.g.
ch. xxiv.) and from fragments of his own writings,
that his view of the conjugal relation was a coarse one,
—that he looked on the wife rather as a necessary
agent for providing the State with children than as
a helpmeet to be tended and revered. And this
being so, we are not surprised to find that men
are already beginning to dislike and avoid marriage;
a most dangerous symptom, with which a century
later Augustus found it impossible to cope. In the
year 131, just after Tiberius Gracchus had been
trying to revive the population of Italy by his
agrarian law, Metellus Macedonicus the censor did

---

[1] Plutarch, *Cato the Elder* 8.

[2] Gellius (x. 23) quotes a fragment of Cato's speech *de Dotibus*, in
which the following sentences occur: "Si quid perverse taetreque factum
est a muliere, multitatur : si vinum bibit, si cum alieno viro probri quid
fecerit, condempnatur. In adulterio uxorem tuam si prehendisses sine
iudicio impune necares : illa te, si adulterares sive tu adulterarere, digito
non auderet contingere, neque ius est." Under such circumstances a bold
woman might take her revenge illegally.

what he could to induce men to marry "liberorum creandorum causa"; and a fragment of a speech of his on this subject became famous afterwards, as quoted by Augustus with the same object. It is equally characteristic of Roman humour and Roman hardness. "If we could do without wives," he said to the people, "we should be rid of that nuisance: but since nature has decreed that we can neither live comfortably with them nor live at all without them, we must e'en look rather to our permanent interests than to a passing pleasure."[1]

Now if we take into account these tendencies, on the part both of men and women in the married state, and further consider the stormy and revolutionary character of the half century that succeeded the Gracchi,—the Social and Civil Wars, the proscriptions of Marius and Sulla,—we shall be prepared to find the ladies of Cicero's time by no means simply feminine in charm or homely in disposition. Most of them are indeed mere names to us, and we have to be careful in weighing what is said of them by later writers. But of two or three of them we do in fact know a good deal.

The one of whom we really know most is the wife of Cicero, Terentia: an ordinary lady, of no particular ability or interest, who may stand as representative of the quieter type of married woman. She lived with her husband about thirty years, and until towards the end of that period, a long one for the age,

[1] Gellius i. 6; cp. Livy, *Epit.* 59.

we find nothing substantial against her. If we had nothing but Cicero's letters to her, more than twenty in number, and his allusions to her in other letters, we should conclude that she was a faithful and on the whole a sensible wife. But more than once he writes of her delicate health,[1] and as the poor lady had at various times a great deal of trouble to go through, it is quite possible that as she grew older she became short in her temper, or trying in other ways to a husband so excitable and vacillating. We find stories of her in Plutarch and elsewhere which represent her as shrewish, too careful of her own money, and so on;[2] but facts are of more account than the gossip of the day, and there is not a sign in the letters that Cicero disliked or mistrusted her until the year 47. Had there really been cause for mistrust it would have slipped out in some letter to Atticus. Then, after his absence during the war, he seems to have believed that she had neglected himself and his interests : his letters to her grow colder and colder, and the last is one which, as has been truly said, a gentleman would not write to his housekeeper. The pity of it is that Cicero, after divorcing her, married a young and rich wife, and does not seem to have behaved very well to her. In a letter to Atticus

---

[1] e.g. *ad Fam.* xiv. 2.

[2] The story of the relations of Cicero, Terentia, Clodius, and Clodia, in Plut. *Cic.* 29 is too full of inaccuracies to be depended on. In the 41st chapter what he says of the divorce and its causes must be received with caution ; it seems to come from some record left by Tiro, Cicero's freedman and devoted friend, and as Cicero obviously loved this man much more than his wife, we can understand why the two should dislike each other.

(xii. 32) he writes that Publilia wanted to come
to him with her mother, when he was at Astura,
devoting himself to grief for his daughter, and that
he had answered that he wished to be let alone. The
letter shows Cicero at his worst, for once heartless
and discourteous ; and if he could be so to a young
lady who wished to do her duty by him, what may
he not have been to Terentia ? I suspect that
Terentia was quite as much sinned against as sinning ;
and may we not believe that of the innumerable
married women who were divorced at this time some
at least were the victims of their husbands' callousness rather than of their own shortcomings ?

The wife of Cicero's brother Quintus does, however,
seem to have been a difficult person to get on with.
She was a sister of Atticus, but she did not share her
brother's tact and universal good-will. Marcus Cicero
has recorded (*ad Att.* v. 1) a scene in which her ill-
temper was so ludicrous that the divorce which took
place afterwards needs no explanation. The two
brothers were travelling together, and Pomponia was
with them ; something had irritated her. When they
stopped to lunch at a place belonging to Quintus at
Arcanum, he asked his wife to invite the ladies of the
party in. "Nothing, as I thought, could be more courteous, and that too not only in the actual words, but
in his intention and the expression of his face. But
she, in the hearing of us all, exclaimed, 'I am only a
stranger here!'" Apparently she had not been asked
by her husband to see after the luncheon ; this had

been done by a freedman, and she was annoyed.
" There," said Quintus, " that is what I have to put up
with every day ! "   When he sent her dishes from the
triclinium, where the gentlemen were, having their
meal, she would not taste them.   This little domestic
contretemps is too good to be neglected, but we
must turn to women of greater note and character.

Terentia and Pomponia and their kind seem to
have had nothing in the way of " higher education,"
nor do their husbands seem to have expected from them
any desire to share in their own intellectual interests.
Not once does Cicero allude to any pleasant social
intercourse in which his wife took part ; and, to say
the truth, he would probably have avoided marriage
with a woman of taste and knowledge.   There were
such women, as we shall see, probably many of
them ; ever since the incoming of wealth and of
Greek education, of theatres and amusements and all
the pleasant out-of-door life of the city, what was
now coming to be called *cultus* had occupied the
minds and affected the habits of Roman ladies as well
as men.   Unfortunately it was seldom that it was
found compatible with the old Roman ideal of the
materfamilias and her duties.   The invasion of new
manners was too sudden, as was the corresponding
invasion of wealth ; such a lady as Cornelia, the
famous mother of the Gracchi, who knew what
education really meant, who had learned men about
her and could write well herself, and yet could
combine with these qualities the careful discharge of

the duties of wife and mother,[1]—such ladies must have been rare, and in Cicero's time hardly to be found.   More and more the notion gained ground that a clever woman who wished to make a figure in society, to be the centre of her own *monde*, could not well realise her ambition simply as a married woman. She would probably marry, play fast and loose with the married state, neglect her children if she had any, and after one or two divorces, die or disappear.   So powerfully did this idea of the incompatibility of culture and wifehood gain possession of the Roman mind in the last century B.C., that Augustus found his struggle with it the most difficult task he had to face; in vain he exiled Ovid for publishing a work in which married women are most frankly and explicitly left out of account, while all that is attractive in the other sex to a man of taste and education is assumed to be found only among those who have, so far at least, eschewed the duties and burdens of married life.   The culta puella and the cultus puer of Ovid's fascinating yet repulsive poem[2] are the products of a society which looks on pleasure, not reason or duty, as the main end of life,—not indeed pleasure simply of the grosser type, but the gratification of one's own wish for enjoyment and excitement, without a thought of the misery all around, or any sense of the self-respect that comes of active well-doing.

[1] Plutarch, *Ti. Gracch.* 1; *Gaius Gracch.* 19. The letters of Cornelia which are extant are quite possibly genuine.

[2] The recent edition of the *Ars amatoria* by Paul Brandt has an introduction in which these points are well expressed.

The most notable example of a woman of *cultus*
in Cicero's day was the famous Clodia, the Lesbia (as
we may now almost assume) who fascinated Catullus
and then threw him over. She had been married to
a man of family and high station, Metellus Celer, who
had died, strange to say, without divorcing her. She
must have been a woman of great beauty and charm,
for she seems to have attracted round her a little
côterie of clever young men and poets, to whom she
could lend money or accord praise as suited the
moment. Whether Cicero himself had once come
within reach of her attractions, and perhaps suffered
by them, is an open question, and depends chiefly on
statements of Plutarch which may (as has been said
above) have no better foundation than the gossip of
society. But we know how two typical young men
of the time, Caelius and Catullus, flew into the candle
and were singed ; we know how fiercely she turned
on Caelius, exposing herself and him without a
moment's hesitation in a public court ; and we know
how cruelly she treated the poet, who hated her for it
even while he still loved her : [1]

> Odi et amo.   Quare id faciam, fortasse requiris ;
> Nescio, sed fieri sentio et excrucior.
>
> CATULL. 85.

She was, as M. Boissier has well said,[2] the exact
counterpart of her still more famous brother : " Elle
apportait dans sa conduite privée, dans ses engage-
ments d'affection, les mêmes emportements et les

---

[1] Catullus 72. 75.   [2] *Cicéron et ses amis*, p. 175.

mêmes ardeurs que son frère dans la vie publique. Prompte à tous les excès et ne rougissant pas de les avouer, aimant et haïssant avec fureur, incapable de se gouverner et détestant toute contrainte, elle ne démentait pas cette grande et fière famille dont elle descendait." All this is true; we need not go beyond it and believe the worst that has been said of her.

We have just a glimpse of another lady of *cultus*, but only a glimpse. This was Sempronia, the wife of an honest man and the mother of another;[1] but according to Sallust, who introduces her to us as a principal in the conspiracy of Catiline, she was one of those who found steady married life incompatible with literary and artistic tastes. " She could play and dance more elegantly than an honest woman should . . . she played fast and loose with her money, and equally so with her good fame."[2] She had no scruples, he says, in denying a debt, or in helping in a murder : yet she had plenty of *esprit*, could write verses and talk brilliantly, and she knew too how to assume an air of modesty on occasion. Sallust loved to colour his portraits highly, and in painting this woman he saw no doubt a chance of literary effect; but that she was really in the conspiracy we cannot doubt, and that she had private ends to gain by it is also probable. She seems to be the first of a series of ladies who during the next century and later were to be a power in politics, and most of whom were at

---

[1] Decimus Brutus, one of the tyrannicides of March 15, 44.

[2] Sall. *Cat*. 25.

least capable of crime, public and private. There is indeed one instance a few years earlier of a woman exercising an almost supreme influence in the State, and a woman too of the worst kind. Plutarch tells us in the most explicit way that when Lucullus in 75 B.C. was trying to secure for himself the command against Mithridates, he found himself compelled to apply to a woman named Praecia, whose social gifts and good nature gave her immense influence, which she used with the pertinacity peculiar to such ladies. Her reputation, however, was very bad, and among other lovers she had enslaved Cethegus (afterwards the conspirator), whose power at the time was immense at Rome. Thus, says Plutarch, the whole power of the State fell into the hands of Praecia, for no public measure was passed if Cethegus was not for it, in other words, if Praecia did not recommend it to him. If the story be true, as it seems to be, Lucullus gained her over by gifts and flattery, and thus Cethegus took up his cause and got him the command.[1]

Even if we put aside as untrustworthy a great deal of what is told us of the relations of men and women in this period, it must be confessed that there is quite sufficient evidence to show that they were loose in the extreme, and show an altogether unhealthy condition of family and social life. The famous tigress of the story of Cluentius, Sassia, as she appears in Cicero's defence of him, was beyond doubt a criminal of the worst kind, however much

---

[1] Plut. *Lucullus* 6.

we may discount the orator's rhetoric ; and her case proves that the evil did not exist only at Rome, but was to be found even in a provincial town of no great importance.   Divorce was so common as to be almost inevitable.   Husbands divorced their wives on the smallest pretexts, and wives divorced their husbands.[1] Even the virtuous Cato seems to have divorced his wife Marcia in order that Hortensius should marry her, and after some years to have married her again as the widow of Hortensius, with a large fortune.[2] Cicero himself writes sometimes in the lightest-hearted way of conjugal relations which we should think most serious ;[3] and we find him telling Atticus how he had met at dinner the actress Cytheris, a woman of notoriously bad character.   "I did not know she was going to be there," he says, " but even the Socratic Aristippus himself did not blush when he was taunted about Lais."[4]   Caesar's reputation in such matters was at all times bad, and though many of the stories about him are manifestly false, his conquest by Cleopatra was a fact, and we learn with regret that the Egyptian queen was living in a villa of his in gardens beyond the Tiber during the year 46, when he was himself in Rome.

It will be a relief to the reader, after spending so

---

[1] Cic. *ad Fam.* viii. 7 : a letter of Caelius, in which he tells of a lady who divorced her husband without pretext on the very day he returned from his province.

[2] Plut. *Cato min.* 25 and 52.   Plutarch seems to be using here the Anti-Cato of Caesar, but the facts must have been well known.

[3] e.g. *ad Att.* xv. 29.   [4] *ad Fam.* ix. 26.

much time in this unwholesome atmosphere, to turn
for a moment in the last place to a record, unique
and entirely credible, of a truly good and wholesome
woman, and of a long period of uninterrupted conjugal
devotion. About the year 8 B.C., not long before Ovid
wrote those poems in which married life was assumed
to be hardly worth living, a husband in high life
at Rome lost the wife who had for forty-one years
been his faithful companion in prosperity, his wise
and courageous counsellor in adversity. He recorded
her praises and the story of her devotion to him in
a long inscription, placed, as we may suppose, on the
wall of the tomb in which he laid her to rest, and
a most fortunate chance has preserved for us a great
part of the marble on which this inscription was
engraved. It is in the form of a laudatio, or funeral
encomium; yet we cannot feel sure that he actually
delivered it as a speech, for throughout it he addresses,
not an audience, but the lost wife herself, in a manner
unique among such documents of the kind as have
come down to us. He speaks to her as though she
were still living, though passed from his sight; and
it is just this that makes it more real and more
touching than any memorial of the dead that has
come down to us from either Italy or Greece.[1]

---

[1] The so-called Laudatio Turiae is well known to all students of Roman
law, as raising a complicated question of Roman legal inheritance; but it
may also be reckoned as a real fragment of Roman literature, valuable, too,
for some points in the history of the time it covers. It was first made
accessible and intelligible by Mommsen in 1863, and the paper he then wrote
about it has lately been reprinted in his *Gesammelte Schriften*, vol. i.

In such a record names are of no great importance; it is no great misfortune that we do not know quite for certain who this man and his wife were. But there is a very strong probability that her name was Turia, and that he was a certain Q. Lucretius Vespillo, who served under Pompeius in Epirus in 48 B.C., whose romantic adventures in the proscriptions of 43 are recorded by Appian,[1] and who eventually became consul under Augustus in 19 B.C. We may venture to use these names in telling the remarkable story. For telling it here no apology is needed, for it has never been told in English as a whole, so far as I am aware.

It begins when the pair were about to be married, probably in 49 B.C., and with a horrible family calamity, not unnatural at the moment of the out-break of a dangerous civil war. Both Turia's parents were murdered suddenly and together at their country residence—perhaps, as Mommsen suggested, by their own slaves. Immediately afterwards Lucretius had to leave with Pompeius' army for Epirus, and Turia was left alone, bereft of both her parents, to do what she could to secure the punishment of the murderers. Alone as she was, or aided only by a married sister, she at once showed the courage and energy which are

together with a new fragment discovered on the same site as the others in 1898. This fragment, and a discussion of its relation to the whole, will be found in the *Classical Review* for June 1905, p. 261 ; the laudatio without the new fragment in *C.I.L.* vi. 1527.

[1] App. *B. C.* iv. 44. The identification has been impugned of late, but, as I think, without due reason. See my article in *Classical Rev.*, 1905, p. 265.

obvious in all we hear of her. She seems to have succeeded in tracking the assassins and bringing them to justice : " even if I had been there myself," says her husband, " I could have done no more."

But this was by no means the only dangerous task she had to undertake in those years of civil war and insecurity. When Lucretius left her they seem to have been staying at the villa where her parents had been murdered ; she had given him all her gold and pearls, and kept him supplied in his absence with money, provisions, and even slaves, which she contrived to smuggle over sea to Epirus.[1] And during the march of Caesar's army through Italy she seems to have been threatened, either in that villa or another, by some detachment of his troops, and to have escaped only through her own courage and the clemency of one whose name is not mentioned, but who can hardly be other than the great Julius himself, a true gentleman, whose instinct and policy alike it was throughout this civil war to be merciful to opponents.

A year later, while Lucretius was still away, yet another peril came upon her. While Caesar was operating round Dyrrhachium, there was a dangerous rising in Campania and Southern Italy, for which our giddy friend Caelius Rufus was chiefly responsible ; gladiators and ruffianly shepherd slaves were enlisted, and by some of these the villa where she was staying

---

[1] This is how I interpret the new fragment.   See *Classical Rev. l.c.* p. 263 foll.

was attacked, and successfully defended by her,—so much at least it seems possible to infer from the fragment recently discovered.

One might think that Turia had already had her full share of trouble and danger, but there is much more to come. About this time she had to defend herself against another attack, not indeed on her person, but on her rights as an heiress. An attempt was made by her relations to upset her father's will, under which she and Lucretius were appointed equal inheritors of his property. The result of this would have been to make her the sole heiress, leaving out her husband and her married sister; but she would have been under the legal *tutela* or guardianship of persons whose motive in attacking the will was to obtain administration of the property.[1] No doubt they meant to administer it for their own advantage; and it was absolutely necessary that she should resist them. How she did it her husband does not tell us, but he says that the enemy retreated from his position, yielding to her firmness and perseverance (constantia). The patrimonium came, as her father had intended, to herself and her husband; and he dwells on the care with which they dealt with it, he exercising a *tutela* over her share, while she exercised a *custodia* over his. Very touchingly he adds, "but of this I leave much unsaid, lest I should seem to be claiming a share in the praise that is due to you alone."

[1] For the legal question see Mommsen, *Gesammelte Schriften*, i. p. 407 foll.

When Lucretius returned to Italy, apparently pardoned by Caesar for the part he had taken against him, the marriage must have been consummated. Then came the murder of the Dictator, which plunged Italy once more into civil war, until in 43 Antony Octavian and Lepidus made their famous compact, and at once proceeded to that abominable work of proscription which made a reign of terror at Rome, and spilt much of the best Roman blood. The happiness of the pair was suddenly destroyed, for Lucretius found himself named in the fatal lists.[1] He seems to have been in the country, not far from Rome, when he received a message from his wife, telling him of impending peril that he might have to face at any moment, and warning him strongly against a certain rash course—perhaps an attempt to escape to Sextus Pompeius in Sicily, a course which cost the lives of many deluded victims. She implored him to return to their own house in Rome, where she had devised a secure hiding-place for him. She meant no doubt to die with him there if he were discovered.

He obeyed his good genius and made for Rome, by night it would seem, with only two faithful slaves. One of these fell lame and had to be left behind; and Lucretius, leaning on the arm of the other, approached the city gate. Suddenly they became

[1] The account that follows is put together from Appian iv. 44, Valerius Maximus vi. 7. 2, and the Laudatio. Appian preserved some fifty stories of escapes at this time, and the only one that fits with the Laudatio is that of Lucretius.

aware of a troop of soldiers issuing from it, and Lucretius took refuge in one of the many tombs that lined the great roads outside the walls. They had not been long in this dismal hiding when they were surprised by a party of tomb-wreckers—ghouls who haunted these roads by night and lived by robbing tombs or travellers. Luckily they wanted rather to rob than to murder, and the slave gave himself up to them to be stripped, while his master, who was no doubt disguised, perhaps as a slave, contrived to slip out of their hands and reached the city gate safely. Here he waited, as we might expect him to do, for his brave companion, and then succeeded in making his way into the city and to his house, where his wife concealed him between the roof and the ceiling of one of their bedrooms, until the storm should blow over.

But neither life nor property was safe until some pardon and restitution were obtained from one at least of the triumvirs. When at last these were conceded by Octavian, he was himself absent in the campaign that ended with Philippi, and Lepidus was consul in charge of Rome. To Lepidus Turia had to go, to beg the confirmation of Octavian's grace, and this brutal man received her with insult and injury. She fell at his feet, as her husband describes with bitter indignation, but instead of being raised and congratulated, she was hustled, beaten like a slave, and driven from his presence. But her perseverance had its ultimate reward. The clemency of Octavian prevailed on his return to Italy, and this treatment of a lady was among the many crimes that called for the eventual degradation of Lepidus.

This was the last of their perilous escapes. A long period of happy married life awaited them, more particularly after the battle of Actium, when "peace and the republic were restored." One thing only was wanting to complete their perfect felicity—they had no children. It was this that caused Turia to make a proposal to her husband which, coming from a truly unselfish woman, and seen in the light of Roman ideas of married life, is far from unnatural; but to us it must seem astonishing, and it filled Lucretius with horror. She urged that he should divorce her, and take another wife in the hope of a son and heir. If there is nothing very surprising in this from a Roman point of view, it is indeed to us both surprising and touching that she should have supported her request by a promise that she would be as much a mother to the expected children as their own mother, and would still be to Lucretius a sister, having nothing apart from him, nothing secret, and taking away with her no part of their inheritance.

To us, reading this proposal in cold blood just nineteen hundred years after it was made, it may seem foolishly impracticable; to her, whose whole life was spent in unselfish devotion to her husband's interests, whose warm love for him was always mingled with discretion, it was simply an act of pietas—of wifely duty.   Yet he could not for a moment think so himself : his indignation at the bare idea of it lives for ever on the marble in glowing words.   " I must confess," he says, " that the anger so burnt within me that my senses almost deserted me : that you should ever have thought it possible that we could be separated but by death, was most horrible to me.   What was the need of children compared with my loyalty to you : why should I exchange certain happiness for an uncertain future ?   But I say no more of this : you remained with me, for I could not yield without disgrace to myself and unhappiness to both of us.   The one sorrow that was in store for me was that I was destined to survive you."

These two, we may feel sure, were wholly worthy of each other.   What she would have said of him, if he had been the first to go, we can only guess ; but he has left a portrait of her, as she lived and worked in his household, which, mutilated though it is, may be inadequately paraphrased as follows :

" You were a faithful wife to me," he says, " and an obedient one : you were kind and gracious, sociable and friendly : you were assiduous at your spinning (lanificia) : you followed the religious rites of your family and your state, and admitted no foreign cults or degraded magic (superstitio) : you did not dress conspicuously, nor seek to make a display in your household arrangements.   Your duty to our whole household was exemplary : you tended my mother

as carefully as if she had been your own. You had
innumerable other excellences, in common with all
other worthy matrons, but these I have mentioned
were peculiarly yours."

No one can study this inscription without becoming convinced that it tells an unvarnished tale of
truth—that here was really a rare and precious
woman; a Roman matron of the very best type,
practical, judicious, courageous, simple in her habits
and courteous to all her guests. And we feel that
there is one human being, and one only, of whom
she is always thinking, to whom she has given her
whole heart—the husband whose words and deeds
show that he was wholly worthy of her.

CHAPTER VI

THE EDUCATION OF THE UPPER CLASSES

FROM what has been said in preceding chapters of the duties and the habits of the two sections of the upper stratum of society, it will readily be inferred that the kind of education called for was one mainly of character. In these men, whether for the work of business or of government, what was wanted was the will to do well and justly, and the instinctive hatred of all evil and unjust dealing. Such an education of the will and character is supplied (whatever be its shortcomings in other ways) by our English public school education, for men whose work in life is in many ways singularly like that of the Roman upper classes. Such an education, too, was outlined by Aristotle for the men of his ideal state; and Mr. Newman's picture of the probable results of it is so suggestive of what was really needed at Rome that I may quote it here.[1]

"As its outcome at the age of twenty-one we may imagine a bronzed and hardy youth, healthy in body and mind, able to bear hunger and hard

---

[1] Newman, *Politics of Aristotle*, i. p. 372.

physical labour . . . not untouched by studies which awake in men the interest of civilised beings, and prepare them for the right use of leisure in future years, and though burdened with little knowledge, possessed of an educated sense of beauty, and an ingrained love of what is noble and hatred of all that is the reverse. He would be more cultivated and human than the best type of young Spartan, more physically vigorous and reverential, though less intellectually developed, than the best type of young Athenian—a nascent soldier and servant of the state, not, like most young Athenians of ability, a nascent orator. And as he would be only half way through his education at an age when many Greeks had finished theirs, he would be more conscious of his own immaturity. We feel at once how different he would be from the clever lads who swarmed at Athens, youths with an infinite capacity for picking holes, and capable of saying something plausible on every subject under the sun."

If we note, with Mr. Newman, that Aristotle here makes if anything too little of intellectual training (as indeed may also be said of our own public schools), and add to his picture something more of that knowledge which, when united with an honest will and healthy body, will almost infallibly produce a sound judgment, we shall have a type of character eminently fitted to share in the duties and the trials of the government of such empires as the Roman and the British. But at Rome, in the age of Cicero,

such a type of character was rare indeed ; and though
this was due to various causes, some of which have
been already noticed,—the building up of a Roman
empire before the Romans were ripe to appreciate
the duties of an imperial state, and the sudden
incoming of wealth in an age when the idea of its
productive use was almost unknown,—yet it will occur
to every reader that there must have been also
something wrong in the upbringing of the youth of
the upper classes to account for the rarity of really
sound character, for the frequent absence of what
we should call the sense of duty, public and private.
I propose in this chapter to deal with the question
of Roman education just so far as to show where in
Cicero's time it was chiefly defective.   It is a subject
that has been very completely worked out, and an
excellent summary of the results will be found in
the little volume on Roman education written by
the late Professor A. S. Wilkins, just before his
lamented death : but he was describing its methods
without special reference to its defects, and it is
these defects on which I wish more particularly to
dwell.[1]

Let us notice, in the first place, how little is said
in the literature of the time, including biographies,

---

[1] A list of the best authorities will be found at the beginning of Professor
Wilkins' book.   Of these by far the most useful for a student is the
section in Marquardt's *Privatleben*, p. 79 foll.   The two volumes of Cramer
(*Geschichte der Erziehung*, etc.), which cover all antiquity, are, as he says,
most valuable for their breadth of view.   See also H. Nettleship, *Lectures
and Essays*, ch. iii. foll.

of that period of life which is now so full of interest
to readers of memoirs, so full of interest to ourselves
as we look back to it in advancing years. It may
be that we now exaggerate the importance of childhood, but it is equally certain that the Romans
undervalued the importance of it. It may be that
we over-estimate the value of our public-school life,
but it is certain that the Romans had no such school
life to be proud of. Biography was at this time a
favourite form of literature, and some of the memoirs
then written were available for use by later writers,
such as Valerius Maximus, Suetonius, and Plutarch;
yet it is curious how little has come down to us of
the childhood or boyhood of the great men of the
time. Plutarch indeed was deeply interested in
education, including that of childhood, and we can
hardly doubt that he would have used in his Roman
Lives any information that came in his way. He
does tell us something, for which we are eternally
indebted to him, of old Cato's method of educating
his son,[1] and something too, in his *Life of Aemilius
Paullus*,[2] of the education of the eldest son of that
family, the great Scipio Aemilianus. But in each
of these Lives we shall find that this information is
used rather to bring out the character of the father
than to illustrate the up-bringing of the son; and as
a rule the Lives begin with the parentage of the hero,
and then pass on at once to his early manhood.

The Life of the younger Cato, however, is an

[1] Plut. *Cato the Elder*, ch. xx.   [2] Plut. *Aem. Paul.* ch. vi.

exception to the rule, which we must ascribe to the attraction which all historians and philosophers felt to this singular character. Plutarch knew the name and character of Cato's paedagogus, Sarpedon,[1] and tells us that he was an obedient child, but would ask for the reason of everything, in those questions beginning with " why " which are often embarrassing to the teacher. Two stories in the second and third chapters of this Life are also found in that insipid medley of fact and fable drawn up in the reign of Tiberius, by Valerius Maximus, for educational purposes ;[2] a third, which is peculiarly significant, and seems to bear the stamp of truth, is only to be found in Plutarch. I give it here in full :

" On another occasion, when a kinsman on his birthday invited some boys to supper and Cato with them, in order to pass the time they played in a part of the house by themselves, younger and older together : and the game consisted of accusations and trials, and the arresting of those who were convicted. Now one of the boys convicted, who was of a handsome presence, being dragged off by an older boy to a chamber and shut up, called on Cato for aid. Cato seeing what was going on came to the door, and pushing through those who were posted in front of it to prevent him, took the boy out ; and went off

---

[1] Plut. *Cato minor* 1 *ad fin.* What is told in the earlier part of this chapter may perhaps be invention, based on the character of the grown man ; but this information at the end may be derived from a contemporary source.

[2] Val. Max. iii. 1. 2.

home with him in a passion, accompanied by other boys."

This is a unique picture of the ways and games of boys in the last century of the Republic. Like the children of all times, they play at that in which they see their fathers most active and interested; and this particular game must have been played in the miserable years of the civil wars and the proscriptions, as Cato was born in 95 B.C. Whether the part played by Cato in the story be true or not, the lesson for us is the same, and we shall find it entirely confirmed in the course of this chapter. The main object of education was the mastery of the art of oratory, and the chief practical use of that art was to enable a man to gain a reputation as an advocate in the criminal courts.[1]

Cicero had one boy, and for several years two, to look after, one his own son Marcus, born in 65 B.C., and the other Quintus, the son of his brother, a year older. Of these boys, until they took the toga virilis, he says hardly anything in his letters to Atticus, though Atticus was the uncle of the elder boy. Only when his brother Quintus was with Caesar in Gaul do we really begin to hear anything about them, and even then more than once, after a brief mention of the young Quintus, he goes off at once to tell his brother about the progress of the villas that are being

---

[1] There is a single story of Cicero's boyhood in Plutarch's *Life* of him, ch. ii., that parents used to visit his school because of his fame as a scholar, etc., but to this I do not attach much importance.

built for him.   But it is clear that the father wished
to know about the boy as well as about the villas ; [1]
and in one letter we find Cicero telling Quintus that
he wishes to teach his boy himself, as he has been
teaching his own son.   " I'll do wonders with him if
I can get him to myself when I am at leisure, for
at Rome there is not time to breathe (nam Romae
respirandi non est locus)." [2]   It is clear that the
boys, who were only eleven and twelve in this year
54, were being educated at home, and as clear too
that Cicero, who was just then very much occupied
in the courts, had no time to attend to them himself.
Young Quintus, we hear, gets on well with his
rhetoric master ; Cicero does not wholly approve the
style in which he is being taught, and thinks he may
be able to teach him his own more learned style,
though the boy himself seems to prefer the declama-
tory method of the teacher. [3]   The last entry in these
letters to the absent father is curious : [4]   " I love your
Cicero as he deserves and as I ought.   But I am
letting him leave me, because I don't want to keep
him from his masters, and because his mother is
going away,—and without her I am nervous about
his greediness ! "   Up to this point he has written
in the warmest terms of the boy, but here, as so
often in Cicero's letters about other people, disappro-
bation is barely hinted in order not to hurt the
feelings of his correspondent.

[1] So in *ad Q.F.* iii. 1. 7 : de Cicerone tuo quod me semper rogas, etc.
    [2] *Ib.*   [3] *Ib.* iii. 3. 4.   [4] *Ib.* iii. 9.

The one thing that is really pleasing in these allusions is the genuine desire of both parents that their boys shall be of good disposition and well educated. But of real training or of home discipline we unluckily get no hint. We must go elsewhere for what little we know about the training of children. Let us now turn to this for a while, remembering that it means parental example and the discipline of the body as well as the acquisition of elementary knowledge. Unfortunately, no book has survived from that age in which the education of children was treated of. Varro wrote such a book, but we know of it little more than its name, *Catus, sive de liberis educandis*.[1] In the fourth book of his *de Republica* Cicero seems to have dealt with "disciplina puerilis," but from the few fragments that survive there is little to be learnt, and we may be pretty sure that Cicero could not write of this with much knowledge or experience. The most famous passage is that in which he quotes Polybius as blaming the Romans for neglecting it;[2] certainly, he adds, they never wished that the State should regulate the education of children, or that it should be all on one model; the Greeks took much unnecessary trouble about it. The Greeks of his own time whom Cicero knew did not inspire him with any exalted idea of the results of Greek education; but we should like to know whether in this book of his

---

[1] See the few fragments in the Appendix to Riese's edition of the remains of Varro's Menippean Satires, p. 248 foll.   [2] *De Rep.* iv. 3. 3.

work on the State he did not express some feeling
that on the children themselves, and therefore on
their training, the fortunes of the State depend.
Such had been the feeling of the old Romans, though
their State laid down no laws for education, but
trusted to the force of tradition and custom. Old
Cato believed himself to be acting like an old Roman
when he looked after the washing and dressing of his
baby, and guided the child with personal care as he
grew up, writing books for his use in large letters
with his own hand.[1] But since Cato's day the idea
of the State had lost strength; and this had an
unfortunate effect on education, as on married life.
The one hope of the age, the Stoic philosophy, was
concerned with those who had attained to reason,
i.e. to those who had reached their fourteenth year;
in the Stoic view the child was indeed potentially
reasonable, and thus a subject of interest, but in
the Stoic ethics education does not take a very
prominent place.[2] We are driven to the conclusion
that a real interest in education as distinct from
the acquisition of knowledge was as much wanting
at Rome in Cicero's day as it has been till lately
in England; and that it was not again awakened
until Christianity had made the children sacred, not
only because the Master so spoke of them, but
because they were inheritors of eternal life.

[1] Plut. *Cato* 20.
[2] There is probably an allusion to the Stoic view, that reason is not
attained till the fourteenth year, in Virgil's line in *Ecl.* 4. 27.

Yet there had once been a Roman home education admirably suited to bring up a race of hardy and dutiful men and women. It was an education in the family virtues, thereafter to be turned to account in the service of the State. The mother nursed her own children and tended them in their earliest years. Then followed an education which we may call one in bodily activity, in demeanour, in religion, and in duty to the State. It is true that we have hardly any evidence of this but tradition; but when Varro, in one of the precious fragments of his book on education, describes his own bringing up in his Sabine home at Reate, we may be fairly sure that it adequately represents that of the old Roman farmer.[1] He tells us that he had a single tunic and toga, was seldom allowed a bath, and was made to learn to ride bareback—which reminds us of the life of the young Boer of the Transvaal before the late war. In another fragment he also tells us that both boys and girls used to wait on their parents at table.[2] Cato the elder, in a fragment preserved by Festus,[3] says that he was brought up from his earliest years to be frugal, hardy, and industrious, and worked steadily on the farm (in the Sabine country), in a stony region where he had to dig and plant the flinty soil. The tradition of such a healthy rearing remained in the memory of the Romans, and associated itself with

---

[1] in Nonius, p. 108, s.v. ephippium. Cp. the account of the education of Cato's young son, Plut. *Cato*, 20. Cp. also Virg. *Æn.* ix. 602 foll.
[2] in Nonius, p. 156, s.v. puerae. [3] p. 281, ed. Müller.

N

the Sabines of central Italy, the type of men who could be called *frugi* :

> rusticorum mascula militum
> proles, Sabellis docta ligonibus
> versare glebas et severae
> matris ad arbitrium recisos
> portare fustis.[1]

It was an education also in demeanour, and especi- ally in obedience[2] and modesty.   In that chapter of Plutarch's *Life of Cato* which has been already quoted, after describing how the father taught his boy to ride, to box, to swim, and so on, he goes on. "And he was as careful not to utter an indecent word before his son, as he would have been in the presence of the Vestal Virgins."   The *pudor* of child- hood was always esteemed at Rome :   "adolescens pudentissimus" is the highest praise that can be given even to a grown youth ;[3] and there are signs that a feeling survived of a certain sacredness of childhood, which Juvenal reflects in his famous words, "Maxima debetur puero reverentia."   The origin of this feeling is probably to be found in the fact that both boys and girls were in ancient times brought up to help in performing the religious duties of the household, as camilli and camillae (acolytes) ; and this is per- haps the reason why they wore, throughout Roman history, the toga praetexta with the purple stripe, like magistrates and sacrificing priests.[4]   It is hardly

---

[1] Hor. *Odes* iii. 6.   [2] Dionys. Hal. ii. 26.
[3] Cic. *pro Cluentio* 60. 165 ; Marq. *Privatleben*, p. 87.
[4] See a paper by the author in *Classical Rev.* vol. x. p. 317, in which

necessary to say that this religious side of education was an education in the practice of cult, and not in any kind of creed or ideas about the gods; but so far as it went its influence was good, as instilling the habit of reverence and the sense of duty from a very early age. Though the Romans of Cicero's time had lost their old conviction of the necessity of propitiating the gods of the State, it is probable that the tradition of family worship still survived in the majority of households.

Again, we may be sure that the idea of duty to the State was not omitted in this old-fashioned education. Cato wrote histories for his son in large letters, "so that without stirring out of the house, he might gain a knowledge of the illustrious actions of the ancient Romans, and of the customs of his country": but it is significant that in the next two or three generations the writers of annals took to glorifying—and falsifying—the achievements of members of their own families, rather than those of the State as a whole. Boys learnt the XII Tables by heart, and Cicero tells us that he did this in his own boyhood, though the practice had since then been dropped.[1] That ancient code of law would have acted, we may imagine, as a kind of catechism of the rules laid down

evidence is collected in support of this view. That the praetexta had a quasi-sacred character seems certain; see e.g. Hor. *Epod.* 5. 7; Persius, v. 30; pseudo-Quintilian, *Declam.* 340. See Henzen, *Acta Fratrum Arvalium* 15, for the pueri patrimi et matrimi, representing in that ancient cult the children of the old Roman family.

[1] Cic. *de Legibus*, ii. 59.

by the State for the conduct of its citizens, and as a reminder that though the State had outgrown the rough legal clothing of its infancy, it had from the very beginning undertaken the duty of regulating the conduct of its citizens in their relations with each other.   Again, when a great Roman died, it is said to have been the practice for parents to take their boys to hear the funeral oration in praise of one who had done great service to the State.[1]

All this was admirable, and if Rome had not become a great imperial state, and if some super-structure of the humanities could have been added in a natural process of development, it might have continued for ages as an invaluable educational basis. But the conditions under which alone it could flourish had long ceased to be.   It is obvious that it depended entirely on the presence of the parents and their interest in the children; as regards the boys it depended chiefly on the father.   Now ever since the Roman dominion was extended beyond sea, i.e. ever since the first two Punic wars, the father of a family must often have been away from home for long periods; he might have to serve in foreign wars for years together, and in numberless cases never saw Italy again.   Even if he remained in Rome, the ever increasing business of the State would occupy him far more than was compatible with a constant per-sonal care for his children.   The conscientious Roman

---

[1] Polyb. vi. 53.   For an account of the practice of laudatio see **Marq.** *Privatleben,* p. 346 foll.   This, too, degenerated into falsification.

father of the last two centuries B.C. must have felt even more keenly than English parents in India the sorrow of parting from their children at an age when they are most in need of parental care. We have to remember that in Cicero's day letter-writing had only recently become possible on an extended scale through the increasing business of the publicani in the provinces (see above, p. 74); the Roman father in Spain or Asia seldom heard of what his wife and children were doing, and the inevitable result was that he began to cease to care. In fact more and more came to depend on the mothers, as with our own hard-working professional classes; and we have seen reason to believe that in the last age of the Republic the average mother was not too often a conscientious or dutiful woman. The constant liability to divorce would naturally diminish her interest in her children, for after separation she had no part or lot in them. And this no doubt is one reason why at this particular period we hear so little of the life of children. There is indeed no reason to suppose that they themselves were unhappy; they had plenty of games, which were so familiar that the poets often allude to them—hoops, tops, dolls, blind man's buff, and the favourite games of "nuts" and "king."[1] But the real question is not whether they could enjoy their young life, but whether they were learning to use their bodies and minds to good purpose.

When a boy was about seven years old, the

---

[1] A full list of games will be found in Marquardt, *Privatleben*, p. 814 foll.

question would arise in most families whether he should remain at home or go to an elementary school.[1] No doubt it was usually decided by the means at the command of the parents. A wealthy father might see his son through his whole education at home by providing a tutor (paedagogus), and more advanced teachers as they were needed. Cato indeed, as we have seen, found time to do much of the work himself, but he also had a slave who taught his own and other children. Aemilius Paullus had several teachers in his house for this purpose, under his own superintendence.[2] Cicero too, as we have seen, seems to have educated his son at home, though he himself is said to have attended a school. But we may suppose that the ordinary boy of the upper classes went to school, under the care of a paedagogus, after the Greek fashion, rising before daylight, and submitting to severe discipline, which, together with the absolute necessity for a free Roman of attaining a certain level of acquirement, effectually compelled him to learn to read, write, and cipher.[3] This elementary work must have been done well; we hear little or nothing of gross ignorance or neglected education.

There were, however, very serious defects in this system of elementary education. Not only the schoolmaster himself, but the paedagogus who was

---

[1] The question is discussed by Quintilian, i. 2.

[2] Plut. *Aem. Paull.* 6.

[3] Full details about elementary schools in Wilkins, ch. iv., and Marq. p. 90 foll.

responsible for the boy's conduct, was almost always either a slave or a freedman ; and neither slave nor freedman could be an object of profound respect for a Roman boy. Hence no doubt the necessity of maintaining discipline rather by means of corporal punishment (to which the Romans never seem to have objected, though Quintilian criticises it)[1] than by moral force; a fact which is attested both in literature and art. The responsibility again which attached to the paedagogus for the boy's morals must have been another inducement to the parents to renounce their proper work of supervision.[2] And once more, the great majority of teachers were Greeks. As the boy was born into a bilingual Graeco-Roman world, of which the Greeks were the only cultured people, this might seem natural and inevitable; but we know that in his heart the Roman despised the Greek. Of witnesses in their favour we might expect Cicero to be the strongest, but Cicero occasionally lets us know what he really thinks of their moral character. In a remarkable passage in his speech for Flaccus, which is fully borne out by remarks in his private letters, he says that he grants them all manner of literary and rhetorical skill, but that the race never understood or cared for the sacred binding force of testimony given in a court of law.[3] Thus the Roman boy was in the anomalous position of

[1] Quintil. i. 3. 14.

[2] Plutarch is careful to tell us that Aem. Paullus exercised this supervision himself (ch. vi.).

[3] *Pro Flacco* 4. 9. Cp. *ad Quint. Fratr.* i. 2. 4.

having to submit to chastisement from men whom as men he despised. Assuredly we should not like our public schoolboys to be taught or punished by men of low station or of an inferior standard of morals. It is men, not methods, that really tell in education; the Roman schoolboy needed some one to believe in, some one to whom to be wholly loyal; the very same overpowering need which was so obvious in the political world of Rome in the last century B.C.[1]

Of this elementary teaching little need be said here, as it did not bear directly on life and conduct. There is, however, one feature of it which may claim our attention for a moment. Both in reading and writing, and also for learning by heart, *sententiae* (γνῶμαι) were used, which remind us of our copy-book maxims. Of these we have a large collection, more than 700, selected from the mimes of Publilius Syrus, who came to Rome from Syria as a slave in the age of which we are writing, and after obtaining his freedom gained great reputation as the author of many popular plays of this kind, in which he contrived to insert these wise saws and maxims. It is not likely that they found their way into the schools all at once, but in the early Empire we find them already alluded to as educational material by Seneca the elder,[2] and we may take them as a fair example of the maxims already in use in Cicero's time,

---

[1] That the boy was not always respectful is shown in an amusing passage in Plautus, *Bacchides*, III. iii. 34 foll.

[2] Sen. *Controversiae*, vii. 3. 8.

making some allowance for their superior neatness and wisdom. Here are a few specimens, taken almost at random ; it will be seen that they convey much shrewd good sense, and occasionally have the true ring of humanity as well as the flavour of Stoic *sapientia*. I quote from the excellent edition by Mr. Bickford-Smith.[1]

> Avarus ipse miseriae causa est suae.
> Audendo virtus crescit, tardando timor.
> Cicatrix conscientiae pro vulnere est.
> Fortunam[2] citius reperias quam retineas.
> Gravissima est probi hominis iracundia.
> Homo totiens moritur, quotiens amittit suos.
> Homo vitae commodatus, non donatus est.
> Humanitatis optima est certatio.
> Iucundum nil est, nisi quod reficit varietas.
> Malum est consilium quod mutari non potest.
> Minus saepe pecces, si scias quod nescias.
> Perpetuo vincit qui utitur clementia.
> Qui ius iurandum servat, quovis pervenit.
> Ubi peccat aetas maior, male discit minor.

I have quoted these to show that Roman children were not without opportunity even in early school-days of laying to heart much that might lead them to good and generous conduct in later life, as well as to practical wisdom. But we know the fate of our own copy-book maxims ; we know that it is not through them that our children become good men and women, but by the example and the un-system-

---

[1] London, C. J. Clay and Sons, 1895.

[2] Fortuna occurs many times, as in the so-called sententiae Varronis printed at the end of Riese's edition of the fragments of Varro's Menippean satires. This is characteristic of the period.

atised precepts of parents and teachers. No such neat γνῶμαι can do much good without a sanction of greater force than any that is inherent in them, and such a sanction was not to be found in the ferula of the grammaticus or the paedagogus. Once more, it is men and not methods that supply the real educational force.

Probably the greatest difficulty which the Roman boy had to face in his school life was the learning of arithmetic; it was this, we may imagine, that made him think of his master, as Horace did of the worthy Orbilius,[1] as a man of blows (plagosus). This is not the place to give an account of the methods of reckoning then used; they will be found fully explained in Marquardt's *Privatleben*, and compressed into a page by Professor Wilkins in his *Roman Education*.[2] It is enough to say that they were as indispensable as they were difficult to learn. "An orator was expected, according to Quintilian (i. 10. 35), not only to be able to make his calculations in court, but also to show clearly to his audience how he arrived at his results." From the small inn-keeper to the great capitalist, every man of business needed to be perfectly at home in reckoning sums of money. The magistrates, especially quaestors and aediles, had staffs of clerks who must have been skilled accountants; the provincial governors and all who were engaged in collecting

---

[1] Hor. *Epist.* i. 1. 70.
[2] Marq. *Privatleben*, p. 95 foll. ; Wilkins, p. 53.

the tributes of the provinces, as well as in lending the money to enable the tax-payers to pay (see above, p. 71 foll.), were constantly busy with their ledgers. The humbler inhabitants of the Empire had long been growing familiar with the Roman aptitude for arithmetic.[1]

> Grais ingenium, Grais dedit ore rotundo
> Musa loqui, praeter laudem nullius avaris.
> Romani pueri longis rationibus assem
> discunt in partes centum diducere.   " Dicat
> filius Albini : si de quincunce remota est
> uncia, quid superat ? poteras dixisse." " triens." " eu !
> rem poteris servare tuam." [2]

This familiar passage may be quoted once more to illustrate the practical nature of the Roman school teaching and the ends which it was to serve. Utilitarian to the backbone, the ordinary Roman, like the ordinary British, parent, wanted his son to get on in life ; it was only the parent of a higher class who sacrificed anything to the Muses, and then chiefly because in a public career it was *de rigueur* that the boy should not be ignorant or boorish.

When the son of well-to-do parents had mastered the necessary elements, he was advanced to the higher type of school kept by a *grammaticus*, and there made his first real acquaintance with literature ; and this was henceforward, until he began to study rhetoric and philosophy, the staple of his work.   We

---

[1] There is a good example of this in the well-known case of Brutus' loan to the Salaminians of Cyprus : see especially Cic. *ad Att.* v. 21. 12.

[2] Hor. *Ars Poet.* 323 foll.

may note, by the way, that science, i.e. the higher mathematics and astronomy, was reckoned under the head of philosophy, while medicine and jurisprudence had become professional studies,[1] to learn which it was necessary to attach yourself to an experienced practitioner, as with the art of war. In the grammar schools, as we may call them, the course was purely literary and humanistic, and it was conducted both in Greek and Latin, but chiefly in Greek, as a natural result of the comparative scantiness of Latin literature.[2] Homer, Hesiod, and Menander were the favourite authors studied; only later on, after the full bloom of the Augustan literature, did Latin poets, especially Virgil and Horace, take a place of almost equal importance. The study of the Greek poets was apparently a thorough one. It included the teaching of language, grammar, metre, style, and subject matter, and was aided by reading aloud, which was reckoned of great importance, and learning by heart, on the part of the pupils. In the discussion of the subject matter any amount of comment was freely allowed to the master, who indeed was expected to have at his fingers' ends explanations of all sorts of allusions, and thus to enable the boys to pick up a great deal of odd knowledge and a certain amount of history, mixed up of course with a large percentage of valueless mythology.

[1] Mommsen, *Hist. of Rome*, iv. p. 563.
[2] Quintilian was of opinion that Greek authors should precede Latin : i. 1. 12.

"In grammaticis," says Cicero, "poetarum pertractatio, historiarum cognitio, verborum interpretatio, pronuntiandi quidam sonus." [1] The method, if such it can be called, was not at all unlike that pursued in our own public schools, Eton, for example, before new methods and subjects came in. Its great defect in each case was that it gave but little opportunity for learning to distinguish fact from fancy, or acquiring that scientific habit of mind which is now becoming essential for success in all departments of life, and which at Rome was so rare that it seems audacious to claim it even for such a man of action as Caesar, or for such a man of letters as Varro. In England this defect was compensated to some extent by the manly tone of school life, but at Rome that side of school education was wanting, and the result was a want of solidity both intellectual and moral.

The one saving feature, given a really good and high-minded teacher, might be the appeal to the example of the great and good men of the past, both Greek and Roman, and the study of their motives in action, in good fortune and ill. This is the kind of teaching which we find illustrated in the book of Valerius Maximus, which has already been alluded to, who takes some special virtue or fine quality as the subject of most of his chapters,[2]—fortitudo, patientia, abstinentia, moderatio, pietas erga parentes, amicitia,

---

[1] *De Oratore*, i. 187.

[2] There are many subjects in the book of other kinds, but all are illustrated in exactly the same way.

and so on, and illustrates them by examples and
stories drawn mainly from Roman history, partly also
from Greek.   This kind of appeal to the young mind
was undoubtedly good, and the finest product of the
method is the immortal work of Plutarch, the Lives
of the great men of Greece and Rome, drawn up for
ethical rather than historical purposes.   But here
again we must note a serious drawback.   Any one who
turns over the pages of Valerius will see that these
stories of the great men of the past are so detached
from their historical surroundings that they could not
possibly serve as helps in the practical conduct of
life ; they might indeed do positive mischief, by
leading a shallow reasoner to suppose that what may
have been justifiable at one time and under certain
circumstances, regicide, for example, or exposure of
oneself in battle, is justifiable at all times and in
all circumstances.   Such an appeal failed also by
discouraging the habit of thinking about the facts
and problems of the day ; and right-minded men like
Cicero and Cato the younger both suffered from this
weakness of a purely literary early training.   Another
drawback is that this teaching inevitably exaggerated
the personal element in history, at the very time too
when personalities were claiming more than their due
share of the world's attention ; and thus the great
lessons which Polybius had tried to teach the Graeco-
Roman world, of seeking for causes in historical
investigation, and of meditating on the phenomena of
the world you live in, were passed over or forgotten.

But so far as the study of language, of artistic diction, of elocution, and intelligent reading could help a boy to prepare himself for life, this education was good; more especially good as laying a foundation for the acquirement of that art of oratory which, from old Cato's time onwards, had been the chief end to be aimed at by all intending to take part in public life. Cato indeed had well said to his son, " Orator est, Marce fili, vir bonus dicendi peritus," [1] thus putting the ethical stamp of the man in the first place; and his " rem tene, verba sequentur " is a valuable bit of advice for all learners and teachers of literature. But more and more the end of all education had come to be the art of oratory, and particularly the art as exercised in the courts of law, where in Cicero's time neither truth nor fact was supreme, and where the first thing required was to be a clever speaker,—a vir bonus by all means if you were so disposed. But to this we shall return directly.

In such schools, if he were not educated at home, the boy remained till he was invested with the toga virilis, or pura. In the late Republic this usually took place between the fourteenth and seventeenth years; [2] thus the two young Ciceros seem both to have been sixteen when they received the toga virilis, while Octavian and Virgil were just fifteen,

[1] H. Jordan, *M. Catonis praeter librum de re rustica quae extant*, p. 80.

[2] Full information on this point will be found in Marquardt, *Privatleben*, p. 131 foll.

and the son of Antony only fourteen. In former times it seems probable that the boy remained "praetextatus" till he was seventeen, the age at which he was legally capable of military service, and that he went straight from the home to the levy;[1] in case of severe military pressure, or if he wished it himself, he might begin his first military exercises and even his active service, in the praetexta. But as in so many other ways, so here the life of the city brought about a change; in a city boys are apt to develop more rapidly in intelligence if not in body, and as the toga virilis was the mark of legal qualification as a man, they might be of more use to the family in the absence of the father if invested with it somewhat earlier than had been the primitive custom. But there was no hard and fast rule; boys develop with much variation both mentally and physically, and, like the Eton collar of our own schoolboys, the toga of childhood might be retained or dropped entirely at the discretion of the parents.

There is, however, a great difference in the two cases in regard to the assumption of the manly dress. With us it does not mean independence; as a rule the boy remains at school for a year or two at least under strict discipline. At Rome it meant, on the contrary, that he was "of age," and in the eye of the law a man, capable of looking after his own education and of holding property. This was a

---

[1] See my *Roman Festivals*, p. 56. The Liberalia (March 17) was the usual day for the change, and a convenient one for the enrolment of tirones.

survival from the time when at the age of puberty the boy, as among all primitive peoples, was solemnly received into the body of citizens and warriors ; and the solemnity of the Roman ceremony fully attests this. After a sacrifice in the house, and the dedication of his boyish toga and bulla to the Lar familiaris, he was invested with the plain toga of manhood (libera, pura), and conducted by his father or guardian, accompanied (in characteristic Roman fashion, see below, p. 271) by friends and relations, to the Forum, and probably also to the tabularium under the Capitol, where his name was entered in the list of full citizens.[1]

With the new arrangement, under which boys might become legally men at an earlier age than in the old days, it is obvious that there must often have been an interval before they were physically or mentally qualified for a profession. As the sole civil profession to which boys of high family would aspire was that of the bar, a father would send his son during that interval to a distinguished advocate to be taken as a pupil. Cicero himself was thus apprenticed to Mucius Scaevola the augur : and in the same way the young Caelius, as soon as he had taken his toga virilis, was brought by his father to Cicero. The relation between the youth and his preceptor was not unlike that of the *contubernium* in military life, in which the general to whom a lad

---

[1] See the very interesting note (11) in Marq. p. 123, as to the enrolment in municipal towns.

was committed was supposed to be responsible for his welfare and conduct as well as for his education in the art of war : thus Cicero says of Caelius [1] that at that period of his life no one ever saw him "except with his father or with me, or in the very well-conducted house of M. Crassus" (who shared with Cicero in the guardianship). "Fuit assiduus mecum," he says a little farther on. This kind of pupilage was called the *tirocinium fori*, in which a lad should be pursuing his studies for the legal profession, and also his bodily exercises in the Campus Martius, so that he might be ready to serve in the army for the single campaign which was still desirable if not absolutely necessary. When he had made his first speech in a court of law, he was said *tirocinium ponere*,[2] and if it were a success, he might devote himself more particularly henceforward to the art and practice of oratory. No doubt all really ambitious young men, who aimed at high office and an eventual provincial government, would, like Caesar, endeavour to qualify themselves for the army as well as the Forum. Cicero, however, whose instincts were not military, served only in one campaign, at the age of seventeen, and apparently he advised Caelius to do no more than this. Caelius served under Q. Pompeius proconsul of Africa, to whom he was attached as *contubernalis*, choosing this province because his father had estates there.[3]

---

[1] *Pro Caelio*, 4. 9.   [2] Livy xlv. 37. 3.

[3] *Pro Caelio*, 30. 72.

It was only on his return with a good character from Pompeius that he proceeded to exhibit his skill as an orator by accusing some distinguished person—in this case the Antonius who was afterwards consul with Cicero.[1]

To attain the skill in oratory which would enable the pupil to make a successful appearance in the Forum, he must have gone through an elaborate training in the art of rhetoric. Cicero does not tell us whether he himself gave Caelius lessons in rhetoric, or whether he sent him to a professional teacher; he had himself written a treatise on a part of the subject—the *de Inventione* of 80 B.C., the earliest of all his prose works—and was therefore quite able to give the necessary instruction if he found time to do so. It is not the object of this chapter to explain the meaning of rhetoric as the Graeco-Roman world then understood it, or the theory of a rhetorical education; for this the reader must be referred to Professor Wilkins' little book,[2] or, better still, to the main source of our knowledge, the *Institutio Oratoris* of Quintilian. Something may, however, be said here of the view taken of a rhetorical training by Cicero himself, very clearly expressed in the exordium of the treatise just mentioned, and often more or less directly reiterated in his later and more mature works on oratory.

" After much meditation," he says, " I have been led to the conclusion that wisdom without eloquence

[1] *Pro Caelio*, 31. 74.   [2] *Roman Education*, ch. v.

is of little use to a state, while eloquence without wisdom is often positively harmful, and never of any value.   Thus if a man, abandoning the study of reason and duty, which is always perfectly straight and honourable, spends his whole time in the practice of speaking, he is being brought up to be a hindrance to his own development, and a dangerous citizen." This reminds us of Cato's saying that an orator is "vir bonus dicendi peritus."   Less strongly expressed, the same view is also found in the exordium of another and more mature treatise on rhetoric, by an author whose name is unknown, written a year or two before that of Cicero: "Non enim parum in se fructus habet copia dicendi et commoditas orationis, si recta intelligentia et definita animi moderatione gubernetur." [1]   We may assume that in Cicero's early years the best men felt that the rhetorical art, if it were to be of real value to the individual and the state, must be used with discretion, and accompanied by high aims and upright conduct.

Yet within a generation of the date when these wise words were written, the letters of Caelius show us that the art was used utterly without discretion, and to the detriment both of state and individual. The high ideal of culture and conduct had been lost in the actual practice of oratory, in a degenerate age, full of petty ambitions and animosities.   We ourselves

---

[1] *Rhetorica ad Herennium, init.*   The date of this work was about 82 B.C. See a paper by the author in *Journal of Philology*, x. 197.

know only too well how a thing good in itself as a means is apt to lose its value if raised into the place of an end;—how the young mind is apt to elevate cricket, football, golf, into the main object of all human activity. So it was with rhetoric; it was the indispensable acquirement to enable a man to enjoy thoroughly the game in the Forum, and thus in education it became the staple commodity. The actual process of acquiring it was no doubt an excellent intellectual exercise,—the learning rules of composition, the exercises in applying these rules, i.e. the writing of themes or essays (proposita, communes loci), in which the pupil had " to find and arrange his own facts," [1] and then the declamatio, or exercise in actual speaking on a given subject, which in Cicero's day was called causa, and was later known as controversia. [2] Such practice must have brought out much talent and ingenuity, like that of our own debating societies at school and college. But there were two great defects in it. First, as Professor Wilkins points out, the subjects of declamation were too often out of all relation to real life, e.g. taken from the Greek mythology; or if less barren than usual, were far more commonplace and flat than those of our debating societies. To harangue on the question whether the life of a lawyer or a soldier is the best, is hardly so inspiring as to debate a question of the day about Ireland or India, which educates in living fact as well

---

[1] H. Nettleship, *Lectures*, etc., p. 111; Wilkins, p. 85; Quintil. xii. 2.
[2] Wilkins, *l.c.*

as in the rules of the orator's art. Secondly, the
whole aim and object of this "finishing" portion of a
boy's education was a false one.   Even the excellent
Quintilian, the best of all Roman teachers, believed
that the statesman (civilis vir) and the orator are
identical : that the statesman must be vir bonus
because the vir bonus makes the best orator; that
he should be sapiens for the same reason.[1] And the
object of oratory is " id agere, ut iudici quae proposita
fuerint, vera et honesta *videantur*" :[2] i.e. the object
is not truth, but persuasion. We might get an idea
of how such a training would fail in forming character, if we could imagine all our liberal education
subordinated to the practice of journalism.   But
fortunately for us, in this scientific age, words and the
use of words no longer serve as the basis of education
or as the chief nurture of young life. We need to
see facts, to understand causes, to distinguish objective
truth from truth reflected in books.   But the perfect
education must be a skilful mingling of the two
methods ; and it may be as well to take care that we
do not lose contact with the best thoughts of the
best men, because they are contained in the literature
we show some signs of neglecting. We may say of
science what Cicero said of rhetoric, that it cannot
do without *sapientia*.

Of schools of philosophy I have already said
something in the last chapter, and as the study of

---

[1] Quintil. i. 4. 5 ; xii. 1. 1 ; xii. 2 and 7.
[2] *Ib.* xii. 1. 11.

philosophy was hardly a part of the regular curriculum of education properly so called, I shall pass it over here. The philosopher was usually to be found in wealthy houses, and if he were a wholesome person, and not a Philodemus, he might assuredly exercise a good influence on a young man. Or a youth might go to Athens or Rhodes or to some other Greek city, to attend the lectures of some famous professor. Cicero heard Phaedrus the Epicurean at Rome and then Philo the Academician, who had a lasting influence on his pupil, and then, at the age of twenty-seven, went to Greece for two years, studying at Athens, Rhodes, and elsewhere. Caesar also went to Rhodes, and he and Cicero both attended the lectures of Molo in rhetoric, in which study, as well as in philosophy, lectures were to be heard in all the great Greek cities.[1] Cicero sent his own son to "the University in Athens" at the age of twenty, giving him an ample allowance and doubtless much good advice. The young man soon outran his allowance and got into debt ; the good advice he seems to have failed to utilise, and in fact gave his father considerable anxiety.

The following letter, which seems to show that a youth who had excellent opportunities might still be lacking in principle and self-control, is the only one which survives of the letters of undergraduates of that day. It was written by the young Cicero, after he had repented and undertaken to reform, not to

---

[1] Plut. *Cic.* 4 ; *Caes.* 3.

his father himself, but to the faithful friend and freedman of his father, Tiro, who afterwards edited the collection of letters in which he inserted it.[1] It is on the whole a pleasing letter, and seems to show real affection for Tiro, who had known the writer from his infancy. It is a little odd in the choice of words, perhaps a trifle rhetorical. The reader shall be left to decide for himself whether it is perfectly straight and genuine. In any case it may aptly conclude this chapter.

" I had been anxiously expecting letter-carriers day after day, when at last they arrived forty-six days after they left you. Their arrival was most welcome to me. I took the greatest possible pleasure in the letter of the kindest and best beloved of fathers, but your own delightful letter put the finishing touch to my joy. So I no longer repent of dropping letter-writing for a time, but am rather glad I did so, for my silence has brought me a great reward in your kindness. I am very glad indeed that you accepted my excuse without hesitation.

"I am sure, my dearest Tiro, that the reports about me which reach you answer your best wishes and hopes. I will make them good, and I will do my best that this beginning of a good report about me may daily be repeated. So you may with perfect confidence fulfil your promise of being the trumpeter (buccinator) of my reputation. For the errors of my youth have caused me so much remorse and suffering,

[1] *ad Fam.* xvi. 21. The translation is based on Mr. Shuckburgh's.

that it is not only my heart that shrinks from what I did—my very ears abhor the mention of it. I know for a fact that you have shared my trouble and sorrow, and I don't wonder; you always wished me to do well not only for my sake but for your own. So as I have been the means of giving you pain, I will now take care that you shall feel double joy on my account.

" Let me tell you that my attachment to Cratippus is that of a son rather than a pupil: I enjoy his lectures, but I am especially charmed by his delightful manners. I spend whole days with him, and often part of the night, for I get him to dine with me as often as I can. We have grown so intimate that he often drops in upon us unexpectedly while we are at dinner, lays aside the stiff air of a philosopher, and joins in our jests with the greatest good will. He is such a man, so delightful, so distinguished, that you ought to make his acquaintance as soon as ever you can. As for Bruttius, I never let him leave me. He is a man of strict and moral life, as well as being the most delightful company. Surely it is not necessary that in our daily literary studies there should never be any fun at all. I have taken a lodging close to him, and as far as I can with my pittance **I subsid**ise his narrow means. I have also begun practising declamation in Greek with Cassius; in Latin I like having my practice with Bruttius. My intimate friends and daily company are those whom Cratippus brought with him

from Mitylene,—good scholars, of whom he has the
highest opinion.   I also see a great deal of Epicrates,
the leading man at Athens, and Leonides, and people
of that sort.   So now you know how I am going on.

"You say something in your letter about Gorgias.
The fact is that I found him very useful in my daily
practice of declamation, but I put my father's injunc-
tions before everything else, and he had written
telling me to give up Gorgias at once.   I wouldn't
shilly-shally about it, for fear my making a fuss
might put some suspicion in my father's head.
Moreover it occurred to me that it would be
offensive for me to express an opinion on a decision
of my father's.   However, your interest and advice
are welcome and acceptable.

"Your apology for want of time I readily accept,
for I know how busy you always are.   I am very
glad you have bought an estate, and you have
my best wishes for the success of your purchase.
Don't be surprised at my congratulations coming
at this point in my letter, for it was at the corresponding point in yours that you told me of this.
You must drop your city manners (urbanitates); you
are a 'rusticus Romanus!'   How clearly I see your
dearest face before me at this moment!   I seem to
see you buying things for the farm, talking to your
bailiff, saving the seeds at dessert in your cloak.
But as to the matter of money, I am sorry I was
not there to help you.   Don't doubt, my dear Tiro,
about my helping you in the future, if fortune will

but stand by me, especially as I know that this estate has been bought for our mutual advantage. As to my commissions about which you are taking trouble, many thanks! I beg you to send me a secretary at the first opportunity, if possible a Greek : for he will save me much trouble in copying out notes. Above all, take care of your health, that we may have some literary talk together some day. I commend Anteros to you. Adieu."

CHAPTER VII

THE SLAVE POPULATION

In the last age of the Republic the employment of slave labour reached its high-water mark in ancient history.[1] We have already met with evidence of this in examining the life of the upper classes; in the present chapter we must try to sketch, first, the conditions under which it was possible for such a vast slave system to arise and flourish, and secondly, the economical and ethical results of it both in city and country. The subject is indeed far too large and complicated to be treated in a single short chapter, but our object throughout this book is only to give such a picture of society in general as may tempt a student to further and more exact inquiry.

We have seen that the two upper classes of society were engaged in business of various kinds, and especially in banking and carrying out public contracts, or in the work of government, and in

---

[1] See *Der Röm. Gutsbetrieb*, by H. Gummerus, reprinted from *Klio*, 1906 : an excellent specimen of economic research, to which I am much indebted in this chapter.—E. Meyer, *Die Sclaverei im Altertum*, p. 46.

Italian agriculture. All this business, public and private, called for a vast amount of labour, and in part, of skilled labour; the great men provided the capital, but the details of the work, as it had gradually developed since the war with Hannibal, created a demand for workmen of every kind such as had never before been known in the Graeco-Roman world. Clerks, accountants, messengers, as well as operatives, were wanted both by the Government and by private capitalists. In the households of the rich the great increase of wealth and luxury had led to a constant demand for helps of all kinds, each with a certain amount of skill in his own particular department; and on the estates in the country, which were steadily growing bigger, and were tending to be worked more and more on capitalistic lines, labour, both skilled and unskilled, was increasingly required. Thus the demand for labour was abnormally great, and had been created with abnormal rapidity, and the supply could not possibly be provided by the free population alone. The lower classes of city and country were not suited to the work wanted, either by capacity or inclination. It was not for a free Roman to be at the beck and call of an employer, like the clerks and underlings of to-day, or to act as servant in a great household; and for a great part of the necessary work he was not sufficiently well educated. Far less was it possible for him to work on the great cattle-runs. And the State wanted the best years of his life for service in the army, which, as has been well remarked, was the real industry of the Roman freeman. But luckily in one sense, and in another unluckily, for Rome, there was an endless supply of labour to be had, of every quality and capacity, for the very same abnormal circumstances which had created the demand also provided the supply. The great wars and the wealth accruing from them in various ways had produced a capitalist class in need of labour, and also created a slave-market on a scale such as the world has never known before or since.

Ever since the time of Alexander and the wars of his successors with each other and their neighbours, it is probable that the supply of captives sold as slaves had been increasing; and in the second century B.C. the little island of Delos had come to be used as a convenient centre for the slave trade. Strabo tells us in a well-known passage that 10,000 slaves might be sold there in a single day.[1] But Rome herself was in the time of Cicero the great emporium for slaves; the wars which were most productive of prisoners had been for long in the centre and the west of the Mediterranean basin. All armies sent out from Rome were accompanied by speculators in this trade, who bought the captives as they were put up to auction after a battle, and then undertook the transport to Rome of all who were suited for employment in Italy or were not bought up in the province which was the seat of war.

[1] Strabo, p. 668.

The enormous number of slaves thus made available, even if we make allowance for the uncertainty of the numbers as they have come down to us, surpasses all belief; we may take a few examples, sufficient to give some idea of a practice which had lasting and lamentable results on Roman society.

After the campaign of Pydna and the overthrow of the Macedonian kingdom, Aemilius Paullus, one of the most humane of Romans, sold into slavery, under orders from the senate, 150,000 free inhabitants of communities in Epirus which had sided with Perseus in the war.[1]   After the war with the Cimbri and Teutones, 90,000 of the latter and 60,000 of the former are said to have been sold;[2] and though the numbers may be open to suspicion, as they amount again to 150,000, the fact of an enormous capture is beyond question.   Caesar, like Aemilius Paullus one of the most humane of Romans, tells us himself that on a single occasion, the capture of the Aduatuci, he sold 53,000 prisoners on the spot.[3]   And of course every war, whether great or small, while it diminished the free population by slaughter, pestilence, or capture, added to the number of slaves. Cicero himself, after his campaign in Cilicia and the capture of the hill stronghold Pindonissus, did of course as all other commanders did; we catch a glimpse of the process in a letter to Atticus: "mancipia venibant Saturnalibus tertiis."[4]   It is

[1] Livy xlv. 34.   [2] Livy, *Epit.* 68.
[3] Caesar, *B.G.* ii. 33.   [4] *ad Att.* v. 20. 5.

hardly necessary to point out that we should be getting our historical perspective quite wrong if we allowed ourselves to expect in these cultured Roman generals any sign of compassion for their victims; it was a part of their mental inheritance to look on men who had surrendered as simply booty, the property of the victors; Roman captives would meet with the same fate, and even for them little pity was ever felt. When Caesar in 49 within a few months dismissed two surrendered armies of Roman soldiers, once at Corfinium and again in Spain, he was doubtless acting from motives of policy, but the enslavement of Roman citizens by their fellows would, we may hope, have been repugnant to him, if not to his own soldiers.[1]

War then was the principal source of the supply of slaves, but it was not the only one. When a slave-trade is in full swing, it will be fostered in all possible ways. Brigandage and kidnapping were rife all over the Empire and in the countries beyond its borders in the disturbed times with which we are dealing. The pirates of Cilicia, until they were suppressed by Pompeius in 66, swarmed all over the Mediterranean, and snapped up victims by raids even on the coasts of Italy, selling them in the market at Delos without hindrance. Cicero, in his

---

[1] Wallon (*Hist. de l'Esclavage*, ii. p. 38) has noted that Virgil alone shows a feeling of tenderness for the lot of the captive, quoting *Aen.* iii. 320 foll. (the speech of Andromache): but this was for the fate of a princess, and a mythical princess. No Latin poet of that age shows any real sympathy with captives or with slaves.

speech in support of the appointment of Pompey,
mentions that well-born children had been carried
off from Misenum under the very eyes of a Roman
praetor.[1] Caesar himself was taken by them when
a young man, and only escaped with difficulty. In
Italy itself, where there was no police protection
until Augustus took the matter in hand, kidnapping
was by no means unknown ; the *grassatores*, as they
were called, often slaves escaped from the prisons
of the great estates, haunted the public roads, and
many a traveller disappeared in this way and passed
the rest of his life in a slave-prison.[2] Varro, in
describing the sort of slaves best suited for work on
the great sheep-runs, says that they should be such
as are strong enough to defend the flocks from wild
beasts and brigands—the latter doubtless quite as
ready to seize human beings as sheep and cattle.
And slave-merchants seem to have been constantly
carrying on their trade in regions where no war was
going on, and where desirable slaves could be procured ; the kingdoms of Asia Minor were ransacked
by them, and when Marius asked Nicomedes king
of Bithynia for soldiers during the struggle with the
Cimbri, the answer he got was that there were none
to send—the slave-dealers had been at work there.[3]
Every one will remember the line of Horace in

---

[1] Cic. *pro lege Manilia* 12. 23. Plutarch, in his *Life of Pompey* 24, adds
that Romans of good standing would join in the pirates' business in order
to make profit in this scandalous way.

[2] Suet. *Aug.* 32, of the period before Augustus.

[3] Varro, *R.R.* ii. 10 ; Diodorus xxxvi. 3. 1.

P

which he calls one of these wretches a "king of Cappadocia." [1]

There were two other sources of the slave supply, of which however little need be said here, as the contribution they made was comparatively small. First, slaves were bred from slaves, and on rural estates this was frequently done as a matter of business.[2] Varro recommends the practice in the large sheep-farms,[3] under certain conditions; and some well-known lines of Horace suggest that on smaller farms, where a better class of slaves would be required, these home-bred ones were looked on as the mark of a rich house, "ditis examen domus." [4] Secondly, a certain number of slaves had become such under the law of debt. This was a common source of slavery in the early periods of Roman history, but in Cicero's day we cannot speak of it with confidence. We have noticed the cry of the distressed freemen of the city in the conspiracy of Catiline, which looks as though the old law were still put in force; and in the country there are signs that small owners who had borrowed from large ones were in Varro's time in some modified condition of slavery,[5] surrendering their labour in lieu of pay-

---

[1] Hor. *Epist*. i. 6. 39 :—

> "Mancipiis locuples eget aeris Cappadocum rex :
> Ne fueris hic tu."

[2] Varro, *R.R.* i. 17.　　　　　　　[3] *Ib*. 2. 10. 3.

[4] Hor. *Epode* 2. 65.　Cp. Tibull. ii. 1. 25 "turbaque vernarum, saturi bona signa coloni."

[5] See Gummerus, *op. cit.* p. 63, who considers the *obaeratus* of Varro as the equivalent of the *addictus* of the Roman law of debt.

ment. But all these internal sources of slavery are
as nothing compared with the supply created by war
and the slave-trade.

This supply being thus practically unlimited,
prices ran comparatively low, and no Roman of
any considerable means at all need be, or was,
entirely without slaves. He had only to go, or to
send his agent, to one of the city slave-markets,
such as the temple of Castor,[1] where the slave-
agents (mangones) exhibited their "goods" under
the supervision of the aediles ; there he could pick
out exactly the kind of slave he wanted at any
price from the equivalent of £10 upwards. The
unfortunate human being was exhibited exactly
as horses are now, and could be stripped, handled,
trotted about, and treated with every kind of indignity,
and of course the same sort of trickery went on in
these human sales as is familiar to all horse-dealers
of the present day.[2] The buyer, if he wanted a
valuable article, a Greek, for example, who could act
as secretary or librarian, like Cicero's beloved Tiro,
or even a household slave with a special character
for skill in cooking or other specialised work of a
luxurious family, would have to give a high price ;
even as long ago as the time of the elder Cato
a very large sum might be given for a single choice

---

[1] See the well-known description of the Forum in Plautus' *Curculio*, iv. 1:
"pone aedem Castoris, ibi sunt subito quibu' credas male " ; Marq. *Privatleben*, p. 168 ; Wallon, *op. cit.* ch. ii.

[2] Gellius iv. 2 gives an extract from the edict of the aediles drawn up
with the object of counteracting such sharp practice.

slave, and Cato as censor in 184 attempted to check such high prices by increasing the duties payable on the sales.[1] Towards the close of the Republican period we have little explicit evidence of prices; Cicero constantly mentions his slaves, but not their values. Doubtless for fancy articles huge prices might be demanded; Pliny tells us that Antony when triumvir bought two boys as twins for more than £800 apiece, who were no doubt intended for handsome pages, perhaps to please Cleopatra.[2] But there can be no doubt that ordinary slaves capable of performing only menial offices in town or country were to be had at this time quite cheap, and the number in the city alone must have been very great.

It is unfortunately quite impossible to make even a probable estimate of the total number in Rome; the data are not forthcoming. Beloch[3] remarks aptly that though some families owned hundreds of slaves, the number of such families was not large, quoting the words of Philippus, tribune in 104 B.C., to the effect that there were not more than two thousand persons of any substance in the State.[4] The great majority of citizens living in Rome had, he thinks, no slaves. He is forced to take as a basis

---

[1] Livy xxxix. 44.

[2] *N.H.* vii. 55. This story affords a good example of the tricks of the trade : the boys were not twins, and came from different countries, though exactly alike.

[3] *Bevölkerung*, p. 403.

[4] Cic. *Off.* ii. 21. 73.

of calculation the proportion of bond to free in the only city of the Empire about which we have certain information on this point; at Pergamum there was one slave to two free persons.[1] Assuming the whole free population to have been about half a million in the time of Augustus, or rather more, including peregrini, he thus arrives at a slave population of something like 280,000 ; this may not be far off the mark, but it must be remembered that it is little more than a guess.

What has been said above will have given the reader some idea of the conditions of life which created a great demand for labour in the last two centuries B.C., and of the circumstances which produced an abundant supply of unfree labour to satisfy that demand.   I propose now to treat the whole question of Roman slavery from three points of view,—the economic, the legal, and the ethical.   In other words, we have to ask: (1) how the abundance of slave labour affected the social economy of the free population; (2) what was the position of the slave in the eye of the law, as regards treatment and chance of manumission; (3) what were the ethical results of this great slave system, both on the slaves themselves and on their masters.

1. From an economical point of view the most interesting question is whether slave labour seriously interfered with the development of free industry ; and unfortunately this question is an extremely

---

[1] Galen v. p. 49, ed. Kuhn ; Galen was a native of this great city.

difficult one to answer. We can all guess easily that the opportunities of free labour must have been limited by the presence of enormous numbers of slaves; but to get at the facts is another matter. In regard to rural slavery we have some evidence to go upon, as we shall see directly, and this has of late been collected and utilised; but as regards labour in the city no such research has as yet been made,[1] and the material is at once less fruitful and more difficult to handle. A few words on this last point must suffice here.

We have seen in Chapter II. that there was plenty of employment at Rome for freemen. Friedländer, than whom no higher authority can be quoted for the social life of the city, goes so far as to assert that even under the early Empire a freeman could always obtain work if he wished for it;[2] and even if we take this as a somewhat exaggerated statement, it may serve to keep us from rushing to the other extreme and picturing a population of idle free paupers. In fact we are bound on general evidence to assume for our own period that he is in the main right; the poor freeman of Rome had to live somehow, and the cheap corn which he enjoyed was not given him gratis until a few years before the Republic came to an end.[3] How did he get the money to pay even the sum of six asses and a third for a modius of corn, or to pay for shelter and clothing, which were

---

[1] Dr. Gummerus promises it.   [2] *Sittengeschichte*, i., ed. 5, p. 264.
[3] Probably by Clodius in 58.

assuredly not to be had for nothing? We know again, that the gilds of trades (see above, p. 45) continued to exist in the last century of the Republic,[1] though the majority had to be suppressed owing to their misuse as political clubs. Supposing that the members of these collegia were small employers of labour, it is reasonable to assume that the labour they employed was at least largely free; for the capital needed to invest, at some risk, in a sufficient number of slaves, who would have to be housed and fed, and whose lives would be uncertain in a crowded and unhealthy city, could not, we must suppose, be easily found by such men. Here and there, no doubt, we find traces of slave labour in factories, e.g. as far back as the time of Plautus, if we can take him as writing of Rome rather than translating from the Greek:

> An te ibi vis inter istas versarier
> Prosedas, pistorum amicas, reginas alicarias,
> Miseras schoeno delibutas servilicolas sordidas?[2]
>
> *Poenulus*, 265 foll.

But on the whole, we may with all due caution, in default of complete investigation of the question, assume that the Roman slaves were confined for the most part to the great and rich families, and were not used by them to any great extent in productive

---

[1] *Asconius ad Cic. pro Cornel.*, ed. Clark, p. 75; Waltzing, *Corporations professionelles*, i. p. 90 foll.

[2] Baking as a trade only came in, as we saw, in 174; Plautus died in 184; some doubt is thus thrown on the Roman character of the passage, or the allusion may not be to a public bakery.

industry, but in supplying the luxurious needs of the household.[1]   In all probability research will show that free labour was far more available than we are apt to think.   We hear of no outbreak of feeling against slave labour, which might suggest a rivalry between the two.   Slave labour, we may think, had filled a gap, created by abnormal circumstances, and did not oust free labour entirely ; but it tended constantly to cramp it, and doubtless started notions of work in general which helped to degrade it.[2]   Those immense *familiae urbanae*, of which the historian of slavery has given a detailed account in his second volume,[3] belong rather to the early Empire than to the last years of the Republic—the evidence for them is drawn chiefly from Seneca, Juvenal, Tacitus, Martial, etc. ; but such evidence as we have for the age of Cicero seems to suggest that the vast palaces of the capitalists, which Sallust describes as being almost like cities,[4] were already beginning to be served by a familia urbana which rendered them almost independent of any aid from without by labour or purchase.   Not only the ordinary domestic helpers of all kinds, but copyists, librarians, paedagogi as tutors for the children, and even doctors might all be found in such households in a servile condition,

[1] See a remarkable passage of Athenaeus (vi. 104) quoted by Marquardt, *Privatleben*, p. 156, on the use of slaves at Rome for unproductive labour.

[2] Sallust, e.g., says of his own life in retirement that he would not engage in "agrum colendo aut venando, servilibus officiis."—*Catil.* 4.

[3] Wallon, *Hist. de l'Esclavage*, vol. ii. ch. iii.

[4] Sall. *Catil.* 12.

without reckoning the great numbers who seem to have been always available as escorts when the great man was travelling in Italy or in the provinces. Valerius Maximus tells us [1] that Cato the censor as proconsul of Spain took only three slaves with him, and that his descendant Cato of Utica during the Civil Wars had twelve; as both these men were extremely frugal, we can form an idea from this passage both of the increasing supply of slaves and of the far larger escorts which accompanied the ordinary wealthy traveller.

As regards the familia rustica, the working population of the farm, the evidence is much more definite. The old Roman farm, in which the pater-familias lived with his wife, children, and slaves, was, no doubt, like the old English holding in a manor, for the most part self-sufficing, doing little in the way of sale or purchase, and worked by all the members of the familia, bond and free. In the middle of the second century B.C., when Cato wrote his treatise on husbandry, we find that a change has taken place; the master can only pay the farm an occasional visit, to see that it is being properly managed by the slave steward [2] (vilicus), and the business is being run upon capitalistic lines, i.e. with a view to realising the utmost possible profit from it by the sale of its products. Thus Cato is most particular in urging

[1] iv. 3. 11 and 12.   Plutarch says that as military tribune Cato the younger had fifteen slaves with him.—*Cato minor* 9.

[2] Cato, *R.R.* 2. 1.

that a farm should be so placed as to have easy communication with market towns, where the wine and oil could be sold, which were the chief products, and where various necessaries could be bought cheap, such as pottery and metal-work of all kinds.[1] Thus the farm does not entirely depend on the labour of its own familia; nevertheless it rests still upon an economic basis of slave labour. For an olivetum of 240 jugera Cato puts the necessary hands as thirteen in number, all non-free; for a vineyard of 100 jugera at sixteen; and these figures are no doubt low, if we remember his character for parsimony and profit-making.[2] Free labour was to be had, and was occasionally needed; at the very outset of his work Cato (ch. 4) insists that the owner should be a good and friendly neighbour, in order that he may easily obtain, not only voluntary help, but hired labourers (operarii). These were needed especially at harvest time, when extra hands were wanted, as in our hop-gardens, for the gathering of olives and for the vintage. Sometimes the work was let out to a contractor, and he gives explicit directions (in chs. 144 and 145) for the choice of these and the contracts to be made with them; whether in this case the contractor (redemptor) used entirely free or slave labour does not appear distinctly, but it seems clear that a proportion at least was

[1] In ch. 135 he mentions towns where many other objects may be bought best and cheapest: at Rome, e.g., clothing and rugs, at Cales and Minturnae farm-instruments of iron, etc. See also Gummerus, *op. cit.* p. 36.

[2] *R.R.* 10 and 11.

free.[1] What the free labourers did at other times of
the year, whether or no they were small cultivators
themselves, Cato does not tell us.

For the age with which we are more specially concerned, we have the evidence of Varro's three books
on husbandry, written in his old age, after the fall of
the Republic.   Here we find the economic condition
of the farm little changed since the time of Cato.
The permanent labour is non-free, but in spite of the
vast increase in the servile labour available in Italy,
there is still a considerable employment of freemen
at certain times, on all farms where the olive and
vine were the chief objects of culture.   In the 17th
chapter of his first book, in which he gives interesting
advice for the purchase of suitable slaves, he begins
by telling us that all land is cultivated either by
slaves or freemen, or both together, and the free are
of three kinds,—either small holders (pauperculi)
with their children ; or labourers who live by wage
(conducticii), and are especially needed in hay harvest
or vintage ; or debtors who give their labour as
payment for what they owe (obaerati).[2] Varro too,
like Cato, recognises the necessity of purchasing
many things which cannot well be manufactured on
a farm of moderate size, and thus the landowner may
in this way also have been indirectly an employer of

---

[1] Assiduos homines quinquaginta praebeto, i.e. the contractor : ch. 144.

[2] See the discussion of this word in Gummerus, p. 62 foll. Varro defines
them as those "qui suas operas in servitutem dant pro pecunia quam
debebant" (de Ling. Lat. vii. 105), i.e. they give their labour as against
servitude.

free labour ; but so far as possible the farm should supply itself with the materials for its own working,[1] for this gives employment to the slaves throughout the year,—and they should never be allowed to be idle.[2]

Thus it is abundantly clear that even in the time of Cicero there was a certain demand for free labour in the ordinary Italian oliveyard and vineyard, and that the necessary supply was forthcoming, though the permanent industrial basis was non-free, and the tendency was to use slave-labour more exclusively. The rule that the slave cannot be allowed to be unemployed was a most important factor in the economical development, and drove the landowner, who never seems to have had any doubt about the comparative cheapness of slave-labour,[3] gradually to make his farm more and more independent of all aid from outside. In the work of Columella, written towards the end of the first century A.D., it is plain that the work of the farm is carried on more exclusively by slave-labour than was the case in the last two centuries B.C.[4]

To this not unpleasant picture of the conditions of Italian agricultural slavery a few words must be added about the great pastoral farms of Southern

[1] *R.R.* i. 22.

[2] Cp. Plut. *Cato the Elder* 21 ; a slave must be at work when he is not asleep.

[3] This is a point on which I cannot enter, but there can hardly be a doubt that in the long run free labour is cheaper. See Cairnes, *Slave Power in America*, ch. iii. ; Salvioli, *Le Capitalisme*, p. 253 ; Columella, *Praefatio*.

[4] Gummerus, p. 81. At the same time the small cultivator is an obvious fact in Columella, cultivating his bit of land without working for others.

Italy. If a man invested his capital in a comparatively small estate of olives and vineyards, such as that which Cato treats of, and which seems to have been his own ; or even in a latifundium of the kind which Varro more vaguely pictures, containing also parks and game and a moderate amount of pasture, he would need slaves mainly of a certain degree of skill. But on the largest areas of pasture, chiefly in the hill districts of Southern Italy, where there was little cultivation except what was necessary for the consumption of the slaves themselves, these were the roughest and wildest type of bondsmen. The work was that of the American ranche, the life harsh, and the workmen dangerous. It was in these districts and from these men that Spartacus drew the material with which he made his last stand against Roman armies in 72-71 B.C. ; and it was in this direction that Caelius and Milo turned in 48 B.C. in quest of revolutionary and warlike bands. These roughs could even be used as galley-slaves ; more than once in the Commentaries on the Civil War Caesar tells us that his opponents drafted them into the vessels which were sent to relieve the siege of Massilia.[1] It was here too, in the neighbourhood of Thurii, that a bloody fight took place between the slaves of two adjoining estates, strong men of courage, as Cicero describes them, of which we learn from the fragments of his lost speech *pro Tullio*. They were

---

[1] For Spartacus, Appian, *B.C.* i. 116 ; for Caelius, Caesar, *B.C.* iii. 22 ; and cp. *B.C.* i. 56.

of course armed, and as we may guess from Varro's
remarks on the kind of slaves suitable for shepherd-
ing,[1] this was usually the practice, in order to defend
the flocks from wild beasts and robbers, particularly
when they were driven up to summer pasture (as
they still are) in the saltus of the Apennines. The
needs of these shepherds would be small, and the
latifundia of this kind were probably almost self-
sufficing, no free labour being required. After their
day's work the slaves were fed and locked up for the
night, and kept in fetters if necessary;[2] they were
in fact simply living tools, to use the expression of
Aristotle, and the economy of such estates was as
simple as that of a workshop. The exclusion of free
labour is here complete : on the agricultural estates
it was approaching a completion which it fortunately
never reached. Had it reached that completion, the
economic influence of slavery would have been
altogether bad ; as it was, the introduction of slave-
labour on a large scale did valuable service to Italian
agriculture in the last century B.C. by contributing
the material for its revival at a time when the
necessary free labour could not have been found.
However lamentable its results may have been in other
ways, especially on the great pastures, the economic
history of Italy, when it comes to be written, will have
to give it credit for an appreciable amount of benefit.

2. The legal and political aspect of slavery. A
slave was in the eye of the law not a *persona*, but a

---

[1] *R.R.* ii. 10.   [2] Columella i. 8.

res, i.e. he had no rights as a human being, could not marry or hold property, but was himself simply a piece of property which could be conveyed (res mancipi).[1] During the Republican period the law left him absolutely at the disposal of his master, who had the power of life and death (jus vitae necisque) over him, and could punish him with chastisement and bonds, and use him for any purpose he pleased, without reference to any higher authority than his own. This was the legal position of all slaves; but it naturally often happened that those who were men of knowledge or skill, as secretaries, for example, librarians, doctors, or even as body-servants, were in intimate and happy relations with their owners,[2] and in the household of a humane man no well-conducted slave need fear bodily degradation. Cicero and his friend Atticus both had slaves whom they valued, not only for their useful service, but as friends. Tiro, who edited Cicero's letters after his death, and to whom we therefore owe an eternal debt of gratitude, was the object of the tenderest affection on the part of his owner, and the letters addressed to him by the latter when he was taken ill at Patrae in 50 B.C. are among the most touching writings that have come down to us from antiquity. "I miss you," he writes in one of them,[3] "yes, but I

[1] Gaius ii. 15.

[2] For examples of slaves' devotion to their masters, Appian, *B.C.* iv. 29; Seneca, *de Benef.* iii. 25.

[3] *ad Fam.* xvi. 1; read also the charming letters which follow. Tiro was manumitted by Cicero at an unknown date.

also love you. Love prompts the wish to see you in good health : the other motive would make me wish to see you as soon as possible,—and the former one is the best." Atticus, too, had his Tiro, Alexis, "imago Tironis," as Cicero calls him in a letter to his friend,[1] and many others who were engaged in the work of copying and transcribing books, which was one of Atticus' many pursuits. All such slaves would sooner or later be manumitted, i.e. transmuted from a *res* to a *persona* ; and in the ease with which this process of transmutation could be effected we have the one redeeming point of the whole system of bondage. According to the oldest and most efficient form (vindicta), a legal ceremony had to be gone through in the presence of a praetor ; but the praetor could easily be found, and there was no other difficulty. This was the form usually adopted by an owner wishing to free a slave in his own lifetime ; but great numbers were constantly manumitted more irregularly, or by the will of the master after his death.[2]

Thus the leading facts in the legal position of the Roman slave were two : (1) he was absolutely at the disposal of his owner, the law never interfering to protect him ; (2) he had a fair prospect of manumission if valuable and well-behaved, and if manumitted he of course became a Roman citizen (libertus or libertinus) with full civil rights,[3] remaining, however,

---

[1] *ad Att.* xii. 10.

[2] See the article "Manumissio" in *Dict. of Antiquities.*

[3] Only in exercising the jus suffragii he was limited with all his fellow libertini to one of the four city tribes.

according to ancient custom, in a certain position of moral subordination to his late master, owing him respect, and aid if necessary. Let us apply these two leading facts to the conditions of Roman life as we have already sketched them. We shall find that they have political results of no small importance.

First, we must try to realise that the city of Rome contained at least 200,000 human beings over whom the State had no direct control whatever. All such crimes, serious or petty, as are now tried and disposed of in our criminal courts, were then, if committed by a slave, punishable only by the master ; and in the majority of cases, if the familia were a large one, they probably never reached his ears. The jurisdiction to which the slave was responsible was a private one, like that of the great feudal lord of the Middle Ages, who had his own prison and his own gallows. The political result was much the same in each case. Just as the feudal lord, with his private jurisdiction and his hosts of retainers, became a peril to good government and national unity until he was brought to order by a strong king like our Henry II. or Henry VII., so the owner of a large familia of many hundreds of slaves may almost be said to have been outside of the State : undoubtedly he became a serious peril to the good order of the capital. The part played by the slaves in the political disturbances of Cicero's time was no mean one. One or two instances will show this. Saturninus, in the year 100. when attacked by

Marius under orders from the senate, had hoisted a
pilleus, or cap of liberty which the emancipated slave
wore, as a signal to the slaves of the city that they
might expect their liberty if they supported him;[1]
and Marius a few years later took the same step
when himself attacked by Sulla. Catiline, in 63,
Sallust assures us, believed it possible to raise the
slaves of the city in aid of his revolutionary plans, and
they flocked to him in great numbers; but he afterwards abandoned his intention, thinking that to mix
up the cause of citizens with that of slaves would
not be judicious.[2] It is here too that the gladiator
slaves first meet us as a political arm; Cicero had
the next spring to defend P. Sulla on the charge,
among others, of having bought gladiators during
the conspiracy with seditious views, and the senate
had to direct that the bands of these dangerous men
should be dispersed to Capua and other municipal
towns at a distance. Later on we frequently hear
of their being used as private soldiery, and the
government in the last years of the Republic ceased
to be able to control them.[3] Again, in defending
Sestius, Cicero asserts that Clodius in his tribunate
had organised a levy of slaves under the name of
collegia, for purposes of violence, slaughter, and
rapine; and even if this is an exaggeration, it shows

[1] Val. Max. viii. 6. 2.

[2] Sall. *Cat.* 24 and 56 ; Wallon, ii. p. 318 foll.

[3] See, e.g., Cic. *ad Att.* ii. 24. 3 ; Asconius, *in Milonianam* (ed. Clark,
p. 31) ; Milo's host of slaves had gladiators among them, and were organised
in military fashion (an antesignanus, p. 32), when he fell in with Clodius.

that such proceedings were not deemed impossible.[1]
And apart from the actual use of slaves for
revolutionary objects, or as private body-guards,
it is clear from Cicero's correspondence that as
an important part of a great man's retinue they
might indirectly have influence in elections and
on other political occasions. Quintus Cicero, in his
little treatise on electioneering,[2] urges his brother
to make himself agreeable to his tribesmen, neighbours, clients, freedmen, and even slaves, "for nearly
all the talk which affects one's public reputation
emanates from domestic sources." And Marcus himself, in the last letter he wrote before he fled into
exile in 58, declares that all his friends are promis-
ing him not only their own aid, but that of their
clients, freedmen, and slaves,—promises which doubtless might have been kept had he stayed to take
advantage of them.[3]

The mention of the freedmen in this letter may
serve to remind us of the political results of manumission, the second fact in the legal aspect of Roman
slavery. The most important of these is the rapid
importation of foreign blood into the Roman citizen
body, which long before the time of Cicero largely
consisted of enfranchised slaves or their descendants;
it was to this that Scipio Aemilianus alluded in his
famous words to the contio he was addressing after
his return from Numantia, "Silence, ye to whom

[1] *Pro Sestio*, 15. 34.   [2] *De Pet. Consulatus*, 5. 17.
[3] *ad Quint. Fratr.* i. 2 *ad fin.*

Italy is but a stepmother " (Val. Max. 6. 2. 3). Had manumission been held in check or in some way superintended by the State, there would have been more good than harm in it. Many men of note, who had an influence on Roman culture, were libertini, such as Livius Andronicus and Caecilius the poets; Terence, Publilius Syrus, whose acquaintance we made in the last chapter; Tiro and Alexis, and rather later Verrius Flaccus, one of the most learned men who ever wrote in Latin. But the great increase in the number of slaves, and the absence of any real difficulty in effecting their manumission, led to the enfranchisement of crowds of rascals as compared with the few valuable men. The most striking example is the enfranchisement of 10,000 by Sulla, who according to custom took his name Cornelius, and, though destined to be a kind of military guarantee for the permanence of the Sullan institutions, only became a source of serious peril to the State at the time of Catiline's conspiracy. Caesar, who was probably more alive to this kind of social danger than his contemporaries, sent out a great number of libertini,—the majority, says Strabo, of his colonists,—to his new foundation at Corinth.[1] But Dionysius of Halicarnassus, writing in the time of Augustus, when he stayed some time in Rome, draws a terrible picture of the evil effects of indiscriminate manumission, unchecked by the law.[2]

" Many," he says, " are indignant when they see

---

[1] Strabo, p. 381.   [2] Dion. Hal. iv. 23.

unworthy men manumitted, and condemn a usage which gives such men the citizenship of a sovereign state whose destiny is to govern the world. As for me, I doubt if the practice should be stopped altogether, lest greater evil should be the result; I would rather that it should be checked as far as possible, so that the state may no longer be invaded by men of such villainous character. The censors, or at least the consuls, should examine all whom it is proposed to manumit, inquiring into their origin and the reasons and mode of their enfranchisement, as in their examination of the equites. Those whom they find worthy of citizenship should have their names inscribed on tables, distributed among the tribes, with leave to reside in the city. As to the crowd of villains and criminals, they should be sent far away, under pretext of founding some colony."

These judicious remarks of a foreigner only expressed what was probably a common feeling among the best men of that time. Augustus made some attempt to limit the enfranchising power of the owner; but the Leges Aelia Sentia and Furia Caninia do not lie within the compass of this book. No great success could attend these efforts; the abnormal circumstances which had brought to Rome the great familiae of slaves reacted inevitably upon the citizen body itself through the process of manumission. Rome had to pay heavily in this, as in so many other ways, for her advancement to the sovereignty of the civilised world. I may be allowed to translate the eloquent words in which the French historian of slavery, in whose great work the history of ancient slavery is treated as only a scholar-statesman can treat it, sums up this aspect of the subject :

"Emancipation, prevalent as it might appear to be towards the beginning of the Empire, was not a step towards the suppression of slavery, but a natural and inevitable sequence of the institution itself, — an outlet for excess in an epoch over-abundant in slaves : a means of renewing the mass, corrupted by the deleterious influence of its own condition, before it should be totally ruined. As water, diverted from its free course, becomes impure in the basin which imprisons it, and when released, will still retain its impurity ; so it is not to be thought that instincts perverted by slavery, habits depraved from childhood, could be reformed and redressed in the slave by a tardy liberation. Thrust into the midst of a society itself vitiated by the admixture of slavery, he only became more unre-strainedly, more dangerously bad. Manumission was thus no remedy for the deterioration of the citizens : it was powerless even to better the condition of the slave." [1]

3. The ethical aspect of Roman slavery. What were the moral effects of the system (1) on the slaves themselves ; (2) on the freemen who owned them ?

First, as regards the slaves themselves, there are

[1] Wallon, *op. cit.* ii. p. 436.

two facts to be fully realised; when this is done, the inferences will be sufficiently obvious. Let us remember that by far the greater number of the slaves, both in the city and on the land, were brought from countries bordering on the Mediterranean, where they had been living in some kind of elementary civilisation, in which the germs of further development were present in the form of the natural ties of race and kinship and locality, of tribe or family or village community, and with their own religion, customs, and government. Permanent captivity in a foreign land and in a servile condition snapped these ties once and for all. To take a single appalling instance, the 150,000 human beings who were sold into slavery in Epirus by the conqueror of Pydna, or as many of them as were transported out of their own country—and these were probably the vast majority,—were thereby deprived for the rest of their lives of all social and family life, of their ancestral worship, in fact of everything that could act as a moral tie, as a restraining influence upon vicious instincts. With the lamentable effect of this on the regions thus depopulated we are not here concerned, but it was beyond doubt most serious, and must be taken into account in reckoning up the various causes which later on brought about the enfeeblement of the whole Roman Empire.[1] The point for us is that a large proportion of the population of Rome and of Italy was now composed of

[1] See Otto Seeck, *Geschichte des Untergangs der antiken Welt*, ch. iv. and v.

human beings destitute of all natural means of moral and social development. The ties that had been once broken could never be replaced. There is no need to dwell on the inevitable result,—the introduction into the Roman State of a poisonous element of terrible volume and power.

The second fact that we have to grasp is this. In the old days, when such slaves as there then were came from Italy itself, and worked under the master's own eye upon the farm, they might and did share to some extent in the social life of the family, and even in its religious rites, and so might under favourable circumstances come within the range of its moral influences.[1] But towards the close of the Republican period those moral influences, as we have seen, were fast vanishing in the majority of families which possessed large numbers of slaves. The common kind of slave in the city, who was not attached to his owner as was a man of culture like Tiro, had no moral standard except implicit obedience ; the highest virtue was to obey orders diligently, and fear of punishment was the only sanction of his conduct. The typical city slave, as he appears in Plautus, though by no means a miserable being without any enjoyment of life, is a liar and a thief, bent on overreaching, and destitute of a conscience.[2] We need

---

[1] See Marquardt, *Privatleben*, p. 172.

[2] Wallon (ii. p. 255 foll.) has collected a number of examples. Plautus' slaves are as much Athenian as Roman, but the conditions would be much the same in each case. Cp. Varro, *Men. Sat.* ed. Riese, p. 220 : "Crede mihi, plures dominos servi comederunt quam canes."

but reflect that the slave must often have had to do vile things in the name of his one virtue, obedience, to realise that the poison was present, and ready to become active, in every Roman household. " Nec turpe est quod dominus iubet." [1]

On the latifundia in the country the master was himself seldom resident, and the slaves were under the control of one or more of their own kind, promoted for good conduct and capacity. The slaves of the great sheep and cattle farms were, as we saw, of the wildest sort, and we may judge of their morality by the story of the Sicilian slave-owner who, when his slaves complained that they were insufficiently clothed, told them that the remedy was to rob the travellers they fell in with. [2] The *ergastula*, where slaves were habitually chained and treated like beasts, were sowing the seeds of permanent moral contamination in Italy. [3] But on the smaller estates of olive-yard and vineyard their condition was better, and a humane owner who chose his overseers carefully might possibly reproduce something of the old feeling of participation in the life as well as the industry of the economic unit. In an interesting chapter Varro advises that the vilicus should be carefully selected, and should be conciliated by being allowed a wife and the means of accumulating a property (*peculium*); he even urges that he should enforce obedience rather

---

[1] Petronius, *Sat.* 75.   [2] Diodorus xxxiv. 38.

[3] "Coli rura ab ergastulis pessimum est et quicquid agitur a desperantibus," wrote Pliny (*Nat. Hist.* xviii. 36) in the famous passage about latifundia.

by words than blows.[1] But of the condition of the
ordinary slave on the farm this is the only hint he
gives us, and it never seems to have occurred to
him, or to any other Roman of his day, that the
work to be done would be better performed by men
not deprived by their condition of a moral sense;
that slave labour is unwillingly and unintelligently
rendered, because the labourer has no hope, no sense
of dutiful conduct leading him to rejoice in the
work of his hands. Nor did any writer recognise the
fact that slaves were potentially moral beings, until
Christianity gave its sanction to dutiful submission
as an act of morality that might be consecrated by a
Divine authority.[2]

Lastly, it is not difficult to realise the mischievous
effects of such a slave system as the Roman upon
the slave-owning class itself. Even those who themselves had no slaves would be affected by it; for
though, as we have seen, free labour was by no means
ousted by it, it must have helped to create an idle
class of freemen, with all its moral worthlessness.
Long ago, in his remarkable book on *The Slave Power*
in America before the Civil War, Professor Cairnes
drew a striking comparison between the "mean whites"
of the Southern States, the result of slave labour on
the plantations, and the idle population of the Roman
capital, fed on cheap corn and ready for any kind of

---

[1] *R.R.* i. 17.

[2] See some excellent remarks on this subject in *Ecce Homo*, towards
the end of ch. xii. ("Universality of the Christian Republic ").

rowdyism.[1] But in the case of the great slave-owners
the mischief was much more serious, though perhaps
more difficult to detect. The master of a horde of
slaves had half his moral sense paralysed, because he
had no feeling of responsibility for so many of those
with whom he came in contact every day and hour.
When most members of a man's household or estate
are absolutely at his mercy, when he has no feeling
of any contractual relation with them, his sense of
duty and obligation is inevitably deadened, even
towards others who are not thus in his power. Can
we doubt that the lack of a sense of justice and
right dealing, more especially towards provincials, but
also towards a man's fellow-citizens, which we have
noticed in the two upper sections of society, was due
in great part to the constant exercise of arbitrary
power at home, to the habit of looking upon the men
who ministered to his luxurious ease as absolutely
without claim upon his respect or his benevolence?
or that the recklessness of human life which was
shown in the growing popularity of bloody gladiatorial shows, and in the incredible cruelty of the
victors in the Civil Wars, was the result of this
unconscious cultivation, from childhood onwards, of
the despotic temper?[2] Even the best men of the
age, such as Cicero, Caesar, Lucretius, show hardly a

---

[1] *The Slave Power*, ch. v., and especially p. 374 foll. A living picture of
the mean white may be found in Mark Twain's *Huckleberry Finn*, drawn
from his own early experience, particularly in ch. xxi.

[2] "Regum nobis induimus animos," wrote Seneca in a well-known letter
about the claims of slaves as human beings, *Ep.* 47.

sign of any sympathy with, or interest in, that vast mass of suffering humanity, both bond and free, with which the Roman dominion was populated; to disregard misery, except when they found it among the privileged classes, had become second nature to them. We can better realise this if we reflect that even at the present day, in spite of the absence of slavery and the presence of philanthropical societies, the average man of wealth gives hardly more than a passing thought to the discomfort and distress of the crowded population of our great cities. The ordinary callousness of human nature had, under the baleful influence of slavery, become absolute blindness, nor were men's eyes to be opened until Christianity began to leaven the world with the doctrine of universal love.

CHAPTER VIII

THE HOUSE OF THE RICH MAN, IN TOWN
AND COUNTRY

WE saw that the poorer classes in Rome were
lodged in huge *insulae*, and enjoyed nothing that
can be called home life. The wealthy families, on
the other hand, lived in *domus*, i.e. separate dwellings, accommodating only one family, often, even in
the Ciceronian period, of great magnificence. But
even these great houses hardly suggest a life such
as that which we associate with the word home.
As Mr. Tucker has pointed out in the case of
Athens,[1] the warmer climates of Greece and Italy
encouraged all classes to spend much more of their
time out of doors and in public places than we do;
and the rapid growth of convenient public buildings,
porticoes, basilicas, baths, and so on, is one of the
most striking features in the history of the city
during the last two centuries B.C. Augustus, part
of whose policy it was to make the city population
comfortable and contented, carried this tendency still

---

[1] *Life in Ancient Athens*, p. 55.

further, and under the Empire the town house played
quite a subordinate part in Roman social life. The
best way to realise this out-of-door life, lazy and
sociable, of the Augustan age, is to read the first
book of Ovid's *Ars Amatoria*,—a fascinating picture
of a beautiful city and its pleasure-loving inhabitants. But with the Augustan age we are not here
concerned.

Yet the Roman house, like the Italian house in
general, was in origin and essence really a home.
The family was the basis of society, and by the
family we must understand not only the head of
the house with his wife, children, and slaves, but
also the divine beings who dwelt there. As the
State comprised both human and divine inhabitants,
so also did the house, which was indeed the germ and
type of the State. Thus the house was in those early
times not less but even more than a house is for us,
for in it was concentrated all that was dear to the
family, all that was essential to its life, both natural
and supernatural. And the two—the natural and
supernatural—were not distinct from each other, but
associated, in fact almost identical; the hearth-fire
was the dwelling of Vesta, the spirit of the flame;
the Penates were the spirits of the stores on which
the family subsisted, and dwelt in the store-cupboard
or larder; the paterfamilias had himself a supernatural side, in the shape of his Genius; and the
Lar familiaris was the protecting spirit of the farm-
land, who had found his way into the house in course

of time, perhaps with the slave labourers, who always had a share in his worship.[1]

It would probably be unjust to the Roman of the late Republic to assume that this beautiful idea of the common life of the human and divine beings in a house was entirely ignored or forgotten by him. No doubt the reality of the belief had vanished; it could not be said of the city family, as Ovid said of the farm-folk :[2]

> ante focos olim scamnis considere longis
> mos erat *et mensae credere adesse deos.*

The great noble or banker of Cicero's day could no longer honestly say that he believed in the real presence of his family deities; the kernel of the old feeling had shrunk away under the influence of Greek philosophy and of new interests in life, new objects and ambitions. But the shell remained, and in some families, or in moments of anxiety and emotion, even the old feeling of *religio* may have returned. Cicero is appealing to a common sentiment, in a passage already once quoted (*de Domo*, 109), when he insists on the real religious character of a house : " hic arae sunt, hic foci, hic di penates : hic sacra, religiones, caerimoniae continentur." And this was in the heart of the city ; in the country-house there was doubtless more leisure and opportunity for such feeling. In the second century B.C. old Cato had described the

---

[1] For this view of the Lar see Wissowa, *Religion und Kultus der Römer*, p. 148 foll. ; and a note by the author in *Archiv für Religionswissenschaft*, 1906, p. 529.

[2] *Fasti*, vi. 299.

paterfamilias, on his arrival at his farm from the
city, saluting the Lar familiaris before he goes about
his round of inspection; and even Horace hardly
shows a trace of the agnostic when he pictures the
slaves of the farm, and the master with them, sitting
at their meal in front of the image of the Lar.[1] We
may perhaps guess that with the renewal of the love of
country life, and with that revival of the cultivation of
the vine and olive, and indeed of husbandry in general,
which is recognisable as a feature of the last years of
the Republic, and which is known to us from Varro's
work on farming, and from Virgil's *Georgics*, the old
religion of the household gained a new life.

It is not necessary here to give any detailed account of the shape and divisions of a Roman house of
the city; full and excellent descriptions may be found
in Middleton's article "Domus" in the *Dictionary
of Antiquities*, and in Lanciani's *Ruins and Excavations of Ancient Rome*; and to these should be added
Mau's work on Pompeii, where the houses were of a
Roman rather than a Greek type. What we are
concerned with is the house as a home or a centre
of life, and it is only in this aspect of it that we
shall discuss it here.

The oldest Italian dwelling was a mere wigwam
with a hearth in the middle of the floor, and a hole
at the top to let the smoke out. But the house of
historical times was rectangular, with one central
room or hall, in which was concentrated the whole

---

[1] Cato, *R.R.*, ch. ii. init.; Horace, *Epode* 2. 65 ; *Sat.* ii. 6. 65.

indoor life of the family, the whole meaning and purpose of the dwelling. Here the human and divine inhabitants originally lived together. Here was the hearth, "the natural altar of the dwelling-room of man," as Aust beautifully expresses it;[1] this was the seat of Vesta, and behind it was the *penus* or store-closet, the seat of the Penates; thus Vesta and the Penates are in the most genuine sense the protecting and nourishing deities of the household. Here, too, was the Lar of the familia with his little altar, behind the entrance, and here was the *lectus genialis*,[2] and the Genius of the paterfamilias. As you looked into the atrium, after passing the *vestibulum* or space between street and doorway, and the *ostium* or doorway with its *janua*, you saw in front of you the *impluvium*, into which the rain-water fell from the *compluvium*, i.e. the square opening in the roof with sloping sides; on either side were recesses (*alae*), which, if the family were noble, contained the images of the ancestors. Opposite you was another recess, the *tablinum*, opening probably into a little garden; here in the warm weather the family might take their meals.

This is the atrium of the old Roman house, and to understand that house nothing more is needed. And indeed architecturally, the atrium never lost its significance as the centre of the house; it is to

---

[1] *Römische Religion*, p. 214.
[2] Or lectulus adversus, i.e. opposite the door; Ascon. ed. Clark, p. 43, a good passage for the contents of an atrium.

the house as the choir is to a cathedral.[1] And it is easy to see how naturally it could develop into a much more complicated but convenient dwelling; for example, the alae could be extended to form separate chambers or sleeping-rooms, the tablinum could be made into a permanent dining-room, or such rooms could be opened out on either side of it. A second story could be added, and in the city, where space was valuable, this was usually the case. The garden could be converted, after the Greek fashion, and under a Greek name, into a *peristylium*, i.e. an open court with a pretty colonnade round it, and if there were space enough, you might add at the rear of this again an *exedra*, or an *oecus*, i.e. open saloons convenient for many purposes. Thus the house came to be practically divided into two parts, the atrium with its belongings, i.e. the Roman part, and the peristylium with its developments, forming the Greek part; and the house reflects the composite character of Roman life in its later period, just as do Roman literature and Roman art. The Roman part was retained for reception rooms, and the Lar, the Penates, and Vesta, with their respective seats, retired into the new apartments for privacy. When the usual crowd of morning callers came to wait upon a great man, they would not as a rule penetrate farther than the atrium, and there he might keep them waiting as long as he pleased. The Greek part of the house, the peristylium and its belongings,

---

[1] See Mau's *Pompeii*, p. 248.

was reserved for his family and his most intimate friends. In Pompeii, which was an old Greek town with Roman life and habits superadded, we find atrium and peristylium both together as early as the second century B.C.[1] At what period exactly the house of the noble in Rome began thus to develop is not so certain. But by the time of Cicero every good domus had without doubt its private apartments at the rear, varying in shape and size according to the ground on which the house stood.[2]

The accompanying plan will give a sufficiently clear idea of the development of the domus from the atrium, and its consequent division into two parts; it is that of "the house of the silver wedding" at Pompeii.

But in spite of all the convenience and comfort of the fully developed dwelling of the rich man at Rome, there was much to make him sigh for a quieter life than he could enjoy in the noisy city. He might indeed, if he could afford it, remove outside the walls to a "domus suburbana," on one of the roads leading out of Rome, or on the hill looking down on the Campus Martius, like the house of Sallust the historian, with its splendid gardens, which still in part exists in the dip between the Quirinal and the Pincian hills.[3] But nowhere within three miles

---

[1] Mau, *Pompeii*, p. 240.

[2] The extent to which this could be carried can be guessed from Sall. *Cat.* 12.

[3] Quintus Cicero, growing rich with Caesar in Gaul, had a fancy for a domus suburbana : Cic. *ad Q. Fr.* iii. 1. 7.   Marcus tells his brother in this letter that he himself had no great fancy for such a residence, and that his

or more of Rome could a man lose his sense of being in a town, or escape from the smoke, the noise, the excitement of the streets. After what has been said

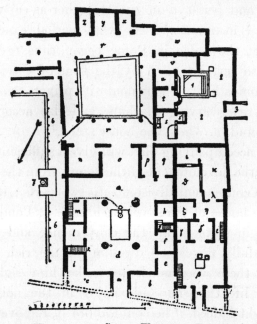

PLAN OF THE HOUSE OF THE SILVER WEDDING.   From Mau's *Pompeii*.

a. Fauces.	1. Open-air swimming tank, in a small garden (2).
d. Tetrastyle atrium.	
n. Dining-room.	3. Corridor leading to another house and to a side street.
o. Tablinum.	
p. Andron.	4. Oecus.
r. Peristyle.	6. Garden, partially excavated.
s. Kitchen.	7. Open-air triclinium.
t-v. Bath. (*v.* Apodyterium. *u.* Tepidarium. *t.* Caldarium.)	*a-ι.* Fauces, atrium, and other rooms of separate dwelling connected with the larger house.
w. Summer dining-room.	
x, z. Sleeping-rooms.	
y. Exedra.	

in previous chapters, the crowd in the Forum and its adjuncts can be left to the reader's imagination ;

house on the Palatine had all the charm of such a suburbana.   His villa at Tusculum, as we shall see, served the purpose of a house close to the city.

but if he wishes to stimulate it, let him look at
the seventh chapter of Cicero's speech for Plancius,
where the orator makes use of the jostling in the
Forum as an illustration so familiar that none can
fail to understand it.[1]   A relief, of which a figure is
given in Burn's *Roman Literature and Roman Art*,
p. 79, gives a good idea of the close crowding,
though no doubt it was habitual with Roman artists
to overcrowd their scenes with human figures.   Even
as early as the first Punic war a lady could complain
of the crowded state of the Forum, and, with the
grim humour peculiar to Romans, could declare that
her brother, who had just lost a great number of
Roman lives in a defeat by the Carthaginians, ought
to be in command of another fleet in order to relieve
the city of more of its surplus population.   What
then must the Forum have been two centuries later,
when half the business of the Empire was daily
transacted there!   And even outside the walls the
trouble did not cease; all night long the wagons
were rolling into the city, which were not allowed in
the day-time, at any rate after Caesar's municipal law
of 46 B.C.   Like the motors of to-day, one might
imagine that their noise would depreciate the value
of houses on the great roads.   The callers and clients
would be here of a morning, as in the house within
the walls; the bore might be met not only in the
Via Sacra, like Horace's immortal friend, but wher-

---

[1] A great number of passages about the noise and crowds of Rome are
collected in Mayor's *Notes to Juvenal*, pp. 173, 203, 207.

ever the stream of life hurried with its busy eddies.[1]
Lucilius drew a graphic picture of this feverish life,
which is fortunately preserved ; it refers of course to
a time before Cicero's birth (Fragm. 9, Baehrens) :

> nunc vero a mani ad noctem, festo atque profesto,
> totus item pariter populus, plebesque patresque,
> iactare indu foro se omnes, decedere nusquam :
> uni se atque eidem studio omnes dedere et arti,
> verba dare ut caute possint, pugnare dolose :
> blanditia certare, bonum simulare virum se :
> insidias facere, ut si hostes sint omnibus omnes.

That this exciting social atmosphere, with its
jostling and over-reaching in the Forum, and its
callers and dinner-parties in the house, had some
sinister influence on men's tempers and nerves, there
can be no doubt. Cicero dearly loved the life of the
city, but he paid for it by a sensibility which is
constantly apparent in his letters, and diminished
his value as a statesman. When he wrote from
Cilicia to his more youthful friend Caelius, urging
him to stick to the city, in words that are almost
pathetic, it never occurred to him that he was
prescribing exactly that course of treatment which
had done himself much damage.[2] The clear sight
and strong nerve of Caesar, as compared with so
many of his contemporaries, was doubtless largely

[1] Some interesting remarks on the general aspect of the city will be found
in the concluding chapter of Lanciani's *Ruins and Excavations*. For the
bore elsewhere than in Rome, see below, p. 256.

[2] *ad Fam.* ii. 12 : "Urbem, Urbem, mi Rufe, cole, et in ista luce vive.
Omnis peregrinatio (foreign travel) obscura et sordida est iis, quorum
industria Roma potest illustris esse," etc.

due to the fact that between 70 and 50 B.C., i.e. in the prime of life, he spent some twelve of the twenty years in the fresher air of Spain and Gaul. Some men were fairly worn out with dissipation and the resulting ennui, and could get no relief even in a country villa. Lucretius has drawn a wonderful picture of such an unfortunate, who hurries from Rome into the country, and finding himself bored there almost as soon as he arrives, orders out his carriage to return to the city. To fill oneself with good things, yet never to be satisfied (explere bonis rebus, satiareque nunquam), was even for the true Epicurean a most dismal fate.[1]

But there was at this time, and had been for many generations, a genuine desire to escape at times from town to country ; and Cicero, in spite of his pathetic exhortation to Caelius, was himself a keen lover of the ease and leisure which he could find only in his country-houses. The first great Roman of whom we know that he had a rural villa, not only or chiefly for farming purposes, but as a refuge from the city and its tumult, was Scipio Africanus the elder. His villa at Liternum on the Campanian coast is described by Seneca in his 86th epistle ; it was small, and without the comforts and conveniences of the later country-house ; but its real significance lies not so much in the increasing wealth that could make a residence possible without a farm

---

[1] Lucr. ii. 22 foll. ; iii. 1060 foll.   Cp. Seneca, *Ep.* 69 : ' Frequens migratio instabilis animi est ! "

attached to it, but in the growing sense of individuality that made men wish for such a retreat. There are other signs that Scipio was a man of strong personality, unlike the typical Roman of his day; he put a value upon his own thoughts and habits, apart from his duty to the State, and retired to Liternum to indulge them. The younger Scipio too (Aemilianus), though no blood-relation of his, had the same instinct, but in his case it was rather the desire for leisure and relaxation,—the same love of a real holiday that we all know so well in our modern life. "Leisure," says Cicero, is not "contentio animi sed relaxatio"; and in a charming passage he goes on to describe Scipio and Laelius gathering shells on the sea-shore, and becoming boys again (repuerascere).[1] This desire for ease and relaxation, for the chance of being for a while your true self,—a self worth something apart from its existence as a citizen, is apparent in the Roman of Cicero's day, and still more in the hard-working functionary of the Empire. Twice in his life the morbid emperor Tiberius shrank from the eyes of men, once at Rhodes and afterwards at Capreae,—a melancholy recluse worn out by hard work.

Every man had to provide his own "health resort" in those days: there was nothing to correspond to the modern hotel. Even at the great luxurious watering-places on the Campanian coast, Baiae and Bauli, the houses, so far as we know, were all private

[1] *de Oratore*, ii. 22.

residences.[1] I do not propose to include in this chapter any account of these centres of luxury and vice, which were far indeed from giving any rest or relief to the weary Roman ; the society of Baiae was the centre of scandal and gossip, where a woman like Clodia, the Lesbia of Catullus, could live in wickedness before the eyes of all men.[2] Let us turn to a more agreeable subject, and illustrate the country-house and the country life of the last age of the Republic by a rapid visit to Cicero's own villas. This has fortunately been made easy for us by the very delightful work of Professor O. E. Schmidt, whose genuine enthusiasm for Cicero took him in person to all these sites, and inspired him to write of them most felicitously.[3]

There being no hotels, among which the change-loving Roman of Cicero's day could pick and choose a retreat for a holiday, he would buy a site for a villa first in one place, then in another, or purchase one ready built, or transform an old farmhouse of his own into a residence with " modern requirements." In choosing his sites he would naturally look south-wards, and find what he sought for either in the choicer parts of Latium, among the hills and woods of the Mons Albanus and Tusculum, or in the rich

---

[1] These houses, with the coast on which they stood, have long sunk into the sea, and we are only now, thanks to the perseverance of Mr. R. T. Günther of Magdalen College, realising their position and former magnificence. See his volume on *Earth Movements in the Bay of Naples.*

[2] See Cic. *pro Caelio*, §§ 48-50.

[3] *Cicero's Villen*, Leipzig, 1889.

Campanian land, the paradise of the lazy Roman ; in the latter case, he would like to be close to the sea on that delicious coast, and even in Latium there were spots where, like Scipio and Laelius, he might wander on the sea-shore.   All this country to the south was beginning to be covered with luxurious and convenient houses ; in the colder and mountain-ous parts of central Italy the villa was still the farmhouse of the older useful type, of which the object was the cultivation of olive and vine, now coming into fashion, as we have already seen.   For Cicero and his friends the word *villa* no longer suggested farming, as it invariably did for the old Roman, and as we find it in Cato's treatise on agricul-ture ; it meant gardens, libraries, baths, and collections of works of art, with plenty of convenient rooms for study or entertainment.   Sometimes the garden might be extended into a park, with fishponds and great abundance of game ; Hortensius had such a park near Laurentum, fifty jugera enclosed in a ring-fence, and full of wild beasts of all sorts and kinds. Varro tells us that the great orator would take his guests to a seat on an eminence in this park, and summon his " Orpheus " thither to sing and play : at the sound of the music a multitude of stags, boars, and other animals would make their appearance— having doubtless been trained to do so by expectation of food prepared for them.[1]   Such was the taste of the great master of " Asiatic " eloquence.   We are

[1] Varro, *R.R.* iii. 13.

reminded of the fairy tale of the Emperor of China and the mechanical nightingale.

His great rival in oratory had simpler tastes, in his country life as in his rhetoric. Cicero had no villa of the vulgar kind of luxury; he preferred to own several of moderate comfort rather than one or two of such magnificence. He had in all six, besides one or two properties which were bought for some special temporary object; and it is interesting to see what relation these houses had to his life and habits. At no point could he afford to be very far from Rome, or from a main road which would take him there easily. The accompanying little map will show that all his villas lay on or near to one or other of the two great roads that led southwards from the capital. The via Latina would take him in an hour or two to Tusculum, where, since the death of Catulus in 68, he owned the villa of that excellent aristocrat.[1] The site of the villa cannot be determined with certainty, but Schmidt gives good reasons for believing that it was where we used formerly to place it, on the slope of the hill above Frascati. That it really stood there, and not in the hollow by Grottaferrata,[2] we would willingly believe, for no one who has ever been there can possibly forget the glorious view or the refreshing air of those flowery slopes. No wonder the owner was fond of it. He tells Atticus, when he first came

---

[1] The villa had once been Sulla's also: and the aristocratic connection gave its owner some trouble. See above, p. 102.

[2] Schmidt, *op. cit.* p. 31.

into possession of it, that he found rest there from
all troubles and toils (*ad Att.* i. 5. 7.), and again that
he is so delighted with it that when he gets there
he is delighted with himself too (*ad Att.* i. 6).   Much
of his literary work was done here, and he had the

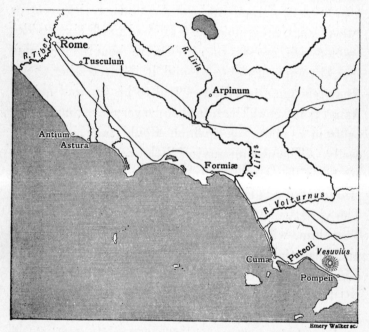

MAP TO ILLUSTRATE THE POSITION OF CICERO'S VILLAS.

great advantage of being close to the splendid library
of Lucullus' neighbouring villa, which was always open
to him.[1]   At Tusculum he spent many a happy day,
until his beloved daughter died there in 45, after
which he would not go there for some time ; but he
got the better of this sorrow, and loved the place
to the end of his life.

[1] *de Finibus*, iii. 2. 7.

If this villa was where we hope it was, the great road passed at no great distance from it, in the valley between Tusculum and the Mons Albanus; and by following this for some fifty miles to the south-east through Latium, Cicero would strike the river Liris not far from Fregellae, and leaving the road there, would soon arrive at his native place Arpinum, and his ancestral property. For this old home he always had the warmest affection; of no other does he write in language showing so clearly that his heart could be moved by natural beauty, especially when combined with the tender associations of his boyhood.[1] In the charming introduction to the second book of his work *de Legibus* (on the Constitution), he dwells with genuine delight on this feeling and these associations; and there too we get a hint of what Dr. Schmidt tells us is the peculiar charm of the spot,—the presence and the sound of water; for if he is right, the villa was placed between two arms of the limpid little river Fibrenus, which here makes a delta as it joins the larger Liris.[2]

But of this house we know for certain neither the site nor the plan,—not so much indeed as we know about a villa of the brother Quintus, not far away, the building of which is described with such exactness in a letter written to the absent owner,[3] that Schmidt thinks himself justified in applying it by

[1] *de Legibus*, ii. 1.
[2] *op. cit.* p. 15. I am assured by a travelling friend that the Fibreno is a delicious stream.　　　[3] *ad Quint. Fratr.* iii. 1.

analogy to the villa of the elder brother. But such reasoning is hardly safe. What we do know about the old house is that it was originally a true villa rustica,—a house with land cultivated by the owner, that Cicero's father, who had weak health and literary tastes, had added to it considerably, and that Cicero himself had made it into a comfortable country residence, with all necessary conveniences. He did not farm the ancestral land attached to it, either himself or by a bailiff, but let it in small holdings [1] (*praediola*), and we could wish that he had told us something of his tenants and what they did with the land. It was not, therefore, a real farmhouse, but a farmhouse made into a pleasant residence, like so many manor-houses still to be seen in England. Its atrium had no doubt retired (so to speak) into the rear of the building, and had become a kitchen, and you entered, as in most country-houses of this period, through a vestibule directly into a peristyle : some idea of such an arrangement may be gained from the accompanying ground-plan of the villa of Diomedes just outside Pompeii, which was a city house adapted to rural conditions (villa pseudurbana). [2]

If Cicero wished to leave Arpinum for one of his villas on the Campanian coast, he would simply have to follow the valley of the Liris until it reached the sea between Minturnae and Formiae, and at

[1] *ad Att.* xiii. 19. 2.
[2] For further details of the amenities of the villa at Arpinum see Schmidt, *op. cit.*

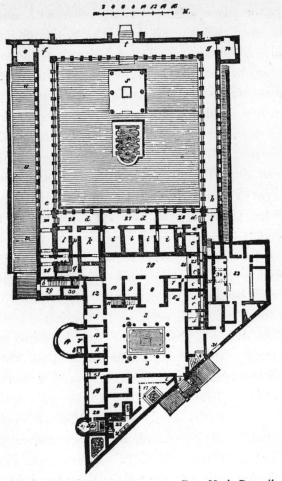

PLAN OF THE VILLA OF DIOMEDES.   From Mau's *Pompeii*.

Steps.
3. Peristyle.
8. Tablinum.
10. Exedra.
12. Dining-room.
14. Sleeping-room, with anteroom (13).
15. Passage leading to a garden at the level of the street.
17. Small court, with hearth (ε) and swimming tank (ζ).
18. Store-room.

19-21. Bath. (19. Apodyterium. 20. Tepidarium. 21. Caldarium.)
22. Kitchen.
26. Colonnade, facing a terrace (28) over the front rooms of the lower part.
e, f, g, h. Colonnade enclosing a large garden.
i, k, l, m. Rooms.
r. Fish-pond.
s. Arbour.

the latter place, a lively little town with charming views over the sea, close to the modern Gaeta, he would find another house of his own,—the next he added to his possessions after he inherited Arpinum. Formiae was a very convenient spot; it lay on the via Appia, and was thus in direct communication both with Rome and the bay of Naples, either by land or sea. When Cicero is not resting, but on the move or expecting to be disturbed, he is often to be found at Formiae, as in the critical mid-winter of 50-49 B.C.; and here at the end of March 49 he had his famous interview with Caesar, who urged him in vain to accompany him to Rome. Here he spent the last weary days of his life, and here he was murdered by Antony's ruffians on December 7, 43.

This villa was in or close to the little town, and therefore did not give him the quiet he liked to have for literary work. It would seem that the *bore* existed elsewhere than at Rome; for in a short letter written from Formiae in April 59, he tells Atticus of his troubles of this kind: "As to literary work, it is impossible! My house is a basilica rather than a villa, owing to the crowds of visitors from Formiae. . . . C. Arrius is my next door neighbour, or rather he almost lives in my house, and even declares that his reason for not going to Rome is that he may spend whole days with me here philosophising. And then, if you please, on the other flank is Sebosus, that friend of Catulus! Which way am I to turn? I declare that I would go at once to Arpinum, if this were not the most convenient place to await your visit : but I will only wait till May 6 : you see what bores are pestering my poor ears." [1]

But his Campanian villas would be almost as easy to reach as Arpinum, if he wished to escape from Formiae and its bores. To the nearest of these, the one at or near Cumae, it was only about forty miles' drive along the coast road, past Minturnae, Sinuessa, and Volturnum, all familiar halting-places. Of this "Cumanum," however, we know very little : that volcanic region has undergone such changes that we cannot recover the site, and its owner never seems to have felt any particular attachment to it. It was in fact too near Baiae and Bauli to suit a quiet literary man ; the great nobles in their vast luxurious palaces were too close at hand for a *novus homo* to be perfectly at his ease there. Yet near the end of his life Cicero added to his possessions another property in this neighbourhood, at or near Puteoli, which was now fast becoming a city of great importance ; but this can be explained by the fact that a banker of Puteoli named Cluvius, an old friend of his, had just died and divided his property by will between Caesar and Cicero,—truly a tremendous will ! Cicero seems to have purchased Caesar's share, and to have looked on the property as a good investment. He began to build a villa here, but had little chance of using it. It may have been here that he entertained Caesar and his retinue at the end of

[1] *ad Att.* ii. 14 and 15.

S

the year 45,[1] as described by him in the famous letter of December 21 (*ad Att.* xiii. 52); when two thousand men had somehow to be provided for, and in spite of literary conversation, Cicero could write that his guest was not exactly one whom you would be in a hurry to see again.

Across the bay, and just within view from the higher ground between Baiae and Cumae, lay the little town of Pompeii, under the sleeping Vesuvius. Here, probably just outside the town, Cicero had a villa of which he seems to have been really fond, and the society of a quiet and gentle friend, M. Marius. Whether we can find the remains of this villa among the excavations of Pompeii is very doubtful: but our excellent guide Schmidt assures us that he has good reason for believing that one particular house, just outside the city on the left side of the road in front of the Porta Herculanea, which has for no very convincing reason ever since its excavation in 1763 been called the Villa di Cicerone, really is the house we wish it to be. But alas! an honest man must confess that the identification wants certainty, and the chance of finding any object or inscription which may confirm it is now very small.

If Cicero were summoned suddenly back to Rome for business, forensic or political, he would hasten first to Formiae and sleep there, and thence hurry, by the via Appia and the route so well known to us from

---

[1] O. E. Schmidt, *Briefwechsel Cicero's*, pp. 66 and 454; but see his *Cicero's Villen*, p. 46, note.

Horace's journey to Brundisium, to another house in the little sea-coast town of Antium. This was his nearest seaside residence, and he often used it when unable to go far from Rome. After the death of his daughter in 45 he seems to have sold this house to Lepidus, and, unable to stay at Tusculum, where she died, he bought a small villa on a little islet called Astura, on the very edge of the Pomptine marshes, and in that melancholy and unwholesome neighbourhood he passed whole days in the woods giving way to his grief. Yet it was a "locus amoenus, et in mari ipso, qui et Antio et Circeiis aspici possit." [1]   It suited his mood, and here he stayed long, writing letter after letter to Atticus about the erection of a shrine to the lost one in some gardens to be purchased near Rome.

This sketch of the country-houses of a man like Cicero may help us to form some idea of the changeful life of a great personage of the period. He did not look for the formation of steady permanent habits in any one place or house; from an early age he was accustomed to travel, going to Greece or Asia Minor for his "higher education," acting perhaps as quaestor, and again as praetor or consul, in some province, then returning to Rome only to leave it for one or other of his villas, and rarely settling down in one of these for any length of time. It was not altogether a wholesome life, so far as the mind was concerned; real thought, the working out of great

[1] *ad Att.* xii. 19 init.

problems of philosophy or politics, is impossible under constant change of scene, and without the opportunity of forming regular habits.[1] And the fact is that no man at this time seriously set himself to think out such problems. Cicero would arrive at Tusculum or Arpinum with some necessary books, and borrowing others as best he could, would sit down to write a treatise on ethics or rhetoric with amazing speed, having an original Greek author constantly before him. At places like Baiae serious work was of course impossible, and would have been ridiculed. There was no original thinker in this age. Caesar himself was probably more suited by nature to reason on facts immediately before him than to speculate on abstract principles. Varro, the rough sensible scholar of Sabine descent, was a diligent collector of facts and traditions, but no more able to grapple hard with problems of philosophy or theology than any other Roman of his time. The life of the average wealthy man was too comfortable, too changeable, to suggest the desirability of real mental exertion.

Nor has this life any direct relation to material usefulness and the productive investment of capital. Cicero and his correspondents never mention farming, never betray any interest in the new movement, if such there was, for the scientific cultivation of the vine and olive.[2] For such things we must go to

---

[1] See Seneca, *Epist.* 69, on the disturbing influence of constant change of scene.

[2] There is an exception in the young Cicero's letter to Tiro, translated above, p. 202.

Varro's treatise, written, some years after Cicero's death, in his extreme old age. In the third book of that invaluable work we shall find all we want to know about the real *villa rustica* of the time,— the working farm-house with its wine-vats and olive-mills, like that recently excavated at Boscoreale near Pompeii. Yet it would be unfair to such men as Cicero and his friends, the wiser and quieter section of the aristocracy, to call their work altogether unproductive. True, it left little permanent impress on human modes of thought; it wrought no material change for the better in Italy or the Empire. We may go so far as to allow that it initiated that habit of dilettantism which we find already exaggerated in the age lately illuminated for us by Professor Dill in his book on *Roman Society from Nero to Marcus Aurelius*, and far more exaggerated in the last age of Roman society, which the same author has depicted in his earlier work. But it may be doubted whether under any circumstances the Romans could have produced a great prophet or a great philosopher; and the most valuable work they did was of another kind. It lay in the humanisation of society by the rational development of law, and by the communication of Greek thought and literature to the western world. This was what occupied the best days of Cicero and Sulpicius Rufus and many others; and they succeeded at the same time in creating for its expression one of the most perfect prose languages that the world has ever known or will know. They

did it too, helping each other by kindly and cheer-
ing intercourse,—the *humanitas* of daily life.   It is
exactly this humanitas that the northern mind of
Mommsen, in spite of its vein of passionate romance,
could not understand; all the softer side of that
pleasant existence among the villas and statues and
libraries was to him simply contemptible.   Let us
hope that he has done no permanent damage to the
credit of Cicero, and of the many lesser men who lived
the same honourable and elegant life.

CHAPTER IX

THE DAILY LIFE OF THE WELL-TO-DO

BEFORE giving some account of the way in which a
Roman of consideration spent his day in the time of
Cicero, it seems necessary to explain briefly how he
reckoned the divisions of the day.

The old Latin farmer knew nothing of hours or
clocks. He simply went about his daily work with
the sun and the light as guides, rising at or before
sunrise, working till noon, and, after a meal and a
rest, resuming his work till sunset. This simple
method of reckoning would suffice in a sunny
climate, even when life and business became more
complicated; and it is a fact that the division of
the day into hours was not known at Rome until
the introduction of the sun-dial in 263 B.C.[1] We may
well find it hard to understand how such business
as the meeting of the senate, of the comitia, or the
exercitus, could have been fixed to particular times
under such circumstances; perhaps the best way of
explaining it is by noting that the Romans were very
early in their habits, and that sunrise is a point of

---

[1] Censorinus, *De die natali*, 23. 6.; Pliny, *N.H.* vii. 213. On the whole
subject of the division of the day see Marquardt, *Privatleben*, p. 246 foll.

time about which there can be no mistake.[1] But in any case the date of the introduction of the sun-dial, which almost exactly corresponds with the beginning of the Punic wars and the vast increase of civil business arising out of them, may suggest at once the primitive condition of the old Roman mind and habit, and the way in which the Romans had to learn from other peoples how to save and arrange the time that was beginning to be so precious.

This first sun-dial came from Catina in Sicily, and was therefore quite unsuited to indicate the hours at Rome. Nevertheless Rome contrived to do with it until nearly a century had elapsed ; at last, in 159 B.C., a dial calculated on the latitude of Rome was placed by the side of it by the censor Q. Marcius Philippus. These two dials were fixed on pillars behind the Rostra in the Forum, the most convenient place for regulating public business, and there they remained even in the time of Cicero.[2] But in the censorship next following that of Philippus the first water-clock was introduced ; this indicated the hours both of day and night, and enabled every one to mark the exact time even on cloudy days.[3]

Thus from the time of the Punic wars the city population reckoned time by hours, i.e. twelve divisions of the day ; but as they continued to reckon the day

---

[1] In the XII Tables only sunrise and sunset were mentioned (Pliny, *l.c.* 212). Later on noon was proclaimed by the Consul's marshal (Varro, *de Ling. Lat.* vi. 5), and also the end of the civil day. Cp. Varro, *L.L.* vi. 89.

[2] Cic. *pro Quinctio*, 18. 59.

[3] See the article "Horologium" in *Dict. of Antiquities*, vol. i.

from sunrise to sunset on the principle of the old agricultural practice, these twelve hours varied in length at different times of the year.   In mid-winter the hours were only about forty-four minutes in length, while at mid-summer they were about seventy-five, and they corresponded with ours only at the two equinoxes.[1] This, of course, made the construction of accurate dials and water-clocks a matter of considerable difficulty.   It is not necessary here to explain how the difficulties were overcome ; the reader may be referred to the article " Horologium " in the *Dictionary of Antiquities*, and especially to the cuts there given of the dial found at Tusculum in 1761.[2]

Sun-dials, once introduced with the proper reckoning for latitude, soon came into general use, and a considerable number still survive which have been found in Rome.   In a fragment of a comedy by an unknown author, ascribed to the last century B.C., Rome is described as " full of sun-dials,"[3] and many have been discovered in other Roman towns, including

---

[1] Our modern hours are called equinoctial, because they are fixed at the length of the natural hour at the equinoxes. This system does not seem to have come in until late in the Empire period.

[2] For the water-clock see Marquardt, *op. cit.* p. 773 foll.

[3] The lines are so good that I may venture to quote them in full from Gell. iii. 3 (cp. Ribbeck, *Fragm. Comicorum*, ii. p. 34) : " parasitus esuriens dicit :

Ut illum di perdant primus qui horas repperit,
Quique adeo primus statuit hic solarium.
Qui mihi comminuit misero articulatim diem,
Nam olim me puero venter erat solarium,
Multo omnium istorum optimum et verissimum :

several at Pompeii. But for the ordinary Roman, who possessed no sun-dial or was not within reach of one, the day fell into four convenient divisions, as with us it falls into three,—morning, afternoon, and evening. As they rose much earlier than we do, the hours up to noon were divided into two parts: (1) *mane*, or morning, which lasted from sunrise to the beginning of the third hour, and (2) *ad meridiem*, or forenoon; then followed *de meridie*, i.e. afternoon, and *suprema*, from about the ninth or tenth hour till sunset. The authority for these handy divisions is Censorinus, *De die natali* (23. 9, 24. 3). There seems to be no doubt that they originated in the management of civil business, and especially in that of the praetor's court, which normally began at the third hour, i.e. the beginning of ad meridiem, and went on till the suprema (tempestas diei), which originally meant sunset, but by a lex Plaetoria was extended to include the hour or two before dark.

The first thing to note in studying the daily life at Rome is that the Romans, like the Greeks, were busy much earlier in the morning than we are. In part this was the result of their comfortable southern climate, where the nights are never so long as with

> Ubivis ste monebat esse, nisi quom nihil erat.
> Nunc etiam quom est, non estur, nisi soli libet.
> Itaque adeo iam oppletum oppidum est solariis,
> Maior pars populi iam aridi reptant fame."

The fourth line contains a truth of human nature, of which illustrations might easily be found at the present day.

us, and where the early mornings are not so chilly and damp in summer or so cold in winter. But it was probably still more the effect of the very imperfect lighting of houses, which made it difficult to carry on work, especially reading and writing, after dark, and suggested early retirement to bed and early rising in the morning. The streets, we must remember, were not lighted except on great occasions, and it was not till late in Roman history that public places and entertainments could be frequented after dark. In early times the oil-lamp with a wick was unknown, and private houses were lighted by torches and rude candles of wax or tallow.[1] The introduction of the use of olive oil, which was first imported from Greece and the East and then produced in Italy, brought with it the manufacture of lamps of various kinds, great and small; and as the cultivation of the valuable tree, so easily grown in Italy, increased in the last century B.C.,[2] the oil-lamp became universal in houses, baths, etc. Even in the small old baths of Pompeii there were found about a thousand lamps, obviously used for illumination after dark.[3] But in spite of this and of the invention of candelabra for extending the use of candles, it was never possible for the Roman to turn night into day as we do in our modern town-life. We must look on the lighting of the streets as quite an

---

[1] Pliny, *N.H.* xv. 1 foll. supplies the history of the oil industry. For the candles see Marquardt, *Privatleben*, p. 690.

[2] See above, p. 93.   [3] Marq. *Privatleben*, p. 264.

exceptional event. This happened, for example, on the night of the famous fifth of December 63 B.C., when Cicero returned to his house after the execution of the conspirators; people placed lamps and torches at their doors, and women showed lights from the roofs of the houses.

An industrious man, especially in winter, when this want of artificial light made time most valuable, would often begin his work before daylight; he might have a speech to prepare for the senate, or a brief for a trial, or letters to write, and, as we shall see, as soon as the sun had well risen it was not likely that he would be altogether his own master. Thus we find Cicero on a February morning writing to his brother before sunrise,[1] and it is not unlikely that the soreness of the eyes of which he sometimes complains may have been the result of reading and writing before the light was good. In his country villas he could do as he liked, but at Rome he knew that he would have the "turba salutantium" upon him as soon as the sun had risen. Cicero is the only man of his own time of whose habits we know much, but in the next generation Horace describes himself as calling for pen and paper before daylight, and later on that insatiable student the elder Pliny would work for hours before daylight, and then go to the Emperor Vespasian, who was also a very early riser.[2] After sunrise the whole population was astir; boys

[1] Cic. *ad Q.F.* ii. 3. 7.   For the lippitudo, *ad Att.* vii. 14.
[2] Hor. *Epist.* ii. 1. 112; Pliny, *Ep.* iii. 5, 8, 9.

were on their way to school, and artisans to their labour.

If Horace is not exaggerating when he says (*Sat.* i. 1. 10) that the barrister might be disturbed by a client at cock-crow, Cicero's studies may have been interrupted even before the crowds came; but this could hardly happen often.   As a rule it was during the first two hours (*mane*) that callers collected.   In the old times it had been the custom to open your house and begin your business at daybreak, and after saluting your familia and asking a blessing of the household gods, to attend to your own affairs and those of your clients.[1]   Although we are not told so explicitly, we must suppose that the same practice held good in Cicero's time; under the Empire it is familiar to all readers of Seneca or Martial, but in a form which was open to much criticism and satire. The client of the Empire was a degraded being; of the client in the last age of the Republic we only know that he existed, and could be useful to his *patronus* in many ways,—in elections and trials especially;[2] but we do not hear of his pressing himself on the attention of his patron every morning, or receiving any "sportula."   All the same, the number of persons, whether clients in this sense or

---

[1] Hor. *Epist.* ii. 1. 103: "Romae dulce diu fuit et solenne reclusa **Mane** domo vigilare, clienti promere iura" etc.   It is curious that all our information on this early business comes from the literature of the Empire.   The single passage of Cicero which Marquardt could find to illustrate it unluckily relates to his practice as governor of Cilicia (*ad Att.* vi. 2. 5).

[2] e.g. *ad Q.F.* i. 2. 16. ; and Q. Cic. *Commentariolum petitionis*, sec. 17.

in the legal sense, or messengers, men of business, and ordinary callers, who would want to see a man like Cicero before he left his house in the morning, would beyond doubt be considerable. Otherwise they would have to catch him in the street or Forum; and though occasionally a man of note might purposely walk in public in order to give his clients their chance, Cicero makes it plain that this was not his way.[1]

Within these two first hours of daylight the busy man had to find time for a morning meal; the idle man, who slept later, might postpone it. This early breakfast, called *ientaculum*,[2] answered to the " coffee and roll" which is usual at the present day in all European countries except our own, and which is fully capable of supporting even a hard-working man for several hours. It is, indeed, quite possible to do work before this breakfast; Antiochus, the great doctor, is said by Galen to have visited such of his patients as lived near him before his breakfast and on foot.[3] But as a rule the meal was taken before a busy man went out to his work, and consisted of bread, either dipped in wine or eaten with honey, olives, or cheese. The breakfast of

[1] See what he says of M'. Manilius in *De Orat.* iii. 133.

[2] The word seems to be connected with ieiunium (Plaut. *Curculio* I. i. 73 ; Festus, p. 346), and thus answers to our break*fast*. The verb is ientare : Afranius : fragm. "ientare nulla invitat."

[3] Galen, vol. vi. p. 332. I take this citation from Marquardt, *Privatleben*, p. 257 ; others will be found in the notes to that page. Marquardt seems to have been the first to bring the evidence of the medical writers to bear on the subject of Roman meals.

Antiochus consisted, for example, of bread and Attic
honey.

The meal over, the man of politics or business
would leave his house, outside which his clients and
friends or other hangers-on would be waiting for him,
and proceed to the Forum,—the centre, as we have
seen, of all his activity — accompanied by these
people in a kind of procession. Some would go
before to make room for him, while others followed
him; if bent on election business, he would have
experienced helpers,[1] either volunteers or in his pay,
to save him from making blunders as to names and
personalities, and in fact to serve him in conducting
himself towards the populace with the indispensable
blanditia.[2] Every Roman of importance liked to
have, and usually had, a train of followers or friends
in descending to the Forum of a morning from his
house, or in going about other public business; what
Q. Cicero urges on his brother in canvassing for the
consulship may hold good in principle for all the public
appearances of a public man,—" I press this strongly
on you, always to be with a multitude." [3] It may
perhaps be paralleled with the love of the Roman
for processions, e.g. the lustrations of farm, city,
and army,[4] and with his instinctive desire for aid
and counsel in all important matters both of public
and private life, shown in the consilium of the

---

[1] See the interesting account of these (salutatores, deductores, assecta-
tores) in the *Commentariolum petitionis* of Q. Cicero, 9. 34 foll.
[2] See above, p. 109.   [3] Q. Cicero, *Comment. Pet.* 9. 37.
[4] See the author's *Roman Festivals*, pp. 125 foll.

paterfamilias and of the magistrate. Examples are easy to find in the literature of this period; an excellent one is the graphic picture of Gaius Gracchus and his train of followers, which Plutarch has preserved from a contemporary writer. "The people looked with admiration on him, seeing him attended by crowds of building-contractors, artificers, ambassadors, magistrates, soldiers, and learned men, to all of whom he was easy of access; while he maintained his dignity, he was gracious to all, and suited his behaviour to the condition of every individual; thus he proved the falsehood of those who called him tyrannical or arrogant." [1]

Arrived at the Forum, if not engaged in a trial, or summoned to a meeting of the senate, or busy in canvassing, he would mingle with the crowd, and spend a social morning in meeting and talking with friends, or in hearing the latest news from the provinces, or in occupying himself with his investments with the aid of his bankers and agents. This is the way in which such a sociable and agreeable man as Cicero was loved to spend his mornings when not deep in the composition of some speech or book,—and at Rome it was indeed hardly possible for him to find the time for steady literary work. It was this social life that he longed for when in Cilicia; "one little walk and talk with you," he could write to Caelius at Rome, "is worth all the profits of a province." [2] But it was also this crowded and talka-

---

[1] Plutarch, *C. Gracchus*, 6.   [2] Cic. *ad Fam.* ii. 12.

tive Forum that Lucilius could describe in a passage
already quoted, as teeming with men who, with the
aid of hypocrisy and blanditia, spent the day from
morning till night in trying to get the better of their
fellows.[1]

After a morning spent in the Forum, our Roman
might return home in time for his lunch (*prandium*),
which had taken the place of the early dinner (*cena*)
of the olden time. Exactly the same thing affected
the hours of these meals as has affected those of our
own within the last century or so ; the great increase
of public business of all kinds has with us pushed
the time of the chief meal later and later, and so it
was at Rome. The senate had an immense amount
of business to transact in the two last centuries B.C.,
and the increase in oratorical skill, as well as the
growing desire to talk in public, extended its sittings
sometimes till nightfall.[2] So too with the law-courts,
which had become the scenes of oratorical display,
and often of that indulgence in personal abuse which
has great attractions for idle people fond of excitement. Thus the dinner hour had come to be postponed from about noon to the ninth or even the
tenth hour,[3] and some kind of a lunch was necessary.
We do not hear much of this meal, which was in fact
for most men little more than the " snack " which

---

[1] Fragm. 9. Baehrens, *Fragm. Poet. Rom.* p. 141. Cp. Galen, vol. x. p. 3
(Kuhn).

[2] Livy xlv. 36 ; Cic. *ad Fam.* i. 2 ; for a famous case of " obstruction "
by lengthy speaking, Gell. iv. 10.

[3] Festus, p. 54.

T

London men of business will take standing at a bar ;
nor do we know whether senators and barristers took
it as they sat in the curia or in court, or whether
there was an adjournment for purposes of refreshment.
Such an adjournment seems to have taken place,
occasionally at least, during the games under the
Empire, for Suetonius (*Claud.* 34) tells us that
Claudius would dismiss the people to take their
prandium and yet remain himself in his seat. A
joke of Cicero's about Caninius Rebilus, who was
appointed consul by Caesar on the last day of the
year 45 at one o'clock, shows that the usual hour
for the prandium was about noon or earlier ; "under
the consulship of Caninius," he wrote to Curius, "no
one ever took luncheon." [1]

After the prandium, if a man were at home and
at leisure, followed the siesta (*meridiatio*). This is
the universal habit in all southern climates, especially
in summer, and indeed, if the mind and body are
active from an early hour, a little repose is useful,
if not necessary, after mid-day. Busy men however like Cicero could not always afford it in the
city, and we find him noting near the end of his
life, when Caesar's absolutism had diminished the
amount of his work both in senate and law-courts,
that he had taken to the siesta which he formerly
dispensed with.[2] Even the sturdy Varro in his old
age declared that in summer he could not possibly

---

[1] *ad Fam.* vii. 30.
[2] *de Divinatione*, ii. 142, written in 44 B.C.

do without his nap in the middle of the day.[1]   On
the other hand, in the famous letter in which Cicero
describes his entertainment of Caesar in mid-winter
45 B.C., nothing is said of a siesta; the Dictator
worked till after mid-day, then walked on the shore,
and returned, not for a nap but for a bath.[2]

Caesar, as he was Cicero's guest, must have taken
his bath in the villa, probably that at Cumae (see
above, p. 257).   Most well-appointed private houses
had by this time a bath-room or set of bath-rooms,
providing every accommodation, according to the
season and the taste of the bather.   This was indeed
a modern improvement; in the old days the Romans
only washed their arms and legs daily, and took a
bath every market-day, i.e. every ninth day.   This is
told us in an amusing letter of Seneca's, who also
gives a description of the bath in the villa of the
elder Scipio at Liternum, which consisted of a single
room without a window, and was supplied with water
which was often thick after rain.[3]   "Nesciit vivere,"
says Seneca, in ironical allusion to the luxury of his
own day.   In Cicero's time every villa doubtless had
its set of baths, with at least three rooms,—the
apodyterium, *caldarium*, and *tepidarium*, sometimes
also an open swimming-bath, as in the House of the

---

[1] Varro, *R.R.* i. 2; the words are put into the mouth of one of the
speakers in the dialogue. See, for examples from later writers, Marq.,
Privatleben, p. 262.

[2] *ad Att.* xiii. 52; the habit may have often been dropped in winter.

[3] Seneca, *Ep.* 86. The whole passage is most interesting, as illustrating
the difference in habits wrought in the course of two centuries.

Silver Wedding at Pompeii.[1] In Cicero's letter to
his brother about the villa at Arcanum, he mentions
the dressing-room (apodyterium) and the caldarium
or hot-air chamber, and doubtless there were others.
Even in the villa rustica of Boscoreale near Pompeii,
which was a working farm-house, we find the bath-
rooms complete, provided, that is, with the three
essentials of dressing-room, tepid-room, and hot-air
room.[2] Caesar probably, as it was winter, used the
last of these, took in fact a Turkish bath, as we should
call it, and then went into a tepidarium, where, as
Cicero tells us, he received some messenger. Here
he was anointed (unctus), i.e. rubbed dry from per-
spiration, with a strigil on which oil was dropped
to soften its action.[3] When this operation was over,
about the ninth hour, which in mid-winter would
begin about half-past one, he was ready for the
dinner which followed immediately.[4]

[1] Mau, *Pompeii*, p. 300. See above, p. 244.

[2] See the plan in Mau, p. 357 ; Marquardt, *Privatleben*, p. 272.

[3] See Professor Purser's explanation and illustrations in the *Dict. of
Antiquities*, vol. i. p. 278.

[4] The subject of the public baths at Rome properly belongs to the period
of the Empire, and is too extensive to be treated in a chapter on the daily
life of the Roman of Cicero's time.   Public baths did exist in Rome already,
but we hear very little of them, which shows that they were not as yet an
indispensable adjunct of social life ; but the fact that Seneca in the letter
already quoted describes the aediles as testing the heat of the water with
their hands shows (1) that the baths were public, (2) that they were of hot
water and not, as later, of hot air (*thermae*).   The latter invention is said to
have come in before the Social war (Val. Max. ix. 1. 1.).   Some baths seem
to have been run as a speculation by private individuals, and bore the
name of their builder (e.g. balneae Seniae, Cic. *pro Cael.* 25. 61).   In
summer the young men still bathed in the Tiber (*pro Cael.* 15. 36).   At

This we may take as the ordinary winter dinner-hour in the country; in summer it would be an hour or so later. In an amusing story given as a rhetorical illustration in the work known as *Rhetorica ad Herennium*, iv. 63, the guests (doomed never to get their dinner that day except in an inn) are invited for the tenth hour. But in the city it must have often happened that the hour was later, owing to the press of business. For example, on one occasion when the senate had been sitting *ad noctem*, Cicero dines with Pompeius after its dismissal (*ad Fam.* i. 2. 3). Another day we find him going to bed after his dinner, and clearly not for a siesta, which, as we saw, he never had time to take in his busy days; this, however, was not actually in Rome but in his villa at Formiae, where he was at that time liable to much interruption from callers (*ad Att.* ii. 16). Probably, like most Romans of his day, he had spent a long time over his dinner, talking if he had guests, or reading and thinking if he were alone or with his family only.

The dinner, *cena*, was in fact the principal private event of the day; it came when all business was over, and you could enjoy the privacy of family life or see your friends and unbend with them. At no other meal do we hear of entertainment, unless the guests were on a journey, as was the case at the lunch at Arcanum when Pomponia's temper got the better of her (see above, p. 52). Even dinner-

Pompeii the oldest public baths (the Stabian; Mau, p. 183) date from the second century B.C.

parties seem to have come into fashion only since the Punic wars, with later hours and a larger staff of slaves to cook and wait at table. In the old days of household simplicity the meals were taken in the atrium, the husband reclining on a *lectus*,[1] the wife sitting by his side, and the children sitting on stools in front of them. The slaves too in the olden time took their meal sitting on benches in the atrium, so that the whole familia was present. This means that the dinner was in those days only a necessary break in the intervals of work, and the sitting posture was always retained for slaves, i.e. those who would go about their work as soon as the meal was over. Columella, writing under the early Empire, urges that the vilicus or overseer should sit at his dinner except on festivals; and Cato the younger would not recline after the battle of Pharsalia for the rest of his life, apparently as a sign that life was no longer enjoyable.[2]

But after the Second Punic war, which changed the habits of the Roman in so many ways, the atrium ceased to be the common dining-place, and special chambers were built, either off the atrium or in the interior part of the house about the peristylium, or even upstairs, for the accommodation of guests, who might be received in different rooms, according to the season and the weather.[3] These *triclinia* were so

[1] The tradition was that the paterfamilias originally also sat instead of reclining. See Marq. *Privatleben*, p. 292 note 3.

[2] Columella, ii. 1. 19, a very interesting chapter; Plutarch, *Cato min.* 56.

[3] Plut. *Lucullus* 40; see above, p. 242.

arranged as to afford the greatest personal comfort and the best opportunities for conversation; they indicate clearly that dinner is no longer an interval in the day's work, but a time of repose and ease at the end of it. The plan here given of a triclinium, as described by Plutarch in his *Quaestiones conviviales*,

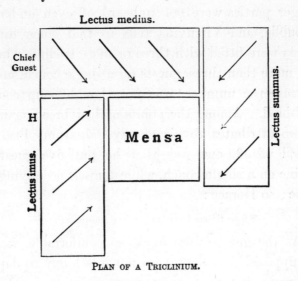

PLAN OF A TRICLINIUM.

will show this sufficiently without elaborate description; but it is necessary to notice that the host always or almost always occupied the couch marked H on the plan, while the one immediately above him, i.e. No. 3 of the *lectus medius*, was reserved for the most important guest, and called *lectus consularis*. Plutarch's account, and a little consideration, will show that the host was thus well placed for the superintendence of the meal, as well as for conversation with his distinguished guest: and that the latter

occupied what Plutarch calls a free corner, so that any
messengers or other persons needing to see him could
get access to him without disturbing the party.[1]
The number that could be accommodated, nine, was
not only a sacred and lucky one, but exactly suited
for convenience of conversation and attendance.
Larger parties were not unheard of, even under the
Republic, and Vitruvius tells us that some dining-
rooms were fitted with three or more triclinia; but to
put more than three guests on a single couch, and so
increase the number, was not thought courteous or
well-bred.   Among the points of bad breeding which
Cicero attributes to his enemy Calpurnius Piso, the
consul of 58, one was that he put five guests to
recline on a single couch, while himself occupying one
alone; so Horace:

Saepe tribus lectis videas cenare quaternos.[2]

As the guests were made so comfortable, it may
be supposed that they were not in a hurry to depart;
the mere fact that they were reclining instead of
sitting would naturally dispose them to stay.   The
triclinia were open at one end, i.e. not shut up as
our dining-rooms are, and the air would not get close
and "dinnery."   Cicero describes old Cato[3] (no doubt
from some passage in Cato's writings) as remaining
in conversation at dinner until late at night.   The
guests would arrive with their slaves, who took off

---

[1] Plut. *Quaest. Conv.* 1. 3 foll.; and Marq. p. 295.
[2] Hor. *Sat.* i. 4. 86; cp. Cic. *in Pisonem*, 27. 67.
[3] Cic. *de Senect.* 14. 46.

their walking shoes, if they had come on foot, and put on their sandals (*soleae*) : each wore a festive dress (*synthesis*), of Greek origin like the other features of the entertainment, and there was no question of changing these again in a hurry. Nothing can better show the difference between the old Roman manners and the new than the character of these parties ; they are the leisurely and comfortable rendezvous of an opulent and educated society, in which politics, literature or philosophy could be discussed with much self-satisfaction. That such discussion did not go too deeply into hard questions was perhaps the result of the comfort.

There was of course another side to this picture of the evening of a Roman gentleman. There was a coarse side to the Roman character, and in the age when wealth, the slave trade, and idle habits encouraged self-indulgence, meals were apt to become ends in themselves instead of necessary aids to a wholesome life. The ordinary three parts or courses (*mensae*) of a dinner,—the gustatio or light preliminary course, the cena proper, with substantial dishes, and the dessert of pastry and fruit, could be amplified and extended to an unlimited extent by the skill of the slave-cooks brought from Greece and the East (see above, p. 209) ; the gourmand had appeared long before the age of Cicero and had been already satirised by Lucilius and Varro.[1] Splendid dinner-services

---

[1] Lucilius, fragm. 30 ; 120 foll. ; 168, 327 etc. Varro wrote a Menippean satire on gluttony, of which a fragment is preserved by Gellius, vi. 16.

might take the place of the old simple ware, and luxurious drapery and rugs covered the couches, instead of the skins of animals, as in the old time.[1] Vulgarity and ostentation, such as Horace satirised, were doubtless too often to be met with. Those who lived for feasting and enjoyment would invite their company quite early in the day (tempestativum convivium) and carry on the revelry till midnight.[2] And lastly, the practice of drinking wine after dinner (*comissatio*), simply for the sake of drinking, under fixed rules according to the Greek fashion, familiar to us all in the *Odes* of Horace, had undoubtedly begun some time before the end of the Republic. In the Actio prima of his Verrine orations Cicero gives a graphic picture of a convivium beginning early, where the proposal was made and agreed to that the drinking should be "more graeco." [3]

But it would be a great mistake to suppose that this kind of self-indulgence was characteristic of the average Roman life of this age. The ordinary student is liable to fall into this error because he reads his Horace and his Juvenal, but dips a very little way into Cicero's correspondence; and he needs to be reminded that the satirists are not deriding the average life of the citizen, any more than the artists who make fun of the foibles of our own day in the pages of *Punch*. Cicero hardly ever mentions his

---

[1] See the interesting passage in Cic. *pro Murena*, 36. 75, about the funeral feast of Scipio Aemilianus.

[2] Catull. 47. 5 : "vos convivia lauta sumptuose De die facitis ?"

[3] 26. 65 foll. ; Hor. *Od.* iii. 19, and the commentators.

meals, his cookery, or his wine, even in his most
chatty letters ; such matters did not interest him,
and do not seem to have interested his friends, so
far as we can judge by their letters.   In one amusing
letter to Poetus, he does indeed tell him what he
had for dinner at a friend's house, but only by way
of explaining that he had been very unwell from
eating mushrooms and such dishes, which his host
had had cooked in order not to contravene a recent
sumptuary law.[1]   The Letters are worth far more as
negative evidence of the usual character of dinners
than either the invectives (vituperationes) against
a Piso or an Antony, or the lively wit of the
satirists.   Let us return for an instant, in conclusion,
to that famous letter, already quoted, in which Cicero
describes the entertainment of Caesar at Cumae in
December, 45.   It contains an expression which has
given rise to very mistaken conclusions both about
Caesar's own habits and those of his day.   After
telling Atticus that his guest sat down to dinner
when the bath was over he goes on: " 'Εμετικὴν
agebat; itaque et edit et bibit ἀδεῶς et iucunde,
opipare sane et apparate, nec id solum, sed

bene cocto
condito, sermone bono, et si quaeri', libenter."

Even good scholars used formerly to make the

---

[1] *ad Fam.* vii. 26, of the year 57 B.C.   The sumptuary law must have
been a certain lex Aemilia of later date than Sulla.   (See Gell. ii. 24 :
"qua lege non sumptus cenarum, sed ciborum genus et modus praefinitus
est.")   This chapter of Gellius, and Macrob. iii. 17, are the safest passages to
consult on the subject of the growth of gourmandism.

mistake of supposing that Caesar, a man habitually
abstemious, or at least temperate, had made up his
mind to over-eat himself on this occasion, as he was
intending to take an emetic afterwards.   And even
now it may be as well to point out that medical
treatment by a course of emetics was a perfectly
well known and valued method at this time;[1] that
Caesar, whose health was always delicate, and at
this time severely tried, was then under this treatment, and could therefore eat his dinner comfortably, without troubling himself about what he
ate and drank: and that the apt quotation from
Lucilius, and the literary conversation which (so
Cicero adds) followed the dinner, prove beyond all
question that this was no glutton's meal, but one of
that ordinary and rational type, in which repose and
pleasant intercourse counted for more than the mere
eating and drinking.

No more work seems to have been done after the
cena was over and the guests had retired.   We found
Cicero on one occasion going to bed soon after the
meal; and, as he was up and active so early in the
morning, we may suppose that he retired at a much
earlier hour than we do.   But of this last act of the
day he tells us nothing.

[1] See Munro, *Elucidations of Catullus*, p. 92 foll.

CHAPTER X

HOLIDAYS AND AMUSEMENTS

THE Italian peoples, of all races, have always had a wonderful capacity for enjoying themselves out of doors. The Italian *festa* of to-day, usually, as in ancient times, linked to some religious festival, is a scene of gaiety, bright dresses, music, dancing, bonfires, races, and improvisation or mummery; and all that we know of the ancient rural festivals of Italy suggests that they were of much the same lively and genial character. Tibullus gives us a good idea of them :

> "Agricola assiduo primum satiatus aratro
> Cantavit certo rustica verba pede ;
> Et satur arenti primum est modulatus avena
> Carmen, ut ornatos diceret ante deos ;
> Agricola et minio suffusus, Bacche, rubenti
> Primus inexperta duxit ab arte choros." [1]

It would be easy to multiply examples of such merry-making from the poets of the Augustan age,

[1] Tibull. ii. 1. 51 foll. Cp. ii. 5. 83 foll. Several are also described by Ovid in his *Fasti*. A charming account of *feste* in a Tuscan village of to-day will be found in *A Nook in the Apennines*, by Leader Scott, chapters xxviii. and xxix. : a book full of value for Italian rural life, ancient and modern.

nearly all of whom were born and bred in the country, and shared Virgil's tenderness for a life of honest work and play among the Italian hills and valleys. But in this chapter we are to deal with the holidays and enjoyments of the great city, and the rural festivals are only mentioned here because almost all the characteristics of the urban holiday-making are to be found in germ there. The Roman calendar of festivals has its origin in the regularly recurring rites of the earliest Latin husbandman. As the city grew, these old agricultural festivities lost of course much of their native simplicity and naïveté; some of them survived merely as religious or priestly performances, some became degraded into licentious enjoyment; but the music and dancing, the gay dresses, the racing, the mumming or acting, are all to be found in the city, developed in one form or another, from the earliest to the latest periods of Roman history.

The Latin word for a holiday was *feriae*, a term which belongs to the language of religious law (*ius divinum*). Strictly speaking, it means a day which the citizen has resigned, either wholly or in part, to the service of the gods.[1] As of old on the farm no work was to be done on such days, so in the city no public business could be transacted. Cicero, drawing up in antique language his idea of the ius divinum, writes thus of feriae : " Feriis iurgia amovento, easque in familiis, operibus patratis, habento " : which he

---

[1] Wissowa, *Religion und Kultus*, p. 366. "Feriae" came in time to be limited to public festivals, while "festus dies" covered all holidays.

afterwards explains as meaning that the citizen must abstain from litigation, and the slave be excused from labour.[1]   The idea then of a holiday was much the same as we find expressed in the Jewish Sabbath, and had its root also in religious observance.   But Cicero, whether he is actually reproducing the words of an old law or inventing it for himself, was certainly not reflecting the custom of the city in his own day ; no such rigid observance of a rule was possible in the capital of an Empire such as the Roman had become. Even on the farm it had long ago been found necessary to make exceptions ; thus Virgil tells us :[2]

> " Quippe etiam festis quaedam exercere diebus
> Fas et iura sinunt : rivos deducere nulla
> Religio vetuit, segeti praetendere saepem,
> Insidias avibus moliri, incendere vepres,
> Balantumque gregem fluvio mersare salubri."

So too in the city it was simply impossible that all work should cease on feriae, of which there were more than a hundred in the year, including the Ides of every month and some of the Kalends and Nones.

As a matter of fact a double change had come about since the city and its dominion began to increase rapidly about the time of the Punic wars. First, many of the old festivals, sacred to deities whose vogue was on the wane, or who had no longer any meaning for a city population, as being deities of husbandry, were almost entirely neglected : even if the priests performed the prescribed rites, no one

---

[1] *de Legibus*, ii. 8. 19 : cp. 12. 29.
[2] *Georg.* i. 268 foll.   Cato had already said the same thing : *R.R.* ii. 4.

knew and no one cared,[1] and it may be doubted
whether the State was at all scrupulous in adhering
to the old sacred rules as to the hours on which
business could be transacted on such days.[2] Secondly,
certain festivals which retained their popularity had
been extended from one day to three or more, in
one or two cases, as we shall see, even to thirteen and
fifteen days, in order to give time for an elaborate
system of public amusement consisting of chariot-
races and stage-plays, and known by the name of
ludi, or, as at the winter Saturnalia, to enable all
classes to enjoy themselves during the short days
for seven mornings instead of one. Obviously this
was a much more convenient and popular arrangement than to have your holidays scattered about
over the whole year as single days ; and it suited the
rich and ambitious, who sought to obtain popular
favour by shows and games on a grand scale,
needing a succession of several days for complete
exhibition.   So the old religious word *feriae* becomes gradually supplanted, in the sense of a public
holiday of amusement, by the word *ludi*, and came
at last to mean, as it still does in Germany, the
holidays of schoolboys.[3] These ludi will form the
chief subject of this chapter ; but we must first

---

[1] Thus Ovid describes the rites performed by the Flamen Quirinalis at
the old agricultural festival of the Robigalia (Robigus, deity of the mildew)
as if it were a curious bit of old practice which most people knew nothing
about.—*Fasti*, iv. 901 foll.

[2] Greenidge, *Legal Procedure in Cicero's time*, p. 457.

[3] It is the same word as our *fair*.

mention one or two of the old feriae which seem always to have remained occasions of holiday-making, at any rate for the lower classes of the population.

One of these occurred on the Ides of March, and must have been going on at the moment when Caesar was assassinated in 44 B.C. It was the festival of Anna Perenna, a mysterious old deity of "the ring of the year." The lower class of the population, Ovid tells us,[1] streamed out to the "festum geniale" of Anna, and spent the whole day in the Campus Martius, lying about in pairs of men and women, indulging in drinking and all kinds of revelry. Some lay in the open ; some constructed tents, or rude huts of boughs, stretching their togas over them for shelter. As they drank they prayed for as many years of life as they could swallow cups of wine. The usual characteristics of the Italian *festa* were to be found there : they sang anything they had picked up in the theatre, with much gesticulation (" et iactant faciles ad sua verba manus "), and they danced, the women letting down their long hair. The result of these performances was naturally that they returned home in a state of intoxication, which roused the mirth of the bystanders. Ovid adds that he had himself met them so returning, and had seen an old woman pulling along an old man, both of them intoxicated. There may have been other popular "jollifications" of this kind, for example at the Neptunalia on July 23, where we find the same curious custom of making temporary huts

---

[1] *Fasti*, iii. 523 foll. ; Fowler, *Roman Festivals*, p. 51.

or shelters ;[1] but this is the only one of which we have any account by an eye-witness. Of the famous Lupercalia in February, and some other festivals which neither died out altogether nor were converted into ludi, we only know the ritual, and cannot tell whether they were still used as popular holidays.

One famous festival of the old religious calendar did, however, always remain a favourite holiday, viz. the Saturnalia on December 17, which was by common usage extended to seven days in all.[2] It was probably the survival of a mid-winter festivity in the life of the farm, at a time when all the farm work of the autumn was over, and when both bond and free might indulge themselves in unlimited enjoyment. Such ancient customs die hard, or, as was the case with the Saturnalia, never die at all; for the same features are still to be found in the Christmas rejoicings of the Italian peasant. Every one knows something of the character of this holiday, and especially of the entertainment of slaves by their masters,[3] which has many parallels in Greek custom, and has been recently supposed to have been borrowed from the Greeks. Various games were played, and among them that of "King," at which we have seen the young Cato playing with his boy

[1] *Roman Festivals*, p. 185. The custom doubtless had a religious origin.

[2] *Ib.* p. 268. Augustus limited the days to three.

[3] Wissowa, *Religion und Kultus*, p. 170. The cult of Saturn was largely affected by Greek usage, but this particular custom was more likely descended from the usage of the Latin farm.

companions.[1] Seneca tells us that in his day all
Rome seemed to go mad on this holiday.

But we must now turn to the real *ludi*, organised
by the State on a large and ever increasing scale.
The oldest and most imposing of these were the
Ludi Romani or Magni, lasting from September 5
to September 19 in Cicero's time. These had their
origin in the return of a victorious army at the end
of the season of war, when king or consul had to
carry out the vows he had made when entering on his
campaign. The usual form of the vow was to entertain the people on his return, in honour of Jupiter,
and thus they were originally called ludi *votivi*,
before they were incorporated as a regularly recurring festival. After they became regular and annual,
any entertainment vowed by a general had to take
place on other days; thus in the year 70 B.C.
Pompey's triumphal ludi votivi immediately pre-
ceded the Ludi Romani of that year,[2] giving the
people in all some thirty days of holiday. The
centre-point, and original day, of the Ludi Romani
was the Ides (13th) of September, which was also
the day of the epulum Jovis,[3] and the dies natalis
(dedication day) of the Capitoline temple of Jupiter;
and the whole ceremonial was closely connected with

[1] See above, p. 172. Marquardt, *Privatleben*, p. 586; Frazer, *Golden
Bough* (ed. 2), vol. iii. p. 138 foll.

[2] Cic. *Verr.* I. 10. 31; where Cicero complains of the difficulties he
experienced in conducting his case in consequence of the number of ludi
from August to November in that year.

Fowler, *Roman Festivals*, p. 217 foll.

that temple and its great deity. The triumphal
procession passed along the Sacra via to the Capitol,
and thence again to the Circus Maximus, where the
ludi were held. The show must have been most
imposing; first marched the boys and youths, on foot
and on horseback, then the chariots and charioteers
about to take part in the racing, with crowds of
dancers and flute-players,[1] and lastly the images of
the Capitoline deities themselves, carried on *fercula*
(biers). All such shows and processions were dear to
the Roman people, and this seems to have become a
permanent feature of the Ludi Romani, whether or
no an actual triumph was to be celebrated, and also
of some other ludi, e.g. the Apollinares and the
Megalenses.[2] Thus the idea was kept up that the
greatness and prosperity of Rome were especially due
to Jupiter Optimus Maximus, who, since the days of
the Tarquinii, had looked down on his people from
his temple on the Capitol.[3]

The Ludi Plebeii in November seem to have been
a kind of plebeian duplicate of the Ludi Romani.
As fully developed at the end of the Republic, they
lasted from the 4th to the 17th; their centre-
point and original day was the Ides (13th), on which,
as on September 13, there was an epulum Jovis in

---

[1] See the account in Dion. Hal. vii. 72, taken from Fabius Pictor.

[2] See Friedländer in Marquardt, *Staatsverwaltung*, iii. p. 508, note 3.

[3] For full accounts of this procession, and the whole question of the Ludi
Romani, see Friedländer, *l.c.* ; Wissowa, *Religion und Kultus*, p. 383 foll. ; or
the article "Triumphus" in the *Dict. of Antiquities*, ed. 2.   All accounts owe
much to Mommsen's essay in *Römische Forschungen*, ii. p. 42 foll.

the Capitol.[1] They are connected with the name of that Flaminius who built the circus Flaminius in the Campus Martius in 220 B.C., the champion of popular rights, killed soon afterwards at Trasimene; and it is probable that his object in erecting this new place of entertainment was to provide a convenient building free of aristocratic associations. But unfortunately we know very little of the history of these ludi.

If we may suppose that the Ludi Plebeii were instituted just before the second Punic war, it is interesting to note that three other great ludi were organised in the course of that war, no doubt with the object of keeping up the drooping spirits of the urban population. The Ludi Apollinares were vowed by a praetor urbanus in 212, when the fate of Rome was hanging in the balance, and celebrated in the Circus Maximus: in 208 they were fixed to a particular day, July 13, and eventually extended to eight, viz. July 6-13.[2] In 204 were instituted the Ludi Megalenses, to celebrate the arrival in Rome of the Magna Mater from Pessinus in Phrygia, i.e. on April 4; but the ludi were eventually extended to April 10.[3] Lastly, in 202 the Ludi Ceriales, which probably existed in some form already, were made permanent and fixed for April 19: they eventually lasted from the 12th to the 19th.[4] After the war was over we only find one more set of ludi per-

---

[1] On the parallelism between the Ludi Plebeii and Romani see Mommsen, *Staatsrecht*, ii. p. 508, note 4.

[2] Fowler, *Roman Festivals*, p. 179 foll.   [3] *Ib.* p. 69.   [4] *Ib.* p. 72 foll.

manently established, viz. the Florales, which date from 173. The original day was April 28, which had long been one of coarse enjoyment for the plebs; like the other ludi, these too were extended, and eventually reached to May 3.[1]   April, we may note, was a month chiefly consisting of holidays : the Ludi Megalenses, Ceriales, and Florales occupied no less than seventeen of its twenty-nine days.

When Sulla wished to commemorate his victory at the Colline gate, he instituted Ludi Victoriae on November 1, the date of the battle, and these seem to have been kept up after most of Sulla's work had been destroyed; they are mentioned by Cicero in the passage quoted above from the Verrines, as Ludi Victoriae, but we hear comparatively little of them.

Before we go on to describe the nature of these numerous entertainments, it may be as well to realise that the spectators had nothing to pay for them; they were provided by the State free of cost, as being part of certain religious festivals which it was the duty of the government to keep up.   Certain sums were set aside for this purpose, differing in amount from time to time; thus in 217 B.C., for the Ludi Romani, on which up to that time 200,000 sesterces (£16,600) had been spent, the sum of 333, $333\frac{1}{3}$ sest. was voted, because the number three had a sacred signification, and the moment was one of extreme peril for the State.[2] On one occasion only before the end of the Republic do we hear of any public collection for the ludi;

[1] Fowler, *Roman Festivals*, p. 91 foll.   [2] Livy xxii. 10. 7 ; Dionys. vii. 71.

in 186 B.C. Pliny tells us that every one was so well
off, owing no doubt to the enormous amount of booty
brought from the war in the East, that all subscribed
some small sum for the games of Scipio Asiaticus.[1]
There was no doubt a growing demand for magnificence in the shows, and thus it came about that
the amount provided by the State had to be
supplemented. But the usual way of supplementing
it was for the magistrate in charge of the ludi to pay
what he could out of his own purse, or to get his
friends to help him; and as all the ludi except the
Apollinares were in charge of the aediles, it became
the practice for these, if they aspired to reach the
praetorship and consulship, to vie with each other in
the recklessness of their expenditure. As early as
176 B.C. the senate had tried to limit this personal
expenditure, for Ti. Sempronius Gracchus as aedile had
that year spent enormous sums on his ludi, and had
squeezed money (it does not appear how) out of the
subject populations of Italy, as well as the provinces,
to entertain the Roman people.[2] But naturally no
decrees of the senate on such matters were likely
to have permanent effect; the great families whose
younger members aimed at popularity in this way
were far too powerful to be easily checked. In the
last age of the Republic it had become a necessary
part of the aedile's duty to supplement the State's
contribution, and as a rule he had to borrow heavily,

---

[1] Pliny, *N.H.* xxxiii. 138. The same thing happened once or twice
under Augustus. [2] Livy xl. 44.

and thus to involve himself financially quite early in his political career. In his *de Officiis*,[1] writing of the virtue of *liberalitas*, Cicero gives a list of men who had been munificent as aediles, including the elder and younger Crassus, Mucius Scaevola (a man, he says, of great self-restraint), the two Luculli, Hortensius, and Silanus; and adds that in his own consulship P. Lentulus outdid all his predecessors, and was imitated by Scaurus in 58 B.C.[2] Cicero himself had to undertake the Ludi Romani, Megalenses, and Florales in his aedileship; how he managed it financially he does not tell us.[3] Caesar undoubtedly borrowed largely, for his expenditure as aedile was enormous,[4] and he had no private fortune of any considerable amount.

Our friend Caelius Rufus was elected curule aedile while he was in correspondence with Cicero, and his letters give us a good idea of the condition of the mind of an ambitious young man who is bent on making the most of himself. He is in a continual state of fidget about his games; he has set his heart on getting panthers to exhibit and hunt, and urges Cicero in letter after letter to procure them for him in Cilicia. "It will be a disgrace to you," he writes in one of them, "that Patiscus has sent ten panthers to Curio, and that you should not send me ten times

[1] ii. 16, 57 foll.

[2] We have some details of the ridiculously lavish expenditure of this aedile in Pliny, *N.H.* xxxvi. 114. He built a temporary theatre, which was decorated as though it were to be a permanent monument of magnificence.

[3] *Verr.* v. 14. 36.   [4] Plut. *Caes.* 5.

as many." [1] The provincial governor, he urges, can
do what he pleases ; let Cicero send for some men of
Cibyra, let him write to Pamphylia, where they are most
abundant, and he will get what he wants, or rather
what Caelius wants.   Even after a letter full of the
most important accounts of public business, including
copies of senatus consulta (*ad Fam.* viii. 8), he harks
back at the end to the inevitable panthers. Cicero tells
Atticus that he rebuked Caelius for pressing him thus
hard to do what his conscience could not approve,
and that it was not right, in his opinion, for a
provincial governor to set the people of Cibyra
hunting for panthers for Roman games. [2] From the
same passage it would seem that Caelius had also
been urging him to take other steps in his province of
which he disapproved, no doubt with the same object
of raising money for the ludi.   This letter to Caelius
is not extant, but we may believe that Cicero had
the courage to reprove his old pupil, and that the
constant worrying for panthers was more than even
his amiability could stand.   But others were less
sensitive ; and it is a well known fact in natural
history that the Roman games had a powerful effect,
from this time forwards, in diminishing the numbers
of wild animals in the countries bordering on the
Mediterranean, and in bringing about the extinction
of species.   In our own day the same work is carried
on by the big-game sportsman, somewhat farther
afield ; the pleasure of slaughter being now confined

[1] Cic. *ad Fam.* viii. 9.   [2] *ad Att.* vi. 1. 21.

to the few rich and adventurous, who shoot for their own delectation, and not to make a London holiday.

Thus to all his ludi the citizen had the right of admission free of cost.[1] An Englishman may find some difficulty at first in realising this; it is as if cricket and football matches and theatres in London were open to the public gratis, and the cost provided by the London County Council. Yet it is not difficult to understand how the Roman government drifted into a practice which was eventually found to have such unfortunate results. It has already been explained that ludi were originally attached to certain religious festivals, which it was the duty of the State and its priests and magistrates to maintain. The Romans, like all Italians, loved shows and out-of-door enjoyment, and as the population increased and became more liable to excitement during the stress of the great wars with Carthage, it became necessary to keep them cheerful and in good humour by developing the old ludi and instituting new ones, for which it would have been contrary to all precedent to make them pay. The government, as we may guess from the history of the ludi which has just been sketched, seems to have been careful at first not to go too far with this policy, and it was some time before any ludi but the Romani were made annual and extended to the length they eventually reached. But the sudden

---

[1] There is no evidence that slaves were admitted under the Republic. Columella, who wrote under Nero, is the first to mention their presence at the games (*R.R.* i. 8. 2), unless we consider the vilicus of Horace, *Epist.* i. 14. 15, as a slave. See Friedländer in Marq. p. 491, note 4.

increase of wealth after the great struggle was over was answerable for this, as for so many other damaging tendencies.   We have seen that the people themselves in 186 were able and willing to contribute ; and now it was possible for aediles to invest their capital in popular undertakings which might, later on, pay them well by carrying them on to higher magistracies and provincial governorships, where fresh fortunes might be made.   The evil results are, of course, as obvious here as in the parallel case of the corn-supply (see above, p. 34) ; enormous amounts of capital were used unproductively, and the people were gradually accustomed to believe that the State was responsible for their enjoyment as well as their food. But we must be most careful not to jump to the con- clusion that this was due to any deliberate policy on the part of the Roman government.   They drifted into these dangerous shoals in spite of the occasional efforts of intelligent steersmen ; and it would indeed have needed a higher political intelligence than was then and there available, to have fully divined the direction of the drift and the dangers ahead of them.

We must now turn in the last place to consider the nature of the entertainments, and see whether there was any improving or educational influence in them.

These had originally consisted entirely of shows of a military character, as we have seen in the case of the Ludi Romani, and especially of chariot-racing in the old Circus Maximus.   The Romans seem always to have been fond of horses and racing, though they never developed a large or thoroughly efficient cavalry force.   It is probable that the position of the Circus Maximus in the vallis Murcia[1] was due to horse-racing near the underground altar of Consus, a harvest deity, and the oldest religious calendar has Equirria (horse-races) on February 27 and March 14, no doubt in connexion with the preparation of the cavalry for the coming season of war.   And in the very curious ancient rite known as " the October horse," there was a two-horse chariot-race in the Campus Martius, when the season of arms was over, and the near horse of the winning pair was sacrificed to Mars.[2]   The Ludi Romani consisted chiefly of chariot-races until 364 B.C. (when plays were first introduced), together with other military evolutions or exercises, such perhaps as the ludus Troiae of the Roman boys, described by Virgil in the fifth Aeneid. Of the Ludi Plebeii we do not know the original character, but it is likely that these also began with *circenses*, the regular word for chariot-races.   The Ludi Cereales certainly included circenses, and plays are only mentioned as forming part of their programme under the Empire ; but on the last day, April 19, there was a curious practice of letting foxes loose in the Circus Maximus with burning firebrands tied to their tails,[3]—a custom undoubtedly ancient, which may have suggested the *venationes* (hunts) of later

---

[1] See above, p. 13 ; Fowler, *Roman Festivals*, p. 208.
[2] *Roman Festivals*, p. 241.   [3] *Ib.* p. 77 foll.

times, for one of which Caelius wanted his panthers. Of the other three ludi, Apollinares, Megalenses, and Florales, we only know that they included both circenses and plays; we must take it as probable that the former were in their programme from the first.

There is no need to describe here in detail the manner of the chariot-racing. We can picture to ourselves the Circus Maximus filled with a dense crowd of some 150,000 people,[1] the senators in reserved places, and the consul or other magistrate presiding; the chariots, usually four in number, painted at this time either red or white, with their drivers in the same colours, issuing from the *carceres* at the end of the circus next to the Forum Boarium and the river, and at the signal racing round a course of about 1600 yards, divided into two halves by a *spina*; at the farther end of this the chariots had to turn sharply and always with a certain amount of danger, which gave the race its chief interest. Seven complete laps of this course constituted a *missus* or race,[2] and the number of races in a day varied from time to time, according to the season of the year and the equipment of the particular ludi. The rivalry between factions and colours, which became so famous later on and lasted throughout the period of the Empire, was only just beginning in Cicero's time. We hear hardly anything of such excitement in the literature of the period; we only know that there

---

[1] Dionys. Hal. iii. 68 gives this number for Augustus' time, and so far as we know Augustus had not enlarged the Circus.   [2] Gell. iii. 10. 16.

were already two rival colours, white and red, and Pliny tells us the strange story that one chariot-owner, a Caecina of Volaterrae, used to bring swallows into the city smeared with his colour, which he let loose to fly home and so bear the news of a victory.[1] Human nature in big cities seems to demand some such artificial stimulus to excitement, and without it the racing must have been monotonous ; but of betting and gambling we as yet hear nothing at all. Gradually, as vast sums of money were laid out by capitalists and even by senators upon the horses and drivers, the colour-factions increased in numbers, and their rivalry came to occupy men's minds as completely as do now the chances of football teams in our own manufacturing towns.[2]

Exhibitions of gladiators (*munera*) did not as yet take place at ludi or on public festivals, but they may be mentioned here, because they were already becoming the favourite amusement of the common people ; Cicero in the *pro Sestio*[3] speaks of them as " that kind of spectacle to which all sorts of people crowd in the greatest numbers, and in which the multitude takes the greatest delight." The consequence was, of course, that candidates for election to magistracies took every opportunity of giving

---

[1] Pliny, *N.H.* x. 71 : he seems to be referring to an earlier time, and this Caecina may have been the friend of Cicero. In another passage of Pliny we hear of the red faction about the time of Sulla (vii. 186 ; Friedl. p. 517). Cp. Tertullian, *de Spectaculis*, 9.

[2] For a graphic picture of the scene in the Circus in Augustus' time see **Ovid**, *Ars Amatoria*, i. 135 foll.   [3] ch. 59.

them ; and Cicero himself in his consulship inserted
a clause in his *lex de ambitu* forbidding candidates
to give such exhibitions within two years of the
election.[1]   They were given exclusively by private
individuals up to 105 B.C., either in the Forum or in
one or other circus : in that year there was an exhibition by the consuls, but there is some evidence that
it was intended to instruct the soldiers in the better
use of their weapons.   This was a year in which the
State was in sore need of efficient soldiers ; Marius
was at the same time introducing a new system of
recruiting and of arming the soldier, and we are told
that the consul Rutilius made use of the best gladiators that were to be found in the training-school
(ludus) of a certain Scaurus, to teach the men a
more skilful use of their weapons.[2]   If gladiators
could have been used only for a rational purpose like
this, as skilful swordsmen and military instructors,
the State might well have maintained some force
of them.   But as it was they remained in private
hands, and no limit could be put on the numbers so
maintained.   They became a permanent menace to
the peace of society, as has already been mentioned
in the chapter on slavery.   Their frequent use in
funeral games is a somewhat loathsome feature of
the age.   These funeral games were an old religious
institution, occurring on the ninth day after the burial,

[1] See Schol. Bob. on the *pro Sestio*, new Teubner ed., p. 105.

[2] Val. Max. ii. 3. 2.   The conjecture as to the object of the exhibition by
the consuls is that of Bücheler, in *Rhein. Mus.* 1883, p. 476 foll.

and known as Ludi Novemdiales; they are familiar
to every one from Virgil's skilful introduction of them,
as a Roman equivalent for the Homeric games, in the
fifth Aeneid, on the anniversary of the funeral of
Anchises. Virgil has naturally omitted the gladiators;
but long before his time it had become common to
use the opportunity of the funeral of a relation to
give munera for the purpose of gaining popularity.[1]
A good example is that of young Curio, who in
53 B.C. ruined himself in this way. Cicero alludes to
this in an interesting letter to Curio.[2] "You may
reach the highest honours," he says, "more easily
by your natural advantages of character, diligence,
and fortune, than by gladiatorial exhibitions. The
power of giving them stirs no feeling of admiration
in any one: it is a question of means and not of
character: and there is no one who is not by this
time sick and tired of them." To Cicero's refined
mind they were naturally repugnant; but young
men like Curio, though they loved Cicero, were not
wont to follow his wholesome advice.[3]

We turn now to the dramatic element in the ludi,
chiefly with the object of determining whether, in
the age of Cicero, it was of any real importance in
the social life of the Roman people. The Roman

[1] The example was set, according to Livy, *Epit.* 16, by a Junius Brutus
at the beginning of the first Punic war. [2] *ad Fam.* ii. 3.

[3] The origin of these bloody shows at funerals needs further investigation.
It may be connected with a primitive and savage custom of sacrificing
captives to the Manes of a chief, of which we have a reminiscence in the
sacrifice of captives by Aeneas, in Virg. *Aen.* xi. 82.

stage had had a great history before the last century
B.C., into which it is not necessary here to enter. It
had always been possible without difficulty for those
who were responsible for the ludi to put on the
stage a tragedy or comedy either written for the
occasion or reproduced, with competent actors and
the necessary music; and there seems to be no
doubt that both tragedies and comedies, whether
adapted from the Greek (fabulae palliatae) or of a
national character (fab. togatae), were enjoyed by
the audiences. In the days of the Punic wars and
afterwards, when everything Greek was popular, a
Roman audience could appreciate stories of the
Greek mythology, as presented in the tragedies of
Ennius, Pacuvius, and Accius, if without learning to
read in them the great problems of human life, at
least as spectacles of the vicissitudes of human
fortune; and had occasionally listened to a tragedy,
or perhaps rather a dramatic history, based on some
familiar legend of their own State. And the conditions of social life in Rome and Athens were not so
different but that in the hands of a real genius like
Plautus the New Athenian comedy could come
home to the Roman people, with their delight in
rather rough fun and comical situations: and
Plautus was followed by Caecilius and the more
refined Terence, before the national comedy of
Afranius and others established itself in the place
of the Greek. It is hardly possible to avoid the
conclusion that in those early days of the Roman

theatre the audiences were really intelligent, and capable of learning something from the pieces they listened to, apart from their natural love of a show, of all acting, and of music.[1]

But before the age with which this book deals, the long succession of great dramatic writers had come to an end. Accius, the nephew of Pacuvius, had died as a very old man when Cicero was a boy;[2] and in the national comedy no one had been found to follow Afranius. The times were disturbed, the population was restless, and continually incorporating heterogeneous elements: much amusement could be found in the life of the Forum, and in rioting and disorder; gladiatorial shows were organised on a large scale. To sit still and watch a good play would become more tiresome as the plebs grew more restless, and probably even the taste of the better educated was degenerating as the natural result of luxury and idleness. Politics and political personages were the really exciting features of the time, and there are signs that audiences took advantage of the plays to express their approval or dislike of a statesman. In a letter to Atticus, written in the summer of 59,[3] the first year of the triumvirate, Cicero describes with enthusiasm how at the Ludi Apollinares the actor Diphilus made an allusion to Pompey in the words (from an unknown tragedy

---

[1] See Lucian Müller's *Ennius*, p. 35 foll., where he maintains against Mommsen the intelligence and taste of the Romans of the 2nd century B.C.

[2] Cic. *Brutus*, 28. 107, where he speaks of having known the poet himself.

[3] *ad Att*. ii. 19.

then being acted), "Nostra miseria tu es—Magnus,'
and was forced to repeat them many times.   When
he delivered the line

"Eandem virtutem istam veniet tempus cum graviter gemes,"

the whole theatre broke out into frantic applause.
So too in a well-known passage of the speech *pro
Sestio* he tells from hearsay how the great tragic
actor Aesopus, acting in the Eurysaces of Accius,
was again and again interrupted by applause as he
cleverly adapted the words to the expected recall
from exile of the orator, his personal friend.[1]   The
famous words "Summum amicum, summo in bello,
summo ingenio praeditum," were among those which
the modest Cicero tells us were taken up by the
people with enthusiasm,—greatly, without doubt, to
the detriment of the play.   The whole passage is
one of great graphic power, and only fails to rouse
us too to enthusiasm when we reflect that Cicero
was not himself present.

From this and other passages we have abundant
evidence that tragedies were still acted; but Cicero
nowhere in his correspondence, where we might
naturally have expected to find it, nor in his philosophical works, gives us any idea of their educational
or aesthetic influence either on himself or others.
He is constantly quoting the old plays, especially
the tragedies, and knows them very well: but he
quotes them almost invariably as literature only.

[1] *Pro Sestio*, 55. 117 foll.

Once or twice, as we shall see, he recalls the gesture
or utterance of a great actor, but as a rule he is
thinking of them as poetry rather than as plays. It
may be noted in this connexion that it was now
becoming the fashion to write plays without any
immediate intention of bringing them on the stage.
We read with astonishment in a letter of Cicero to
his brother Quintus, then in Gaul, that the latter
had taken to play-writing, and accomplished four
tragedies in sixteen days, and this apparently in
the course of the campaign.[1] One, the *Erigona*, was
sent to his brother from Britain, and lost on the
way. We hear no more of these plays, and have no
reason to suppose that they were worthy to survive.
No man of literary eminence in that day wrote
plays for acting, and in fact the only person of note,
so far as we know, who did so, was the younger
Cornelius Balbus, son of the intimate friend and
secretary of Caesar. This man wrote one in Latin
about his journey to his native town of Gades, had
it put on the stage there, and shed tears during its
performance.[2]

When we hear of plays being written without
being acted, and of tragedies being made the occasion
of expressing political opinions, we may be pretty
sure that the drama is in its nonage. An interesting proof of the same tendency is to be found in the

[1] *ad Q. Fratr.* iii. 5.

[2] It is only fair to say that this information comes from a letter of Asinius
Pollio to Cicero (*ad Fam.* x. 32. 3), and as Pollio was one who had a word of
mockery for every one, we may discount the story of the tears.

first book of the *Ars Amatoria* of Ovid, though
it belongs to the age of Augustus.   In this book
Ovid describes the various resorts in the city where
the youth may look out for his girl; and when he
comes to the theatre, draws a pretty picture of the
ladies of taste and fashion crowding thither,—but

Spectatum veniunt : veniunt spectentur ut ipsae.

And then, without a word about the play, or the
smallest hint that he or the ladies really cared about
such things, he goes off into the familiar story of the
rape of the Sabine women, supposed to have taken
place when Romulus was holding his ludi.

It is curious, in view of what thus seems to be a
flagging interest in the drama as such, to find that
the most remarkable event in the theatrical history
of this time is the building of the first permanent
stone theatre.   During the whole long period of the
popularity of the drama the government had never
consented to the erection of a permanent theatre
after the Greek fashion; though it was impossible
to prohibit the production of plays adapted from
the Greek, there seems to have been some strange
scruple felt about giving Rome this outward token
of a Greek city.   Temporary stages were erected in
the Forum or the circus, the audience at first standing,
but afterwards accommodated with seats in a *cavea*
of wood erected for the occasion.   The whole show,
including play, actors, and pipe-players[1] to accom-

---

[1] Tibicines, usually mistranslated flute-players; this characteristic Italian

pany the voices where necessary, was contracted for, like all such undertakings,[1] on each occasion of Ludi scaenici being produced. At last, in the year 154 B.C., the censors had actually set about the building of a theatre, apparently of stone, when the reactionary Scipio Nasica, acting under the influence of a temporary anti-Greek movement, persuaded the senate to put a stop to this symptom of degeneracy, and to pass a decree that no seats were in future to be provided, "ut scilicet remissioni animorum standi virilitas propria Romanae gentis iuncta esset."[2] Whether this extraordinary decree, of which the legality might have been questioned a generation later, had any permanent effect, we do not know; certainly the senators, and after the time of Gaius Gracchus the equites, sat on seats appropriated to them. But Rome continued to be without a stone theatre until Pompey, in the year of his second consulship, 55 B.C., built one on a grand scale, capable of holding 40,000 people. Even he, we are told, could not accomplish this without some criticism from the old and old-fashioned,—so lasting was the prejudice against anything that might seem to be turning Rome into a Greek city.[3] There was a story too, of which it is difficult to make out the real origin, that he was compelled by popular feel-

---

instrument was really a primitive oboe played with a reed, and usually of the double form (two pipes with a connected mouthpiece), still sometimes seen in Italy.

[1] See above, p. 70.　　　　[2] Val. Max. ii. 4. 2 ; Livy, *Epit.* 48.

[3] Tacitus, *Ann.* xiv. 20.

ing to conceal his design by building, immediately
behind the theatre, a temple of Venus Victrix, the
steps of which were in some way connected with his
auditorium.[1] The theatre was placed in the Campus
Martius, and its shape is fairly well known to us from
fragments of the Capitoline plan of the city;[2] adjoining it Pompey also built a magnificent *porticus* for
the convenience of the audience, and a *curia*, in which
the senate could meet, and where, eleven years later,
the great Dictator was murdered at the feet of
Pompey's statue.

In spite of the magnificence of this building, it
was by no means destined to revive the earlier
prosperity of the tragic and comic drama. Even
at the opening of it the signs of degeneracy are
apparent. Luckily for us Cicero was in Rome at
the time, and in a letter to a friend in the country
he congratulates him on being too unwell to come to
Rome and see the spoiling of old tragedies by over-
display.[3] "The ludi," he says, "had not even that
charm which games on a moderate scale generally
have; the spectacle was so elaborate as to leave no
room for cheerful enjoyment, and I think you need
feel no regret at having missed it. What is the
pleasure of a train of six hundred mules in the

---

[1] Tertullian, *de Spectaculis*, 10 ; Pliny, *N.H.* viii. 20.

[2] See the excellent account in Hülsen, vol. iii. of Jordan's *Topographie*,
p. 524 foll. Some of the arches of the supporting arcade are still visible.

[3] *ad Fam.* vii. 1. Professor Tyrrell calls this letter a rhetorical exercise ;
is it not rather one of those in which Cicero is taking pains to write, therefore writing less easily and naturally than usual ?

Clytemnestra (of Accius), or three thousand bowls (craterae) in the Trojan Horse (of Livius), or gay-coloured armour of infantry and cavalry in some mimic battle ?   These things roused the admiration of the vulgar : to you they would have brought no delight." This ostentatious stage-display finds its counterpart to some extent at the present day, and may remind us also of the huge orchestras of blaring sound which are the delight of the modern composer and the modern musical audience.   And the plays were by no means the only part of the show.   There were displays of athletes ; but these never seem to have greatly interested a Roman audience, and Cicero says that Pompey confessed that they were a failure ; but to make up for that there were wild-beast shows for five whole days (*venationes*)—"magnificent," the letter goes on, "no one denies it, yet what pleasure can it be to a man of refinement, when a weak man is torn by a very powerful animal, or a splendid animal is transfixed by a hunting-spear ? . . . The last day was that of the elephants, about which there was a good deal of astonishment on the part of the vulgar crowd, but no pleasure whatever.   Nay, there was even a feeling of compassion aroused by them, and a notion that this animal has something in common with mankind." [1]   This last interesting sentence is confirmed by a passage in Pliny's *Natural History*, in which he asserts that the people were so much

[1] I have used Mr. Shuckburgh's translation, with one or two verbal changes.

moved that they actually execrated Pompey.[1] The
last age of the Republic is a transitional one, in this,
as in other ways ; the people are not yet thoroughly
inured to bloodshed and cruelty to animals, as they
afterwards became when deprived of political excite-
ments, and left with nothing violent to amuse them
but the displays of the amphitheatre.

Earlier in this same letter Cicero had told his
friend Marius that on this occasion certain old actors
had re-appeared on the stage, who, as he thought, had
left it for good. The only one he mentions is the
great tragic actor Aesopus, who " was in such a state
that no one could say a word against his retiring
from the profession." At one important point his
voice failed him. This may conveniently remind us
that Aesopus was the last of the great actors of
tragedy, and that his best days were in the early
half of this century—another sign of the decay of
the legitimate drama. He was an intimate friend of
Cicero, and from a few references to him in the
Ciceronian writings we can form some idea of his
genius. In one passage Cicero writes of having seen
him looking so wild and gesticulating so excitedly,
that he seemed almost to have lost command of himself.[2] In the description, already quoted from the
speech *pro Sestio*, of the scene in the theatre before
his recall from exile, he speaks of this "summus
artifex" as delivering his allusions to the exile with

---

[1] Pliny, *Nat. Hist.* viii. 21.
[2] *de Div.* i. 37. 80. Cp. the story in Plut. *Cic.* 5.

infinite force and passion. Yet the later tradition of his acting was rather that he was serious and self-restrained; Horace calls him *gravis*, and Quintilian too speaks of his *gravitas*.[1] Probably, like Garrick, he was capable of a great variety of moods and parts. How carefully he studied the varieties of gesticulation is indicated by a curious story preserved by Valerius Maximus, that he and Roscius the great comedian used to go and sit in the courts in order to observe the action of the orator Hortensius.[2]

Roscius too was an early intimate friend of Cicero, who, like Caesar, seems to have valued the friendship of all men of genius, without regard to their origin or profession. Roscius seems to have been a freed-man;[3] his great days were in Cicero's early life, and he died in 61 B.C., to the deep grief of all his friends.[4] So wonderfully finished was his acting that it became a common practice to call any one a Roscius whose work was more than usually perfect. He never could find a pupil of whom he could entirely approve; many had good points, but if there were a single blot, the master could not bear it.[5] In the *de Oratore* Cicero tells us several interesting things about him,— how he laid the proper emphasis on the right words, reserving his gesticulation until he came to them; and how he was never so much admired when acting

---

[1] Hor. *Ep.* ii. 82 ; Quintil. ii. 3. 111.

[2] Val. Max. viii. 10. 2. Cicero was said to have learnt gesticulation both from Aesopus and Roscius.—Plut. *Cic.* 5.

[3] Pliny, *N.H.* vii. 128.   [4] *Pro Archia*, 8.

[5] *De Oratore*, i. 28. 129.

with a mask on, because the expression of his face was so full of meaning.[1]

In Cicero's later years, when Roscius was dead and Aesopus retired, we hear no more of great actors of this type. With these two remarkable men the great days of the Roman drama come to an end, and henceforward the favourite plays are merely farces, of which a word must here be said in the last place.

The origin of these farces, as indeed of all kinds of Latin comedy, and probably also of the literary satura, is to be found in the jokes and rude fun of the country festivals, and especially perhaps, as Horace tells us of the harvest amusements :[2]

> Fescennina per hunc inventa licentia morem
> Versibus alternis opprobria rustica fudit,
> Libertasque recurrentis accepta per annos
> Lusit amabiliter, etc.
>
> *Epist.* ii. 1. 145 foll.

These amusements were always accompanied with the music and dancing so dear to the Italian peoples, and it is easy to divine how they may have gradually developed into plays of a rude but tolerably fixed type, with improvised dialogue, acted in the streets, or later in the intervals between acts at the theatre, and eventually as afterpieces, more after our own fashion.

In Cicero's day two kinds of farces were in vogue. In his earlier life the so-called Atellan plays (fabulae

---

[1] *De Oratore*, iii. 27, 59.

[2] A useful succinct account of the literature of this difficult subject will be found in Schanz, *Gesch. der röm. Litteratur*, vol. i. (ed. 3) p. 21 foll.

Atellanae) were the favourites : these were of indi-
genous Latin origin, and probably took their name
from the ruined town Atella, which might provide a
permanent scenery as the background of the plays
without offending the jealousy of any of the other
Latin cities.[1] They were doubtless very comic, but
it was possible to get tired of them, for the number
of stock characters was limited, and the masks were
always the same for each character—the old man
Pappus, the glutton Bucco, Dossennus the sharper, etc.
About the time of Sulla the *mimes* seem to have dis-
placed these old farces in popular favour, perhaps
because their fun was more varied ; the mere fact that
the actors did not wear masks shows that the improvisation could be freer and less stereotyped. But both
kinds were alike coarse, and may be called the comedy
of low life in country towns and in the great city.
Sulla's tastes seem to have been low in the matter
of plays, if we may trust Plutarch, who asserts that
when he was young he spent much of his time among
mimi and jesters, and that when he was dictator
he " daily got together from the theatre the lewdest
persons, with whom he would drink and enter into
a contest of coarse witticisms." [2] This may be due
to the evidence of an enemy, but it is not improbable;
and it is possible that both Sulla and Caesar, who
also patronised the mimes, may have wished to avoid

---

[1] This is the view of Mommsen, *Hist.* iii. p. 455, which is generally
accepted.   For further information see Teuffel, *Hist. of Roman Literature*,
i. (ed. 2) p. 9.   That they were in fashion before the mimus is gathered
from Cic. *ad Fam.* ix. 16.   [2] Plut. *Sulla*, 2 : cp. 36.

the personal allusions which, as we have seen, were so often made or imagined in the exhibition of tragedies, and have aimed at confining the plays to such as would give less opportunity for unwelcome criticism.[1]

About the year 50 B.C., as we have seen in the chapter on education, there came to Italy the Syrian Publilius, who began to write mimes in verse, thus for the first time giving them a literary turn. Caesar, always on the look-out for talent, summoned him to Rome, and awarded him the palm for his plays.[2] These must have been, as regards wit and style, of a much higher order than any previous mimes, and in fact not far removed from the older Roman comedy (fabula togata) in manner. Cicero alludes to them twice: and writing to Cornificius from Rome in October 45 he says that at Caesar's ludi he listened to the poems of Publilius and Laberius with a well-pleased mind.[3] "Nihil mihi tamen deesse scito quam quicum haec familiariter docteque rideam"; here the word *docte* seems to suggest that the performance was at least worthy of the attention of a cultivated man. Laberius, also a Roman knight, wrote mimes at the same time as Publilius, and was beaten by him in competition; of him it is told that he was induced

---

[1] Political allusions in mimes, were, however, not unknown. Cp. Cic. *ad Att.* xiv. 3, written in 44 B.C., after Caesar's death.

[2] All the passages about Publilius are collected in Mr. Bickford Smith's edition of his *Sententiae*, p. 10 foll. On mimes generally the reader may be referred to Professor Purser's excellent article in Smith's *Dict. of Antiq.* ed. 2.

[3] Animo aequissimo, *ad Fam.* xii. 19. He means perhaps rather that flattering allusions to Caesar did not hurt his feelings.

by Caesar to act in his own mime, and revenged himself for the insult, as it was then felt to be by a Roman of good birth, in a prologue which has come down to us.[1] We may suppose that his plays were of the same type as those of Publilius, and interspersed with those wise sayings, *sententiae*, which the Roman people were still capable of appreciating. Even in the time of Seneca applause was given to any words which the audience felt at once to be true and to hit the mark.[2]

Thus the mime was lifted from the level of the lowest farcical improvisation to a recognised position in literature, and quite incidentally became useful in education. But the coarseness remained; the dancing was grotesque and the fun ribald, and, as Professor Purser says, the plots nearly always involved "some incident of an amorous nature in which ordinary morality was set at defiance." The Roman audience of the early Empire enjoyed these things, and all sorts of dancing, singing, and instrumental music, and above all the *pantomimus*,[3] in which the actor only gesticulated, without speaking; this and the fact that the real drama never again had a fair chance is one of the many signs that the city population was losing both virility and intelligence.

---

[1] See Ribbeck, *Fragm. Comic. Lat.* p. 295 foll.

[2] Seneca, *Epist.* 108. 8.

[3] See another excellent article of Professor Purser's in the *Dict. of Antiq.*

CHAPTER XI

RELIGION

It is easy to write the word "religion" at the head of this chapter, but by no means easy to find anything in this materialistic period which answers to our use of the word. In the whole mass, for example, of the Ciceronian correspondence, there is hardly anything to show that Cicero and his friends, and therefore, as we may presume, the average educated man of the day, were affected in their thinking or their conduct by any sense of dependence on, or responsibility to, a Supreme Being. If, however, it had been possible to substitute for the English word the Latin *religio*, it would have made a far more appropriate title to this chapter, for *religio* meant primarily awe, nervousness, scruple—much the same in fact as that feeling which in these days we call superstition; and secondarily the means taken, under the authority of the State, to quiet such feelings by the performance of rites meant to propitiate the gods.[1] In both of these senses *religio* is to be found in the last age of

---

[1] See the *Hibbert Journal* for July 1907, p. 847. In the second sense Cicero often uses the plural "religiones," esp. in *de Legibus,* ii.

the Republic ; but, as we shall see, the tendency to superstitious nervousness was very imperfectly allayed, and the worship that should have allayed it was in great measure neglected.

It may be, indeed, that in quiet country districts the joyous rural festivals went on—we have many allusions and a few descriptions of them in the literature of the Augustan period,—and also the worship of the household deities, in which there perhaps survived a feeling of *pietas* more nearly akin to what we call religious feeling than in any of the cults (*sacra publica*) undertaken by the State for the people. Even in the city the cult of the dead, or what may perhaps be better called the religious attention paid to their resting-places, and the religious ceremonies attending birth, puberty, and marriage, were kept up as matters of form and custom among the upper and wealthier classes. But the great mass of the population of Rome, we may be almost sure, knew nothing of these rites ; the poor man, for example, could no more afford a tomb for himself than a house, and his body was thrown into some *puticulus* or common burying-place,[1] where it was impossible that any yearly ceremonies could be performed to his memory, even if any one cared to do so. And among the higher strata of society, outside of these *sacra privata*, carelessness and negligence of the old State cults were steadily on the increase.

---

[1] See Middleton, *Rome in 1887*, p. 423 ; Horace, *Sat.* i. 8. 8 foll. ; Nissen, *Italische Landeskunde*, ii. p. 522.

Neither Cicero nor any of his contemporaries but Varro has anything to tell us of their details, and the decay had gone so far that Varro himself knew little or nothing about many of the deities of the old religious calendar,[1] or of the ways in which they had at one time been worshipped. Vesta, with her simple cult and her virgin priestesses, was almost the only deity who was not either forgotten or metamorphosed in one way or another under the influence of Greek literature and mythology; Vesta was too well recognised as a symbol of the State's vitality to be subject to neglect like other and less significant cults. The old sacrificing priesthoods, such as the Fratres Arvales and the lesser Flamines, seem not to have been filled up by the pontifices whose duty it was to do so: and the Flamen Dialis, the priest of Jupiter himself, is not heard of from 89 to 11 B.C., when he appears again as a part of the Augustan religious restoration. The explanation is probably that these offices could not be held together with any secular one which might take the holder away from Rome; and as every man of good family had business in the provinces, no qualified person could be found willing to put himself under the restriction. The temples too seem to have been sadly neglected; Augustus tells us himself[2] that he had to restore no less than eighty-two; and from Cicero we actually hear of thefts of statues and other temple property[3]—sacrileges which may be

---

[1] Fowler, *Roman Festivals*, p. 336 foll.

[2] *Monumentum Ancyranum* (Lat.), 4. 17.   [3] *de Nat. Deor.* i. 29. 82.

Y

attributed to the general demoralisation caused by the Social and Civil Wars.   At the same time there seems to have been a strong tendency to go after strange gods, with whose worship Roman soldiers had made acquaintance in the course of their numerous eastern campaigns.   It is a remarkable fact that no less than four times in a single decade the worship of Isis had to be suppressed,—in 58, 53, 50, and 48 B.C.   In the year 50 we are told that the consul Aemilius Paullus, a conservative of the old type, actually threw off his toga praetexta and took an axe to begin destroying the temple, because no workmen could be found to venture on the work.[1] These are indeed strange times ; the beautiful religion of Isis, which assuredly had some power to purify a man and strengthen his conscience,[2] was to be driven out of a city where the old local religion had never had any such power, and where the masses were now left without a particle of aid or comfort from any religious source.   The story seems to ring true, and gives us a most valuable glimpse into the mental condition of the Roman workman of the time.

Of such foreign worships, and of the general neglect of the old cults, Cicero tells us nothing; we have to learn or to guess at these facts from evidence supplied by later writers.   His interest in religious practice was confined to ceremonies which had some political importance.   He was himself an augur, and

---

[1] Valerius Maximus, *Eptt.* 3. 4 ; Wissowa, *Rel. und Kult.* p. 293.

[2] See, e.g. Dill, *Roman Society from Nero to Marcus Aurelius*, ch. v.

was much pleased with his election to that ancient
college; but, like most other augurs of the time, he
knew nothing **of** augural "science," and only cared
to speculate philosophically on the question whether
it is possible to foretell the future. He looked
upon the right of the magistrate to "observe the
heaven" as a part of an excellent constitution,[1] and
could not forgive Caesar for refusing in 59 B.C. to have
his legislation paralysed by the fanatical declarations
of his colleague that he was going to "look for
lightning." He firmly believed in the value of the
ius divinum of the State. In his treatise on the
constitution (*de Legibus*) he devotes a whole book to
this religious side of constitutional law, and gives a
sketch of it in quasi-legal language from which it
appears that he entirely accepted the duty of the
State to keep the citizen in right relation to the gods,
on whose goodwill his welfare depended. He seems
never to have noticed that the State was neglecting
this duty, and that, as we saw just now, temples and
cults were falling into decay, strange forms of religion
pressing in. Such things did not interest him; in
public life the State religion was to him a piece of
the constitution, to be maintained where it was
clearly essential; in his own study it was a matter of
philosophical discussion. In his young days he was
intimate with the famous Pontifex Maximus, Mucius
Scaevola, who held that there were three religions,—
that of the poets, that of the philosophers, and that of

[1] See, e.g., *pro Sestio*, 15. 32; *in Vatinium*, 7. 18.

the statesman, of which the last must be accepted and acted on, whether it be true or not.[1] Cicero could hardly have complained if this saying had been attributed to himself.

This attitude of mind, the combination of perfect freedom of thought with full recognition of the legal obligations of the State and its citizens in matters of religion, is not difficult for any one to understand who is acquainted with the nature of the ius divinum and the priesthood administering it. That ius divinum was a part of the ius civile, the law of the Roman city-state; as the ius civile, exclusive of the ius divinum, regulated the relations of citizen to citizen, so did the ius divinum regulate the relations of the citizen to the deities of the community. The priesthoods administering this law consisted not of sacrificing priests, attached to the cult of a particular god and temple, but of lay officials in charge of that part of the law of the State; it was no concern of theirs (so indeed they might quite well argue) whether the gods really existed or not, provided the law were maintained. When in 61 B.C. Clodius was caught in disguise at the women's festival of the Bona Dea, the pontifices declared the act to be *nefas*,—crime against the ius divinum; but we may doubt whether any of those pontifices really believed in the existence of such a deity. The idea of the *mos maiorum* was still so strong in the mind of every true Roman, his con-

---

[1] Augustine, *Civ. Dei*, iv. 27.

servative instincts were so powerful, that long after
all real life had left the divine inhabitants of his
city, so that they survived only as the dead stalks
of plants that had once been green and flourishing,
he was quite capable of being horrified at any open
contempt of them. And he was right, as Augustus
afterwards saw clearly; for the masses, who had no
share in the education described in the sixth chapter,
who knew nothing of Greek literature or philosophy,
and were full of superstitious fancies, were already
losing confidence in the authorities set over them,
and in their power to secure the good-will of the
gods and their favour in matters of material well-
being. This is the only way in which we can
satisfactorily account for the systematic efforts of
Augustus to renovate the old religious rites and
priesthoods, and we can fairly argue back from it to
the tendencies of the generation immediately before
him. He knew that the proletariate of Rome and
Italy still believed, as their ancestors had always
believed, that state and individual would alike suffer
unless the gods were properly propitiated; and that
in order to keep them quiet and comfortable the
sense of duty to the gods must be kept alive even
among those who had long ceased to believe in them.
It was fortunate indeed for Augustus that he found
in the great poet of Mantua one who was in some
sense a prophet as well as a poet, who could urge the
Roman by an imaginative example to return to a
living pietas,—not merely to the old religious forms,

but to the intelligent sense of duty to God and man which had built up his character and his empire. In Cicero's day there was also a great poet, he too in some sense a prophet; but Lucretius could only appeal to the Roman to shake off the slough of his old religion, and such an appeal was at the time both futile and dangerous. Looking at the matter historically, and not theologically, we ought to sympathise with the attitude of Cicero and Scaevola towards the religion of the State. It was based on a statesmanlike instinct; and had it been possible for that instinct to express itself practically in a positive policy like that of Augustus, instead of showing itself in philosophical treatises like the *de Legibus*, or on occasional moments of danger like that of the Bona Dea sacrilege, it is quite possible that much mischief might have been averted. But in that generation no one had the shrewdness or experience of Augustus, and no one but Julius had the necessary free hand; and we may be almost sure that Julius, Pontifex Maximus though he was, was entirely unfitted by nature and experience to undertake a work that called for such delicate handling, such insight into the working of the ignorant Italian mind.

This attitude of inconsistency and compromise must seem to a modern unsatisfactory and strained, and he turns with relief to the courageous out-spokenness of the great poem of Lucretius on the Nature of Things, of which the main object was to persuade the Romans to renounce for good all the

mass of superstition, in which he included the religion
of the State, by which their minds were kept in a
prison of darkness, terror, and ignorance. Lucretius
took no part whatever in public life; he could afford
to be in earnest; he felt no shadow of responsibility
for the welfare of the State as such. The Epicurean
tenets which he held so passionately had always
ranked the individual before the community, and
suggested a life of individual quietism; Lucretius in
his study could contemplate the "rerum natura" without troubling himself about the "natura hominum"
as it existed in the Italy of his day. "Felix qui
potuit rerum cognoscere causas,"—so wrote of him
his great successor and admirer, yet added, with a
tinge of pathos which touches us even now,
"Fortunatus et ille deos qui novit agrestes." Even
at the present day an uncompromising unbeliever
may be touched by the simple worship, half pagan
though it may seem to him, of a village in the
Apennines; but in the eyes of Lucretius all worship
seemed prompted by fear and based on ignorance of
natural law. Virgil's tender and sympathetic soul
went out to the peasant as he prayed to his gods for
plenty or prosperity, as it went out to all living
creatures in trouble or in joy.

But it is nevertheless true that Lucretius was a
great religious poet. He was a prophet, in deadly
earnest, calling men to renounce their errors both of
thought and conduct. He saw around him a world
full of wickedness and folly; a world of vanity,

vexation, fear, ambition, cruelty, and lust.   He saw
men fearing death and fearing the gods; overvaluing
life, yet weary of it; unable to use it well, because
steeped in ignorance of the wonderful working of
Nature.[1] He saw them, as we have already seen
them, the helpless victims of ambition and avarice,
ever, like Sisyphus, rolling the stone uphill and never
reaching the summit.[2] Of cruelty and bloodshed in
civil strife that age had seen enough, and on this
too the poet dwells with bitter emphasis;[3] on the
unwholesome luxury and restlessness of the upper
classes,[4] and on their unrestrained indulgence of
bodily appetites.   In his magnificent scorn he probably exaggerated the evils of his day, yet we have
seen enough in previous chapters to suggest that he
was not a mere pessimist; there is no trace in his
poem of cynicism, or of a soured temperament.   We
may be certain that he was absolutely convinced of
the truth of all he wrote.

So far Lucretius may be called a religious poet,
in that with profound conviction and passionate
utterance he denounced the wickedness of his age, and,
like the Hebrew prophets, called on mankind to put
away their false gods and degrading superstitions,
and learn the true secret of guidance in this life.   It
is only when we come to ask what that secret was,
that we feel that this extraordinary man knew far too

[1] Cp. i. 63 foll.; iii. 87 and 894; v. 72 and 1218; and many other
passages.   [2] iii. 995 foll.; v. 1120 foll.
   [3] iii. 70; v. 1126.   [4] ii. 22 foll.; iii. 1003; v. 1116.

little of ordinary human nature to be either a religious reformer or an effective prophet : as Sellar has said of him,[1] he had no sympathy with human activity. His secret, the remedy for all the world's evil and misery, was only a philosophical creed, which he had learnt from Epicurus and Democritus. His profound belief in it is one of the most singular facts in literary history ; no man ever put such poetic passion into a dogma, and no such imperious dogma was ever built upon a scientific theory of the universe. He seems to have combined two Italian types of character, which never have been united before or since,—that of the ecclesiastic, earnest and dogmatic, seeing human nature from a doctrinal platform, not working and thinking with it ; and secondly the poetic type, of which Dante is the noblest example, perfectly clear and definite in inward and outward vision, and illuminating all that it touches with an indescribable glow of pure poetic imagination.

Lucretius' secret then is knowledge,[2]—not the dilettanteism of the day, but real scientific knowledge of a single philosophical attempt to explain the universe,—the atomic theory of the Epicurean school. Democritus and Epicurus are the only saviours,—of this Lucretius never had the shadow of a doubt. As the result of this knowledge, the whole supernatural and spiritual world of fancy vanishes, together with

---

[1] *Roman Poets of the Republic,* p. 306.

[2] The secret may be found in the last 250 lines of Bk. iii., and at the beginning and end of Bk. v.

all futile hopes or fears of a future life. The gods, if they exist, will cease to be of any importance to mankind, as having no interest in him, and doing him neither good nor harm. Chimaeras, portents, ghosts, death, and all that frightens the ignorant and paralyses their energies, will vanish in the pure light of this knowledge; man will have nothing to be afraid of but himself. Nor indeed need he fear himself when he has mastered "the truth." By that time, as the scales of fear fall from his eyes, his moral balance will be recovered; the blind man will see. What will he see? What is the moral standard that will become clear to him, the sanction of right living that will grip his conscience?

It is simply the conviction that as this life is all we have in past, present, or future, it *must be used well.* After all then, Lucretius is reduced to ordinary moral suasion, and finds no new power or sanction that could keep erring human nature in the right path. And we must sadly allow that no real moral end is enunciated by him; his ideal seems to be quietism in this life, and annihilation afterwards.[1] It is a purely self-regarding rule of life. It is not even a social creed; neither family nor State seems to have any part in it, much less the unfortunate in this life, the poor, and the suffering. The poet never mentions slavery, or the crowded populations of great cities. It might almost be called a creed of fatalism, in which Natura plays much the same part as Fortuna

---

[1] v. 1203; ii. 48-54.

did in the creed of many less noble spirits of that age.[1] Nature fights on ; we cannot resist her, and cannot improve on her ; it is better to acquiesce and obey than to try and rule her.

Thus Lucretius' remedy fails utterly ; it is that of an aristocratic intellect, not of a saviour of mankind.[2] So far as we know, it was entirely fruitless ; like the constitution of Sulla his contemporary, the doctrine of Lucretius roused no sense of loyalty in Roman or Italian, because it was constructed with imperfect knowledge of the Roman and Italian nature. But it was a noble effort of a noble mind; and, apart from its literary greatness, it has incidentally a lasting value for all students of religious history, as showing better than anything else that has survived from that age the need of a real consecration of morality by the life and example of a Divine man.

Thus while the Roman statesman found it necessary to maintain the ius divinum without troubling himself to attempt to put any new life into the details of the worship it prescribed, content to let much of it sink into oblivion as no longer essential to the good government of the State, the greatest poetical genius of the age was proclaiming in trumpet tones that if a man would make good use of his life he must abandon absolutely and without a scruple the old religious ideas of the Graeco-Roman world. But there was another

[1] v. 1129.

[2] "Philosophy has never touched the mass of mankind except through religion" (*Decadence*, by Rt. Hon. A. J. Balfour, p. 53). This is a truth of which Lucretius was profoundly, though not surprisingly, ignorant.

school of thought which had long been occupied with these difficulties, and had reached conclusions far better suited than the dogmatism of Lucretius to the conservative character of the Roman mind, for it found a place for the deities of the State, and therefore for the ius divinum, in a philosophical system already widely accepted by educated men. This school may be described as Stoic, though its theology was often accepted by men who did not actually call themselves Stoics; for example, by Cicero himself, who, as an adherent of the New Academy, the school which repudiated dogmatism and occupied itself with dialectic and criticism, was perfectly entitled to adopt the tenets of other schools if he thought them the most convincing. Its most elaborate exponent in this period was Varro, and behind both Varro and Cicero there stands the great figure of the Rhodian Posidonius,[1] of whose writings hardly anything has come down to us. It is worth while to trace briefly the history of this school at Rome, for it is in itself extremely interesting, as an attempt to reconcile the old theology—if the term may be used—with philosophical thought, and it probably had an appreciable influence on the later quasi-religious Stoicism of the Empire.

We must go back for a moment to the period succeeding the war with Hannibal. The awful experience of that war had done much to discredit the old Roman religious system, which had been

[1] See above, p. 115.

found insufficient of itself to preserve the State. The people, excited and despairing, had been quieted by what may be called new religious prescriptions, innumerable examples of which are to be found in Livy's books. The Sibylline books were constantly consulted, and *lectisternia, supplicationes, ludi,* in which Greek deities were prominent, were ordered and carried out. Finally, in 204 B.C., there was brought to Rome the sacred stone of the Magna Mater Idaea, the great deity of Pessinus in Phrygia, and a festival was established in her honour, called by the Greek name Megalesia. All this means, as can be seen clearly from Livy's language,[1] that the governing classes were trying to quiet the minds of the people by convincing them that no effort was being spared to set right their relations with the unseen powers; they had invoked in vain their own local and native deities, and had been compelled to seek help elsewhere; they had found their own narrow system of religion quite inadequate to express their religious experience of the last twenty years. And indeed that old system of religion never really recovered from the discredit thus cast on it. The temper of the people is well shown by the rapidity with which the orgiastic worship of the Greek Dionysus spread over Italy a few years later; and the fact that it was allowed to remain, though under strict supervision, shows that the State religion no longer had the power to satisfy the cravings of the masses. And

[1] e.g. xxi. 62.

the educated class too was rapidly coming under the influence of Greek thought, which could hardly act otherwise than as a solvent of the old religious ideas. Ennius, the great literary figure of this period, was the first to strike a direct blow at the popular belief in the efficacy of prayer and sacrifice, by openly declaring that the gods did not interest themselves in mankind,[1]—the same Epicurean doctrine preached afterwards by Lucretius. It may indeed be doubted whether this doctrine became popular, or acceptable even to the cultured classes ; but the fact remains that the same man who did more than any one before Virgil to glorify the Roman character and dominion, was the first to impugn the belief that Rome owed her greatness to her divine inhabitants.

But in the next generation there arrived in Rome a man whose teaching had so great an influence on the best type of educated Roman that, as we have already said, he may almost be regarded as a missionary.[2] We do not know for certain whether Panaetius wrote or taught about the nature or existence of the gods ; but we do know that he discussed the question of divination[3] in a work Περὶ προνοίας, where he could hardly have avoided the subject. In any case the Stoic doctrines which he held, themselves ultimately derived from Plato and the Old Academy, were found

[1] Ribbeck, *Fragm. Trag. Rom.* p. 54 : Ego deum genus esse semper dixi et dicam coelitum, Sed eos non curare opinor quid agat humanum genus.

[2] See above, p. 114.

[3] See H. N. Fowler, *Panaetii et Hecatonis librorum fragmenta*, p. 10 ; Hirzel, *Untersuchungen zu Cicero's philosophischen Schriften*, i. p. 194 foll.

capable in the hands of his great successor Posidonius
of Rhodes of supplying a philosophical basis for the
activity as well as the existence of the gods. These
men, it must be repeated, were not merely professed
philosophers, but men of the world, travellers, writing
on a great variety of subjects; they were profoundly
interested, like Polybius, in the Roman character and
government; they became intimate with the finer
Roman minds, from Scipio the younger to Cicero and
Varro, and seem to have seen clearly that the old rigid
Stoicism must be widened and humanised, and its
ethical and theological aspects modified, if it were to
gain a real hold on the practical Roman understanding. We have already seen [1] how their modified
Stoic ethics acted for good on the best Romans of
our period. In theology also they left a permanent
mark on Roman thought; Posidonius wrote a work
on the gods, which formed the basis of the speculative
part of Varro's *Antiquitates divinae*, and almost
certainly also of the second book of Cicero's *de
Natura Deorum*.[2] Other philosophers of the period,
even if not professed Stoics, may have discussed the
same subjects in their lectures and writings, arriving
at conclusions of the same kind.

It is chiefly from the fragments of Varro's work
that we learn something of the Stoic attempt to
harmonise the old religious beliefs with philosophic

---

[1] See above, p. 115.

[2] Schmekel, *Die Mittlere Stoa*, p. 85 foll.; Hirzel, *Untersuchungen*, etc.,
i. p. 194 foll.

theories of the universe.[1]   Varro, following his
teacher, held the Stoic doctrine of the *animus mundi*,
the Divine principle permeating all material things,
which, in combination with them, constitutes the
universe, and is Nature, Reason, God, Destiny, or
whatever name the philosopher might choose to give
it.   The universe is divine, the various parts of it
are, therefore, also divine, in virtue of this informing
principle.   Now in the sixteenth book of his great
work Varro co-ordinated this Stoic theory with the
Graeco-Roman religion of the State as it existed in
his time.   The chief gods represented the *partes
mundi* in various ways ; even the difference of sex
among the deities was explained by regarding male
gods as emanating from the heaven and female ones
from the earth, according to a familiar ancient idea
of the active and passive principle in generation.
The Stoic doctrine of δαίμονες was also utilised to
find an explanation for semi-deities, lares, genii,
etc., and thus another character of the old Italian
religious mind was to be saved from contempt and
oblivion.   The old Italian tendency to see the supernatural manifesting itself in many different ways
expressed by adjectival titles, e.g. Mars Silvanus,
Jupiter Elicius, Juno Lucina, etc., also found an
explanation in Varro's doctrine ; for the divine element
existing in sky, earth, sea, or other parts of the
mundus, and manifesting itself in many different

---

[1] The fragments are collected by R. Agahd, Leipzig, 1898. The great
majority are found in St. Augustine, *de Civitate Dei*.

forms of activity, might be thus made obvious to the ordinary human intellect without the interposition of philosophical terms.

At the head of the whole system was Jupiter, the greatest of Roman gods, whose title of Optimus Maximus might well have suggested that no other deity could occupy this place. Without him it would have been practically impossible for Varro to carry out his difficult and perilous task. Every Roman recognised in Jupiter the god who condescended to dwell on the Capitol in a temple made with hands, and who, beyond all other gods, watched over the destinies of the Roman State; every Roman also knew that Jupiter was the great god of the heaven above him, for in many expressions of his ordinary speech he used the god's name as a synonym for the open sky.[1] The position now accorded to the heaven-god in the new Stoic system is so curious and interesting that we must dwell on it for a moment.

Varro held, or at any rate taught, that Jupiter was himself that soul of the world (animus mundi) which fills and moves the whole material universe.[2] He is the one universal causal agent,[3] from whom all

---

[1] As Wissowa says (*Religion und Kultus der Römer*, p. 100), Jupiter does not appear in Roman language and literature as a personality who thunders or rains, but rather as the heaven itself combining these various manifestations of activity. The most familiar illustration of the usage alluded to in the text is the line of Horace in *Odes* i. 1. 25 : "manet sub Iove frigido venator."

[2] ap. Aug. *Civ. Dei*, iv. 11.   [3] *Ib.* vii. 9.

Z

the forces of nature are derived;[1] or he may be called, in language which would be intelligible to the ordinary Roman, the universal Genius.[2] Further, he is himself all the other gods and goddesses, who may be described as parts, or powers, or virtues, existing in him.[3] And Varro makes it plain that he wishes to identify this great god of gods with the Jupiter at Rome, whose temple was on the Capitol; St. Augustine quotes him as holding that the Romans had dedicated the Capitol to Jupiter, who by his spirit breathes life into everything in the universe :[4] or in less philosophical language, "The Romans wish to recognise Jupiter as king of gods and men, and this is shown by his sceptre and his seat on the Capitol." Thus the god who dwelt on the Capitol, and in the temple which was the centre-point of the Roman Empire, was also the life-giving ruler and centre of the whole universe. Nay, he goes one step further, and identifies him with the one God of the monotheistic peoples of the East, and in particular with the God of the Jews.[5]

Thus Varro had arrived, with the help of Posidonius and the Stoics, at a monotheistic view of the Deity, which is at the same time a kind of pantheism, and yet, strange to say, is able to accommodate itself to the polytheism of the Graeco-Roman world. But

---

[1] ap. Aug. *Civ. Dei*, vii. 13 : animus mundi is here so called, but evidently identified with Jupiter.

[2] *Ib.* vii. 9.   [3] *Ib.* iv. 11, 13.

[4] Aug. *de consensu evangel.* i. 23. 24.   Cp. *Civ. Dei*, iv. 9.

[5] *Ib.* i. 22. 30 ; *Civ. Dei*, xix. 22.

without Jupiter, god of the heaven both for Greeks and Romans, and now too in the eyes of both peoples the god who watched over the destiny of the Roman Empire, this wonderful feat could not have been performed. The identification of the heaven-god with the animus mundi of the Stoics was not indeed a new idea; it may be traced up Stoic channels even to Plato. What is really new and astonishing is that it should have been possible for a conservative Roman like Varro, in that age of carelessness and doubt, to bring the heaven-god, so to speak, down to the Roman Capitol, where his statue was to be seen sitting between Juno and Minerva, and yet to teach the doctrine that he was the same deity as the Jewish Jehovah, and that both were identical with the Stoic animus mundi.

But did Varro also conceive of this Jupiter as a deity "making for righteousness," or acting as a sanction for morality? It would not have been impossible or unnatural for a Roman so to think of him, for of all the Roman deities Jupiter is the one whose name from the most ancient times had been used in oaths and treaties, and whose *numen* was felt to be violated by any public or private breach of faith.[1] We cannot tell how far Varro himself followed out this line of thought, for the fragments of his great work are few and far between. But we know that the Roman Stoics saw in that same universal Power or Mind which Varro identified with

[1] See Wissowa, *Religion und Kultus*, p. 103.

Jupiter the source and strength of law, and therefore
of morality ; here it is usually called reason, *ratio*,
the working of the eternal and immutable Mind of
the universe. "True law is right reason," says
Cicero in a noble passage ;[1] and goes on to teach
that this law transcends all human codes of law, em-
bracing and sanctioning them all ; and that the spirit
inherent in it, which gives it its universal force, is
God Himself. In another passage, written towards
the end of his life, and certainly later than the publication of Varro's work, he goes further and identifies
this God with Jupiter.[2] "This law," he says, "came
into being simultaneously with the Divine Mind"
(i.e. the Stoic Reason): "wherefore that true and
paramount law, commanding and forbidding, is the
right reason of almighty Jupiter" (summi Iovis). Once
more, in the first book of his treatise on the gods,
he quotes the Stoic Chrysippus as teaching that the
eternal Power, which is as it were a guide in the
duties of life, is Jupiter himself.[3] It is characteristic
of the Roman that he should think, in speculations
like these, rather of the law of his State than of the
morality of the individual, as emanating from that
Right Reason to which he might give the name of
Jupiter: I have been unable to find a passage in

[1] *de Rep.* iii. 22. See above, p. 117.
[2] *de Legibus*, ii. 10.
[3] *de Nat. Deor.* i. 15. 40 : "idem etiam legis perpetuae et eternae vim,
quae quasi dux vitae et magistra officiorum sit, Iovem dicit esse, eandemque
fatalem necessitatem appellat, sempiternam rerum futurarum veritatem."
Chrysippus of course was speaking of the Greek Zeus.

which Cicero attributes to this deity the sanction for
individual goodness, though there are many that
assert the belief that justice and the whole system
of social life depend on the gods and our belief in
them.[1] But the Roman had never been conscious
of individual duty, except in relation to his State, or
to the family, which was a living cell in the organism
of the State. In his eyes law was rather the source
of morality than morality the cause and the reason
of law; and as his religion was a part of the law of
his State, and thus had but an indirect connection
with morality, it would not naturally occur to him that
even the great Jupiter himself, thus glorified as the
Reason in the universe, could really help him in the
conduct of his life *qua* individual. It is only as the
source of legalised morality that we can think of
Varro's Jupiter as " making for righteousness."

Less than twenty-five years after Cicero's death,
in the imagination of the greatest of Roman poets,
Jupiter was once more brought before the Roman
world, and now in a form comprehensible by all
educated men, whether or no they had dabbled in
philosophy. What are we to say of the Jupiter of
the *Aeneid*? We do not need to read far in the first
book of the poem to find him spoken of in terms
which remind us of Varro: " O qui res hominumque
deumque Aeternis regis imperiis," are the opening
words of the address of Venus; and when she has
finished,

---

[1] e.g. *de Off.* iii. 28 ; *de Nat. Deor.* i. 116.

Olli subridens hominum sator atque deorum
Vultu, quo caelum tempestatesque serenat,
Oscula libavit natae, dehinc talia fatur ;
" Parce metu, Cytherea, manent immota tuorum
Fata tibi."

Jupiter is here, as in Varro's system, the prime cause
and ruler of all things, and he also holds in his hand
the destiny of Rome and the fortunes of the hero
who was to lay the first foundation of Rome's
dominion.   It is in the knowledge of his will that
Aeneas walks, with hesitating steps, in the earlier
books, in the later ones with assured confidence,
towards the goal that is set before him.   But the
lines just quoted serve well to show how different is
the Jupiter of Virgil from the universal deity of the
Roman Stoic.   Beyond doubt Virgil had felt the
power of the Stoic creed; but he was essaying an
epic poem, and he could not possibly dispense with
the divine machinery as it stood in his great Homeric
model.   His Jupiter is indeed, as has been lately
said,[1] " a great and wise god, free from the tyrannical
and sensuous characteristics of the Homeric Zeus,"
in other words, he is a Roman deity, and sometimes
acts and speaks like a grave Roman consul of the
olden time.   But still he is an anthropomorphic deity,
a purely human conception of a personal god-king;
in these lines he smiles on his daughter Venus
and kisses her.   This is the reason why Virgil has
throughout his poem placed the Fates, or Destiny,
in close relation to him, without definitely explaining

[1] Glover, *Studies in Virgil*, p. 275.

that relation. Fate, as it appears in the Aeneid, is the Stoic εἱμαρμένη applied to the idea of Rome and her Empire; that Stoic conception could not take the form of Jupiter, as in Varro's hands, for the god had to be modelled on the Homeric pattern, not on the Stoic. It is perhaps not going too far to say that the god, as a theological conception, never recovered from this treatment; any chance he ever had of becoming the centre of a real religious system was destroyed by the Aeneid, the *pietas* of whose hero is indeed nominally due to him, but in reality to the decrees of Fate.[1]

While philosophers and poets were thus performing intellectual and imaginative feats with the gods of the State, the strong tendency to superstition, un-tutored fear of the supernatural, which had always been characteristic of the Italian peoples, so far from losing power, was actually gaining it, and that not only among the lower classes. As Lucretius mock-ingly said, even those who think and speak with contempt of the gods will in moments of trouble slay black sheep and sacrifice them to the Manes. This feeling of fear or nervousness, which lies at the root of the meaning of the word *religio*,[2] had been

---

[1] It is interesting to note that in the religious revival of Augustus Jupiter by no means has a leading place. See Carter, *Religion of Numa*, p. 160, where, however, the attitude of Augustus towards the great god is perhaps over-emphasised. On the relation of Virgil's Jupiter to Fate, see E. Norden, *Virgils epische Technik*, p. 286 foll. Seneca, it is worth noting, never mentions Jupiter as the centre of the Stoic Pantheon.—Dill, *Roman Society from Nero to M. Aurelius*, p. 331.

[2] See an article by the author in *Hibbert Journal*, July 1907, p. 847.

quieted in the old days by the prescriptions of the
pontifices and their jus divinum, but it was always
ready to break out again; as we have seen, in the
long and awful struggle of the Hannibalic war, it
was necessary to go far beyond the ordinary pharma-
copœia within reach of the priesthoods in order to
convince the people that all possible means were
being taken for their salvation.   Again, in this last
age of the Republic, there are obvious signs that
both ignorant and educated were affected by the
gloom and uncertainty of the times.   Increasing
uncertainty in the political world, increasing doubt
in the world of thought, very naturally combined to
produce an emotional tendency which took different
forms in men of different temperament.   We can
trace this (1) in the importance attached to omens,
portents, dreams; (2) in a certain vague thought of
a future life, which takes a positive shape in the
deification of human beings; (3) at the close of the
period, in something approaching to a sense of sin,
of neglected duty, bringing down upon State and
individual the anger of the gods.

1. If we glance over the latter part of the book of
prodigies, compiled by the otherwise unknown writer
Julius Obsequens from the records of the pontifices
quoted in Livy's history, we can get a fair idea of
the kind of portent that was troubling the popular
mind.   They are much the same as they always
had been in Roman history,—earthquakes, monstrous
births, temples struck by lightning, statues over-

thrown, wolves entering the city, and so on; they
are extremely abundant in the terrible years of the
Social and Civil Wars, become less frequent after the
death of Sulla, and break out again in full force with
the murder of Caesar. They were reported to the
pontifices from the places where they were supposed
to have occurred, and if thought worthy of expiation
were entered in the pontifical books. We may
suppose that they were sent in chiefly by the unedu-
cated. But among men of education we have many
examples of this same nervousness, of which two
or three must suffice. Sulla, as we know from his
own Memoirs, which were used directly or indirectly
by Plutarch, had a strong vein of superstition in his
nature, and made no attempt to control it. In
dedicating his Memoirs to Lucullus he advised him
" to think no course so safe as that which is enjoined
by the δαίμων (perhaps his genius) in the night";[1]
and Plutarch tells us several tales of portents on
which he acted, evidently drawn from this same
autobiography. We are told of him that he always
carried a small image of Apollo, which he kissed from
time to time, and to which he prayed silently in
moments of danger.[2] Again, Cicero tells us a curious
story of himself, Varro, and Cato, which shows that
those three men of philosophical learning were quite
liable to be frightened by a prophecy which to us
would not seem to have much claim to respect.[3] He

---

[1] Plut. *Sulla*, 6.   [2] Valerius Maximus ii. 3.
[3] *de Div.* i. 32. 68.

tells how when the three were at Dyrrachium, after Caesar's defeat there and the departure of the armies into Thessaly, news was brought them by the commander of the Rhodian fleet that a certain rower had foretold that within thirty days Greece would be weltering in blood ; how all three were terribly frightened, and how a few days later the news of the battle at Pharsalia reached them. Lastly, we all remember the vision which appeared to Brutus on the eve of the battle of Philippi, of a huge and fearsome figure standing by him in silence, which Shakespeare has made into the ghost of Caesar and used to unify his play. According to Plutarch, the Epicurean Cassius, as Lucretius would have done, attempted to convince his friend on rational grounds that the vision need not alarm him, but apparently in vain.[1]

2. Lucretius had denied the doctrine of the immortality of the soul, as the cause of so much of the misery which he believed it to be his mission to avert. Caesar, in the speech put into his mouth by Sallust, in the debate on the execution of the conspirators on December 5, 63, seems to be of the same opinion, and as Cicero alludes to his words in the speech with which he followed Caesar, we may suppose that Sallust was reporting him rightly.[2] The poet and the statesman were not unlike in the way in which they looked at facts ; both were of clear strong vision, without a trace of mysticism. But such men were

[1] Plut. *Brutus.* 36, 37.   [2] Sall. *Cat.* 51 ; Cic. *Cat.* iv. 4. 7.

the exception rather than the rule; Cicero probably represents better the average thinking man of his time. Cicero was indeed too full of life, too deeply interested in the living world around him, to think much of such questions as the immortality of the soul; and as a professed follower of the Academic school, he assuredly did not hold any dogmatic opinion on it. He was at no time really affected by Pythagoreanism, like his friend Nigidius Figulus, whose works, now lost, had a great vogue in the later years of Cicero's life, and much influence on the age that followed. In the first book of his Tusculan Disputations Cicero discusses the question from the Academic point of view, coming to no definite conclusion, except that whether we are immortal or not we must be grateful to death for releasing us from the bondage of the body. This book was written in the last year of his life; but ten years earlier, in the beautiful myth, imitated from the myths of Plato, which he appended to his treatise *de Republica*, he had emphatically asserted the doctrine. There the spirit of the elder Scipio appears to his great namesake, Cicero's ideal Roman, and assures him that the road to heaven (caelum) lies open to those who do their duty in this life, and especially their duty to the State. " Know thyself to be a god; as the god of gods rules the universe, so the god within us rules the body, and as that great god is eternal, so does an eternal soul govern this frail body." [1]

[1] Cic. *de Rep.* iv. 24.

The *Somnium Scipionis* was an inspiration, written under the influence of Plato at one of those emotional moments of Cicero's life which make it possible to say of him that there was a religious element in his mind.[1] Some years later the poignancy of his grief at the death of his daughter Tullia had the effect of putting him again in a strong emotional mood. For many weeks he lived alone at Astura, on the edge of the Pomptine marshes, out of reach of all friends, forbidding even his young wife and her mother to come near him; brooding, as it would seem, on the survival of the godlike element in his daughter. These sad meditations took a practical form which at first astonishes us, but is not hard to understand when we have to come to know Cicero well, and to follow the tendencies of thought in these years. He might erect a tomb to her memory,—but that would not satisfy him; it would not express his feeling that the immortal godlike spark within her survived. He earnestly entreats Atticus to find and buy him a piece of ground where he can build a *fanum*, i.e. a shrine, to her spirit. " I wish to have a shrine built, and that wish cannot be rooted out of my heart. I am anxious to avoid any likeness to a tomb . . . in order to attain as nearly as possible to an apotheosis." [2] A little further on he calls these foolish ideas; but this is doubtless only because he is writing to Atticus, a man of the world, not given to emotion or mysticism.

[1] Reid, *The Academics of Cicero*, Introduction, p. 18.
[2] *ad Att.* xii. 36.

Cicero is really speaking the language of the Italian mind, for the moment free from philosophical speculation; he believes that his beloved dead lived on, though he could not have proved it in argument. So firmly does he believe it that he wishes others to know that he believes it, and insists that the shrine shall be erected in a frequented place![1]

Though the great Dictator did not believe in another world, he consented at the end of his life to become Jupiter Julius, and after his death was duly canonised as Divus, and had a temple erected to him. But the many-sided question of the deification of the Caesars cannot be discussed here; it is only mentioned as showing in another way the trend of thought in this dark age of Roman history. Whatever some philosophers may have thought, there cannot be a doubt that the ordinary Roman believed in the godhead of Julius.[2]

3. We saw in an earlier chapter with what gay and heedless frivolity young men like Caelius were amusing themselves even on the very eve of civil war. In strange contrast with this is the gloom that overspread all classes during the war itself, and more especially after the assassination of the Dictator. Caesar seemed irresistible and godlike, and men were probably beginning to hope for some new and more stable order of things, when he was suddenly struck down, and the world plunged again into confusion and

---

[1] *ad Att.* xii. 37.
[2] Suetonius, *Jul.* 88. See E. Kornemann in *Klio*, vol. i. p. 95.

doubt; and it was not till after the final victory of
Octavian at Actium, and the destruction of the
elements of disunion with the deaths of Antony and
Cleopatra, that men really began to hope for better
times. The literature of those melancholy years
shows distinct signs of the general depression, which
was perhaps something more than weariness and
material discomfort; there was almost what we may
call a dim sense of sin, or at least of moral evil, such
a feeling, though far less real and intense, as that
which their prophets aroused from time to time in the
Jewish people, and one not unknown in the history of
Hellas.

The most touching expression of this feeling is to
be found in the preface which Livy prefixed to his
history—a wonderful example of the truth that when
a great prose writer is greatly moved, his language reflects his emotion in its beauty and earnestness. Every
student knows the sentence in which he describes the
gradual decay of all that was good in the Roman
character: "donec ad haec tempora, quibus nec vitia
nostra nec remedia pati possumus, perventum est";
but it is not every student who can recognise in it a
real sigh of despair, an unmistakable token of the
sadness of the age.[1] In the introductory chapters
which serve the purpose of prefaces to the *Jugurtha*
and *Catiline* of Sallust, we find something of the

---

[1] We do not know exactly when this preface was written. Prefaces are
now composed, as a rule, when a work is finished: but this does not seem to
have been the practice in antiquity, and internal evidence is here strongly in
favour of an early date.

same sad tone, but it does not ring true like Livy's
exordium ; Sallust was a man of altogether coarser
fibre, and seems to be rather assuming than expressing
the genuine feeling of a saddened onlooker.   In one
of his earliest poems, written perhaps after the
Perusian war of 41 B.C.[1] even the lively Horace was
moved to voice the prevailing depression, fancifully
urging that the Italian people should migrate, like
the Phocaeans of old, to the far west, where, as
Sertorius had been told in Spain, lay the islands of
the blest, where the earth, as in the golden age, yields
all her produce untilled :

> Iuppiter illa piae secrevit litora genti
> Ut inquinavit aere tempus aureum ;
> Aere, dehinc ferro duravit saecula, quorum
> Piis secunda vate me datur fuga.

It may be, as has recently been suggested, that
the famous fourth Eclogue of Virgil, "the Messianic
Eclogue," was in some sense meant as an answer to
this poem of Horace.   "There is no need," he seems
to say in that poem, written in the year 39, "to seek
the better age in a fabled island of the west.   It is
here and now with us.   The period upon which Italy
is now entering more than fulfils in real life the dream
of a Golden Age.   A marvellous child is even now
coming into the world who will see and inaugurate
an era of peace and prosperity : darkness and despair
will after a while pass entirely away, and a regenerate
Italy,—regenerate in religion and morals as in fertility

[1] *Epode* 16. 54 ; cp. 30 foll.

and wealth,—will lead the world in a new era of happiness and good government." [1]

But the Golden Age, so fondly hoped for, so vaguely and poetically conceived, was not to come in the sense in which Virgil, or any other serious thinker of the day, could dream of it. I may conclude this chapter with a few sentences which express this most truly and eloquently. " When there is a fervent aspiration after better things, springing from a strong feeling of human brotherhood, and a firm belief in the goodness and righteousness of God, such aspiration carries with it an invincible confidence that some how, some where, some when, it must receive its complete fulfilment, for it is prompted by the Spirit which fills and orders the Universe throughout its whole development. But if the human organ of inspiration goes on to fix the how, the where, and the when, and attributes to some nearer object the glory of the final blessedness, then it inevitably falls into such mistakes as Virgil's, and finds its golden age in the rule of the Caesars (which was indeed an essential feature of Christianity), or perhaps, as in later days, in the establishment of socialism or imperialism. Well for the seer if he remembers that the kingdom of God is within us, and that the true golden age must have its foundation in penitence for misdoing, and be built up in righteousness and lovingkindness." [2]

[1] Sir W. M. Ramsay, quoted in *Virgil's Messianic Eclogue*, p. 54.
[2] Dr. J. B. Mayor, in *Virgil's Messianic Eclogue*, p. 118 foll.

EPILOGUE

THESE sketches of social life at the close of the Republican period have been written without any intention of proving a point, or any pre-conceived idea of the extent of demoralisation, social, moral, or political, which the Roman people had then reached. But a perusal of Mr. Balfour's suggestive lecture on "Decadence" has put me upon making a very succinct diagnosis of the condition of the patient whose life and habits I have been describing. The Romans, and the Italians, with whom they were now socially and politically amalgamated, were not in the last two centuries B.C. an old or worn-out people. It is at any rate certain that for a century after the war with Hannibal Rome and her allies, under the guidance of the Roman senate, achieved an amount of work in the way of war and organisation such as has hardly been performed by any people before or since; and even in the period dealt with in this book, in spite of much cause for misgiving at home, the work done by Roman and Italian armies both in East and West shows beyond doubt that under healthy discipline the native vigour of the population could assert itself.

2 A

We must not forget, however severely we may condemn the way in which the work was done, that it is to these armies, in all human probability, that we owe not only the preservation of Graeco-Italian culture and civilisation, but the opportunity for further progress. The establishment of definite frontiers by Pompeius and Caesar, and afterwards by Augustus and Tiberius, brought peace to the region of the Mediterranean, and with it made possible the development of Roman law and the growth of a new and life-giving religion.

But peoples, like individuals, if offered opportunities of doing themselves physical or moral damage, are only too ready to accept them. Time after time in these chapters we have had to look back to the age following the war with Hannibal in order to see what those opportunities were; and in each case we have found the acceptance rapid and eager. We have seen wealth coming in suddenly, and misused; slave-labour available in an abnormal degree, and utilised with results in the main unfortunate; the population of the city increasing far too quickly, yet the difficulties arising from this increase either ignored or misapprehended. We have noticed the decay of wholesome family life, of the useful influence of the Roman matron, of the old forms of the State religion; the misconception of the true end of education, the result partly of Greek culture, partly of political life; and to these may perhaps be added an increasing liability to diseases, and especially to malaria, arising from

economic blunders in Italy and insanitary conditions
of life in the city. All these opportunities of damage
to the fibre of the people had been freely accepted,
and with the result that in the age of Cicero we cannot mistake the signs and symptoms of degeneracy.

But it would be a mistake to jump to the conclusion
that this degeneracy had as yet gone too far to be
arrested. It was assuredly not that degeneracy of
senility which Mr. Balfour is inclined to postulate as
an explanation of decadence. So far as I can judge,
the Romans were at that stage when, in spite of
unhealthy conditions of life and obstinate persistence
in dangerous habits, it was not too late to reform and
recover. To me the main interest of the history of
the early Empire lies in seeking the answer to the
question how far that recovery was made. If these
chapters should have helped any student to prepare
the ground for the solution of this problem their
object will have been fully achieved.

INDEX

357

THE END

APPENDIX

Page 1, l. 12. *totam aestimare Romam:* to appreciate Rome in its entirety.

Page 3, l. 12. *Hinc ad Tarpeiam,* etc.: he leads him next to the Tarpeian Rock and to the Capitol, now of gold, once thick with wild bushes.

Page 4, l. 24. *Hinc septem,* etc.: from here you may see the seven hills of the sovereign city, and appreciate Rome as a whole, the Alban and the Tusculan hills, and all the cool suburban retreats.

Page 10, l. 1. *rerum,* etc. Rome became a supreme thing of beauty.

Page 10, l. 13. *nativa praesidia:* natural defences.

Page 10, l. 21. *regionum,* etc. A site in the middle of Italy, singularly fitted by nature for the development of the city.

Page 17, l. 2. *nec ferrea,* etc.: nor has he seen the hardships of the law, the mad forum, or the archives of the people.

Page 22, l. 2. *Ille, ille,* etc.: he it was, Jupiter himself, who withstood the attack, he who willed it that the Capitol, that these temples, that the whole city and you all should be safe.

Page 29, footnote 1. *in montibus,* etc.: built between mountains and valleys, raised and almost suspended on high, through the stones of its buildings, with its back streets.

Page 39, l. 6. *ubi semel,* etc.: he who has once strayed from the right path will come to calamity.

Page 52, l. 11. *lanificium:* the working of wool.

Page 55, l. 26. *graffiti:* ancient scribblings, scratched, painted, o. otherwise marked on a wall, column, tablet, or other surface.

Page 61, l. 4. *quaestio de repetundis:* court for extortion.

Page 64, l. 15. *familiarem,* etc.: intimate with L. Lucullus, wealthy, of intractable character.

Page 73, l. 14. *qui de censoribus,* etc.: whosoever shall have secured a contract from the censors shall not be accepted as associate or shareholder.

Page 73, footnote 2. *Asiatici,* etc.: of the public revenue of Asia, he had a very small share.

Page 91, l. 3. *fortissimus,* etc.: a most powerful and important farmer of the public revenue.

Page 93, l. 20. *insanum forum:* the forum in its maddening bustle.

Page 116, l. 12. *doctissimus,* etc. the most learned of that time.

Page 121, l. 11. *monumentum,* etc.: a monument more enduring than bronze.

Page 123, l. 20. *vere humanus:* truly refined.

Page 127, l. 23. *omnia,* etc.: he transforms himself into all portentous shapes.

Page 130, l. 20. *ménager ses transitions:* to pass gradually over to the other side.

Page 132, l. 18. *de vi:* of criminal violence.

Page 133, l. 9. *Uni se,* etc.: they are addicted to one and the same practice, that they may cautiously cheat and craftily contend, outdo each other in blandishments, feign honesty, set snares as if they were all enemies to each other.

Page 133, l. 28. *rari nantes,* etc.: few and scattered swimmers in the vast abyss.

Page 142 (bottom). *Claudite,* etc.: close the doors, maidens, enough have we sung. And you, noble couple, live happily and apply your vigorous youth to the assiduous task of wedlock.

Page 149, footnote 2. *Si quid,* etc.: if a woman act reprehensibly or disgracefully, he punishes her ; if she has drunk wine, if she has done something wrong with a stranger, he condemns her. If you surprise your wife in the act of adultery, you may with impunity kill her without any form of judgment ; but if she caught you in adultery, she would not dare touch you, for she has no right.

Page 150, l. 11. *liberorum,* etc.: in order to have children.

Page 155, l. 22. *Odi,* etc.: I hate and I love. You ask perhaps how that can be. I do not know, I feel it, and am distressed.

Page 155 (bottom). *Elle apportait,* etc.: she revealed in her private behavior, in her affections, the same vehemence and the same passion which her brother showed in public life. Ready for all excesses, and not blushing to confess them, loving and hating with fury, incapable of controlling herself, and opposed to all constraint, she did not belie the great and haughty family from which she was sprung.

Page 178, l. 3. *rusticorum,* etc.:

> The farmer-soldier's manly brood
> Was trained to delve the Sabine sod,
> And at an austere mother's nod
> To hew and fetch the fagot wood.

Page 178, l. 20. *Maxima,* etc.: the greatest concern must be shown for children.

Page 185, l. 8. *Avarus,* etc.:

> The covetous is the cause of his own misery.
> Bravery is increased by daring and fear by hesitation.
> You can more easily discover fortune than cling to it.
> The wrath of the just is to be dreaded.
> A man dies every time that he is bereft of his kin.

Man is loaned, not given to life.
The best strife is rivalry in benignity.
Nothing is pleasing unless renewed by variety.
Bad is the plan which cannot be altered.
Less often would you err if you knew how much you don't know.
He who shows clemency always comes out victorious.
He who respects his oath succeeds in everything.
Where old age is at fault youth is badly trained.

Page 187, l. 7. *Grais*, etc.: the muse gave genius to the Greeks and the pride of language, covetous of nothing but of praise. But the Roman youths by long reckonings learn to split the coin into a hundred parts. Let young Albinus say: "If you take one away from five pence, what results?" "A groat." Good, you'll thrive.

Page 189, l. 1. *In grammaticis*, etc.: in the study of literature, the perusal of the poets, the knowledge of history, the interpretation of words, the peculiar tone of pronunciation.

Page 191, l. 9. *Orator est*, etc.: an orator, my son, is an upright man skilled in speaking.

Page 191, l. 11. *Rem tene*, etc.: master the subject; the words will follow.

Page 196, l. 9. *vir bonus*, etc.: see page 191, l. 9.

Page 196, l. 13. *Non enim*, etc.: eloquence and oratorical aptness obtain good results if they be swayed by a right understanding and by the discretion and control of the mind.

Page 210, footnote 1. *Mancipiis*, etc.: avoid being like the Cappadocian monarch, rich in slaves and penniless in purse.

Page 211, footnote 1. *pone aedem*, etc.: behind the temple of Castor are those to whom you'd be sorry to lend money.

Page 215, l. 18. *An te ibi*, etc.: would you stay there among those harlots, prostitutes of bakers, leavings of the breadmakers, smeared with rank cosmetics, nasty devotees of slaves?

Page 216, footnote 2. *agrum*, etc.: in cultivating the fields or in hunting, servile occupations, etc.

Page 233, l. 5. *Nec turpe*, etc.: what a master commands cannot be disgraceful.

Page 233, footnote 3. *Coli rura*, etc.: it is a bad practice to fill the fields with men from the workhouse, or to have anything done by men who are forsaken by hope.

Page 235, footnote 2. *Regum*, etc.: we have taken the tyrant's temper.

Page 239, l. 10. *ante focos*, etc.: it was customary once to take places in the long benches before the fireplace, and to trust that the gods were present at our table.

Page 246, l. 5. *nunc vero*, etc.: but now from morning till evening, on holidays and working days, the whole people, senators and commoners, busy themselves in the forum and retire nowhere, etc. (See page 133, l. 9, and translation of that passage.)

Page 246, footnote 2. *Urbem*, etc.: remain in the city, Rufus ; stay there and live in that light. All foreign travel is humble and lowly for those that can work for the greatness of Rome.

Page 247, footnote 1. *Frequens*, etc.: constant change of abode is a sign of unstable mind.

Page 248, l. 12. *contentio*, etc.: not a straining of the mind, but a relaxation.

Page 259, l. 12. *locus*, etc.: a pleasant site, on the sea itself, and can be seen from Antium and Circeii.

Page 265, footnote 3. *Ut illum*, etc.: may the gods confound him who first invented the hours, and who first placed a sundial in this city. Pity on me! They have cut up my day in compartments. Once when I was a boy my stomach was my clock, and it was much more fitting and reliable; it never failed to warn me except when there was nothing; now, even when there is something, there is no eating unless it so please the sun. For the whole city is full of sundials, and most of the people crawl on in need of food and drink.

Page 269, footnote 1. *Romae*, etc.: in Rome it was for a long time a joy and a pride to open up the house at early morning and attend to the legal needs of the clients.

Page 275, l. 20. *Nesciit vivere:* he did not know how to live.

Page 277, l. 10. *ad noctem:* late into the night.

Page 280, l. 17. *Saepe tribus*, etc.: often you would see three couches with four guests apiece.

Page 283, l. 21. Ἐμετικὴν, etc.: he was under the emetic cure, and consequently ate and drank freely and with much satisfaction; and everything certainly was good and well served; nay more, I may say that

> "Though the cook was good,
> 'Twas Attic salt that flavored best the food."

Page 283, footnote 1. *qua lege*, etc.: which law did not determine the expense, but the kind of victuals and the manner of cooking them.

Page 285, l. 11. *Agricolo*, etc.: the farmer is the first who after a long day of toil in the fields adapted rustic songs to the laws of metre ; the first in satisfied leisure to modulate a song on his reed, which he would say before the gods decked with flowers. It was the farmer, O Bacchus, who with his face colored with reddish minium, taught his untrained feet the first movements of the dance.

Page 287, l. 18. *Quippe etiam*, etc.: for even on holy days, divine and human laws allow us to perform certain works. No religion has forbidden to clear the channels, to raise a fence before the corn, to lay snares for birds, to fire the thorns, and plunge in the wholesome river a flock of bleating sheep.

Page 303, l. 2. *lex de ambitu:* law concerning the courting of popular favor in canvassing.

Page 307, l. 4. *Eandem,* etc.: a time will come when you will bewail that valor of yours.

Page 309, l. 7. *Spectatum,* etc.: they come to see, but they come also to be seen.

Page 313, l. 27. *summus artifex:* consummate artist.

Page 314, l. 3. *gravis:* serious.

Page 314, l. 4. *gravitas:* seriousness.

Page 315, l. 14. *Fescennina,* etc.: the rude Fescennine farce grew from rites like these, where rustic taunts were hurled in alternate verse ; and the pleasing license, tolerated from year to year, gambolled, etc.

Page 317, l. 18. *Nihil mihi,* etc.: know well that I lacked nothing except company with whom to laugh in a friendly way and intelligently over these things.

Page 324, l. 28. *mos maiorum:* the customs of our ancestors.

Page 327, l. 12. *Felix,* etc.: blessed is he who succeeded in knowing the causes of events.

Page 327, l. 16. *Fortunatus,* etc.: fortunate he also who knows the rustic gods.

Page 333, l. 6. *lectisternia:* a feast of the gods during which their images on pillars were placed in the streets.

Page 333, l. 6. *supplicationes:* religious solemnities for supplication.

Page 333, l. 6. *ludi:* games.

Page 339, l. 23. *numen:* godhead, deity.

Page 340, footnote 3. *idem etiam,* etc.: he says also that Jupiter is the power of this law, eternal and immutable, which is the guide, so to speak, of our life and the principle of our duties ; a law which he calls a fatal necessity, an eternal truth of future things.

Page 341, l. 15. *qua:* as.

Page 341, l. 26. *O qui res,* etc.: thou who rulest with eternal sway the doings of men and gods.

Page 342, l. 1. *Olli,* etc.: the sire of men and gods, smiling to her with that aspect wherewith he clears the tempestuous sky, gently kissed his daughter's lips ; then thus replies: Cytherea, cease from fear; immovable to thee remain the fates of thy people.

Page 351, l. 13. *Iuppiter,* etc.: Jove reserved these shores for the just, when he alloyed the golden age with brass; with brass, then with iron he hardened the ages, from which there shall be a happy escape according to my predictions.

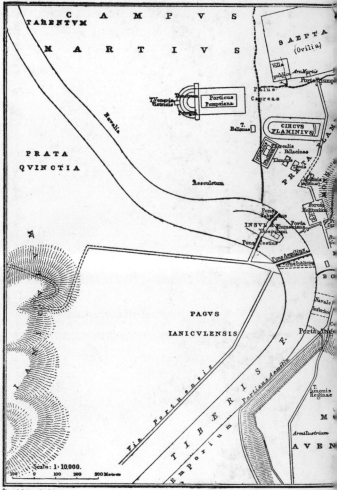

Scale : 1·10,000.

100   0   100   200   300 Metres

London : M

ROME IN THE LAST